Positive Psychology for Your Hero's Journey

Discovering True and Lasting Happiness

First Edition

Bruce W. Smith

ISBN-13: 978-1983486609

ISBN-10: 1983486604

Grateful acknowledgement to the VIA Institute on Character
for permission to use the VIA classification and definitions.
© Copyright 2004-2018, VIA Institute on Character.
Used with permission. All rights reserved. www.viacharacter.org,

iv

Brief Table of Contents

Detailed Table of Contents

Preface

A journey of a thousand miles begins with a single step.

— Lao-Tzu[1]

This book grew out of what may be the happiest and most fulfilling experiences of my life. During the fall of 2005, I was given the opportunity to teach positive psychology at the University of New Mexico in Albuquerque. A couple weeks before the course was to start, I was awarded a research grant that meant I would no longer need to teach it. After not being able to find anyone else to teach the course, I had no choice but to teach it—and now am so glad I did.

The course was full with 30 undergraduates jammed in a small classroom in the basement of the psychology building. At the time, the Iraq war was raging and hurricane Katrina had just flooded New Orleans. The students included a soldier home after a tour in Iraq and a young woman displaced after her university in New Orleans was flooded. The class also contained what I originally thought of as the "fearsome foursome." This included another young woman and three men of different ethnicities who seemed to want to hide together in the back row. I was sure they were there to harass me during the semester.

I thought the cards were already stacked against me in teaching a course with the word "positive" in it. I grew up in what I thought was an overly positive family. I thought that my parents often looked at the bright side to avoid the dark and scary things that seemed only too real to me as a child. Little did I know that positive psychology was not about avoiding or denying the dark side, but bringing the power of science to find joy and happiness in the midst of and even in spite of it.

After 16 weeks with those 30 students, I was transformed in my understanding of positive psychology and the power of science to bring us hope. The class and the students in it came to embody a primary goal of positive psychology—to enable us to live life fully and be at our best. The soldier gave a moving personal account of his courage and integrity in going to Iraq. The refugee from New Orleans became a living example of how stress and trauma can lead to the most surprising and profound personal growth. And one of the fearsome foursome shared the unforgettable story of how the class inspired him to reach out for the first time to the father who had hurt him—and find a way to forgive him.

Our final meeting was not in the classroom but around a bonfire at the home of one of the four who I thought were there to harass me. While I had been afraid that I would have to teach a group of unmotivated students about superficial happiness, I discovered the surprising power of a new scientific focus on the good life that not only transformed individuals but created a life-giving community. I expected that I would be imparting cold academic knowledge to bored and unmotivated students, but found that the students came to life as they saw themselves anew and shared their own stories of the best of what was possible for them. I couldn't help but wonder what the hell had happened.

Now, after teaching positive psychology for 12 years, having the class grow from 30 students to 200 every semester, and having the students voting it the best class at the university, I think I am beginning to understand. In each of the times I taught positive psychology, I have seen the same kind of engagement, enthusiasm, and positive transformation of so many students. Each time I have tried to learn from the over 3,000 students that I have had in class. Now, I think I have a better understanding of what it is that calls them to such a great new adventure.

The moving stories of students in the early classes got me thinking about Joseph Campbell's idea of a hero's journey. He wrote about how our favorite stories contain a similar pattern involving leaving a comfort zone, facing great challenges, and returning with a gift for others. He believed that we love great stories because they speak to us and reflect our own stories. Thus, I began to teach positive psychology as a hero's journey to what may make students happy. I saw how the idea of a hero's journey motivated and inspired them to use positive psychology to become their best and make the most of their lives.

After years of hearing students say how much the class meant to them, my research lab began a study to see if the data supported this. We have examined changes in happiness and well-being for students in the class relative to students in other classes. After several semesters, we have consistently found that the positive psychology students have had significant increases in happiness, positive emotions, meaning and purpose in life, accomplishing goals, and in the quality of their relationships, and significant decreases in negative emotions and loneliness.[2]

My goal for this book is to take the very best of what I've learned teaching this class and make it available so you can make the same journey and reap the same benefits. I wouldn't be surprised if you have some of the same skepticism and doubt I had when I first began teaching positive psychology. We are all too familiar with superficial self-help books and self-promoting gurus who are more about selling something than genuine human transformation. But I can't help but wonder if you too may be on the verge of discovering a whole new world of good about yourself and the life that is possible for you. I can't help but think that you too might be in for a wonderful journey.

Bruce W. Smith
January 1, 2018

Chapter 1

Introduction to the Adventure

The big question is whether you are going to be able to say a hearty yes to your adventure.

—Joseph Campbell[1]

At the beginning of every great story, there is a call to adventure. Your own life can be a great story and reading these words can be the beginning of a wonderful new adventure. Just as Hedwig the owl came with the letters to invite Harry Potter to *Hogwarts* and Gandalf in *The Lord of the Rings* came to invite Frodo to begin a great journey, so this can be a call to you to go on what may be the greatest adventure of your life.

This book is not about superficial happiness or the pleasures that only feel good for a moment and quickly pass through our fingers. It is about the true and lasting happiness that comes with the kind of joy that we can experience even in the midst of stress and suffering, the kind of love that makes our life worth living, and the kind of fulfillment that comes from living to the best of what we can be. It is about the opportunity for something more—to make the most of our lives and what we have been given.

If you are not looking for that, you can put this book down right now and go back to whatever you were doing. This kind of journey is not for the faint of heart or those who are looking to be—as the *Pink Floyd* song says—"comfortably numb." If you do want to hear a new call, then read on and be prepared to blaze a new trail like Harry and Frodo and all of our greatest heroes to discovering a kind of happiness you may have not thought possible. The love that you have for your favorite stories is the same that you can experience for your own hero's journey that you can begin today.

Just as the Force enabled Luke Skywalker to accomplish more than he ever dreamed, so there is a new force that is available to us all. This force is not fiction and it is not magic, but the same force that has enabled us to harness nuclear energy and go to the moon. This force is the power of science as it has come to be expressed in our ability to develop and test new theories. This is a force that enables us to learn from our mistakes and continue to refine our ideas to do what we never before thought possible.

Only this time science is not being used in the service of creating bombs or flying to distant planets. Now, science has finally directed its power and potential to what may be to us the most important thing of all. This time science has turned toward understanding what it is that may bring us true and lasting happiness. Despite all the suffering and darkness in the world today, there is truly a new hope for unleashing the scientific method on this most life-giving task.

Is it really possible to use the scientific method to help us become happy? Psychology has been defined as a science focused on understanding human thought, emotion, and behavior. However, until recently the focus of psychology has been primarily on the kinds of thoughts, emotions, and behaviors that get us into problems and trouble. While there were some notable exceptions, the greatest emphasis was on what is abnormal and pathological and what goes wrong with us. During almost all of the 20th century, there were many more studies on what makes us anxious and depressed than on what makes us happy and well.

Then something very unusual happened. In 1998, Martin Seligman, the new president of the American Psychological

Association, started an initiative for what he called "positive psychology."[2] Rather than focusing on what goes wrong with us, positive psychology has become the science of what can go right with us and enable us to function at our best. Rather than just focusing on how we get anxious and depressed, positive psychology is concerned with what enables us to live with the greatest joy, happiness, meaning, and fulfillment. The positive psychology movement became the catalyst for studying what makes life worth living.

Over the last 20 years, the positive psychology movement has grown into a community of researchers and practitioners with new professional organizations and journals. Like never before, the positive psychology movement has brought the power of science to focus on how to live the good life rather than just how to avoid psychopathology. While before we could get lost in the often confusing and contradictory advice of self-help gurus, motivational speakers, and misinformed common sense, now science is testing these and other ideas to see what really works.

The Scientific Method and This Book

Positive psychology is the application of the scientific method to enable us to make the most of our lives and live them to the fullest. In philosophy, epistemology is the study of how we come to know something. In this book, the primary way of knowing is the scientific method which involves using critical thinking and doing research to determine what is true and what works. There are many ways to think about using the scientific method and here are four principles for how it will be used here:

1. *The ideas about what happiness is and how to achieve it will be grounded in the scientific method which involves research to test ideas and the possibility of being proven wrong.*

4

Positive psychology is not like what has been called "pop psychology" or "self-help." Pop psychology is short for "popular psychology" and includes ideas about human behavior that are widespread and uncritically held by the general population. "Self-help" has been associated with "self-help books" that present the ideas of different authors about how people can help themselves overcome various problems and challenges or be happy and successful.

Both popular psychology and self-help can be based in scientific research or theory but are not necessarily so. They are often based on the kind of common sense or conventional wisdom that is frequently thoughtlessly shared between family members and friends. The critical difference between positive psychology and self-help or pop psychology is that it has been subjected to the possibility of being proven wrong by scientific research. As much as possible, I will attempt to ground this book in the ideas, theories, and practices that have withstood the test of modern science.

2. *When questions have not been fully tested, critical thinking will be used to apply psychological theories that have been tested or broadly supported.*

Because human beings are so diverse and complex and because the time and funds for psychological research are limited, there are many important questions relevant for happiness and well-being that have not and probably will not be directly tested. For example, there is no direct experiment to tell you whether dating or marrying a particular person will make you happy or whether working at a particular job or going to a particular school will be best for you in the long run.

However, there are certain general principles that have been supported by research such as the value of acceptance and the dangers of contempt in romantic relationships that can serve as guides in making such a decision.[3] As another example, research has generally shown that married people are happier than single people in the United States. However, the level of happiness in a marriage depends on many factors that also need to be considered such as age, maturity, and matches in values and beliefs.

For many of the most important decisions we make, it may be necessary to think critically about a variety of scientific findings and theories to make a reasonably informed and satisfying choice. It is also often necessary to make decisions even when we are lacking important information or when there is a great deal of uncertainty. We will be covering the ways that psychology has begun to use a scientific approach to help us make difficult choices through critical thinking, moral decision-making, and what is now studied under the rubric of "wisdom."

3. *When certain questions may not be subject to experimental testing, every attempt will be made to identify the basic assumptions, values, and beliefs that underlie different answers.*

There are certain questions about human happiness and a life worth living that may be difficult or even impossible to address by the scientific method. Although new scientific techniques, such as functional neuroimaging, have made it possible to study the physiological bases of our thoughts and emotions in a way never before possible, there are still many topics that may be beyond the scope of science as we know it. Some examples are questions such as, "What does it mean to be conscious?", "Is there a God or a supreme being?", and "What is the ultimate meaning of life?"

When considering these kinds of questions, my approach will be to be as clear as possible about how our responses may be informed by our basic assumptions, values, and beliefs. As another example, while science can help us determine how we make decisions about what is morally right and wrong, it may not actually tell us what is the most moral or just choice. These might be thought of as "value judgments" that depend more on our underlying beliefs and assumptions than something that can be determined by the scientific method.

4. *We can take a scientific approach to our own lives to see what works for us while trying to be aware of the expectations and biases that may affect our thinking.*

Here is where science can start to get really fun—and sometimes really challenging. I have already talked about the fact that there may be questions, problems, and dilemmas that are difficult to address by science. Part of the problem is that each of us is so unique in who we are and in the situations in which we find ourselves. Rather than go to graduate school and spend our careers trying to discover what generally makes most people happy, we can actually do case study experiments with ourselves to discover what makes *us* happy. We can learn to take a more critical approach to observing and analyzing our own life experience.

Just as Sherlock Holmes learned to use his mind to pay close attention to the details in solving a murder mystery, so can we learn to use our own powers of observation and critical thinking to discover what makes us most happy. This is where positive psychology has come into its own by offering a variety of exercises and activities that can serve as catalysts for improving our lives. But while we may know what generally works for most people, we do not know as much about when, where, and for whom it works best. Thus, I am going to give you many opportunities to do your own personal experiments and see what works for you.

In doing this, there are a couple of important cautions to keep in mind. First, there is the placebo effect. As you learn in any introductory psychology course, the placebo effect refers to the extent that the expectation of something good happening may explain why something good actually happens. You take a pill that you think is an aspirin and your headache gets better even though it was really only a sugar pill. If the placebo effect could explain part of why one of your personal experiments works, it will be important for you to pay attention to your expectations and compare the effects of different exercises for which you have similar expectations.

Second, there are a variety of cognitive biases that influence whether we think something is working for us or not. As the Nobel Prize winning psychologist Daniel Kahneman demonstrates in his best-selling book *Thinking, Fast and Slow*,[4] many of these biases evolved to help us make quick decisions but may get us into trouble when more reflection is required. For example, a *confirmation bias* is the tendency to interpret new evidence as the confirmation of our existing beliefs. If we already believe that money is important for happiness, then we may exaggerate any evidence we see for it and discount any evidence that we see against it. I will do my best to raise your awareness of these cognitive biases and give you ways to defend against them.

The Organization of This Book

Now that I have talked about how the scientific method will be our primary tool for understanding what may bring us the greatest happiness and fulfillment, I want to tell you how this book is organized to help make this possible for you. The chapters are organized into three parts that address the questions: (1) What can make us happy? (2) What can we do to become happier? and (3) How can we best use what we learn in the future?

In addressing the first question, I will not only present what we are learning about what makes us happy in the more superficial sense of feeling pleasure, but also in the sense of living a life that is meaningful, fulfilling, and worthwhile. In addition, I will not only talk about what makes people happy in general, but also how different things make different people happy. I will also give you questions that will help you identify the unique things that may make you most happy.

Can you think of a song that you really love? Whereas another person may listen to it one time and never want to hear it again, you may be able to listen over and over without getting tired of it. Part of what I want to help you do is to find that kind of song, sport, hobby, job, relationship, or activity that will consistently make you happy. The science of positive psychology has developed a variety of new tools to help you do just that. Once you get a better idea of what makes you happy, you can use the rest of the book to bring it more into your life and make it play a larger role in your life.

Thus, while the first part of the book is about what enables us to be most happy and fulfilled, the second and largest part of the book is about what you can do to move towards that kind of life. I will begin by framing the path to greater happiness as a kind of hero's journey to inspire and motivate you to learn about all the things that can help you. The idea is that achieving lasting happiness is like a journey that involves a call to adventure and facing many challenges just like our favorite fictional and real-life heroes.

Next, I will present an overview of the basic theories and approaches in psychology that we can use on our journey. These will include basic ways to change our thoughts and behavior such as those used in cognitive and behavioral therapies and fundamental qualities that we all need every day such as mindfulness and resilience. Finally, I will present what we know about how to increase happiness under a comprehensive classification of human strengths that includes things like wisdom, creativity, courage, kindness, self-control, gratitude, hope, and humor.

The chapters about these strengths will focus on how and why these qualities may be important for happiness and what we can do to increase them and put them into practice. They will include examples of the strengths in action in the lives of famous people, fictional heroes, and people like you. Think about the people that you love, look up to, and admire the most. These may be some of the best examples for you in your own journey towards a happier and more satisfying life.

The final part of the book will include the last chapter and several appendices designed to enable you to best use what you have learned in the future. The focus will be on enabling you to continue your journey to happiness and making the most of your life. This will include ways to remember and remind yourself about what you have learned and also ways to continue to learn and grow in your own hero's journey in the future.

The last chapter will also help you identify ways that you might use your own path to benefit those you care about and find ways to make a difference in your larger community and the world. The aim is to enable you to make happiness a "win-win" proposition where both you and those around you benefit. As opposed to the vicious cycle we often hear about where bad things beget bad results, the goal is to create a virtuous cycle where finding happiness in contributing to the well-being of others also comes back to make your life better.

Using Books and Movies

What else can help you on the road to greater happiness? Appendix A contains a list of books that I have found to be particularly useful for a variety of people. Included are books by authors closely associated with the positive psychology movement begun by Martin Seligman in 1998. There are also books written before 1998 or which have not been directly associated with the positive psychology movement. A prime example is the classic *Man's Search for Meaning*[5] by the German psychiatrist Viktor Frankl, which was in one poll voted the best "positive psychology" book. Although this book was originally written in 1946, it is directly relevant to positive psychology in enabling people to lead lives that can be meaningful and fulfilling even in the midst of great stress and trauma.

Appendix B has a list of TED Talks that are also relevant for specific chapters and topics. TED Talks are brief talks by people who discuss "ideas worth spreading" that can be watched online. I have found TED Talks to be particularly useful in understanding positive psychology because many of the ideas are directly relevant for increasing human happiness and well-being. I would encourage you to try to listen to at least one TED Talk for each chapter or topic you find interesting and feel free to search the Internet for more.

Appendix C has a list of movies that I have found to be useful to show students which illustrate the idea of "the hero's journey" that is central to this book. This list is only suggestive and in no way intended to be exhaustive. Ryan Niemiec and Danny Wedding have written an excellent book that provides thorough reviews of the many movies that may illustrate different aspects of positive psychology.[6]

Using Personal Exercises

One of the most important goals of positive psychology has been to identify activities that can be catalysts for positive change and a happier life. The idea is to find things that are simple and small but are so enjoyable and rewarding that they become a habit and eventually lead to a happier way of life. These have included specific and practical ways to increase things like gratitude and hope that lead to greater happiness, better relationships, and a more meaningful and fulfilling life.

Most of these activities have been tested in research and all have a strong foundation in psychological theory. In Chapters 7-13, when I talk about the strengths that can bring us a better life, there are specific suggestions for building them and putting them into practice. Several examples are provided so you can try the ones that appeal to you the most and that you think will work best for you.

Appendix D contains 14 exercises that have come to be the best weekly assignments in my positive psychology class. They have been refined and highly rated by students and have been designed as a logical progression to complete during the semester. You may want to read the whole book first or pick and choose which of the exercises you want to try first. Alternately, you could read a chapter a week and do the exercises in order which would reflect the experience of the class and be a 98-day plan to increase your happiness and well-being.

When I was growing up, I often had to make a choice about whether to watch or to play football on Sunday afternoon. I almost always chose to go outside and play because it was usually a lot more fun and I could play an active role in determining the outcome. When I teach positive psychology, I like to say that it is much more of a participatory sport compared to other classes that are more like spectator sports. The best way to learn about positive psychology is not to sit passively reading or listening to someone lecture, but to dare to do something different and see what effect it has on you. So I would strongly encourage you to try as many of the exercises and activities as you can.

And now, finally, back to that call to adventure. I would remind you of the call to adventure in the well-known stories of *Harry Potter, The Lord of the Rings, Star Wars,* and *Wonder Woman.* In each of these stories, the main characters were called to fight against the powers of darkness and fight for the things that bring us joy, happiness, love, and a better world. The call to adventure in the book is not unlike these calls and the challenges that we face can sometimes be just as frightening—but also just as rewarding.

As a child or even as an adult, you may have sometimes longed for the great gifts or magical powers of your favorite fictional heroes. But here the "force" is not fictional and the power is not magic—but the very real power of science. Not the power to create weapons and destroy, but the power of science as it is now being brought to bear on bringing us happiness and is both true and lasting. What might be possible if we—if you—answer the call in seeing and exploring what this new focus in science can offer to you. You may never go to *Hogwarts* or become a Jedi warrior, but this may be the chance for something even better.

Chapter 2

The Foundations of Positive Psychology

When I turned five, I decided not to whine anymore.
That was the hardest thing I've ever done.
And if I can stop whining, you can stop being such a grouch.

—*Nikki Seligman*[1]

In the last chapter, I invited you to respond to a new call to adventure: the call to the adventure of discovering how science may help us move towards a better life. I talked about how this adventure may be not so unlike the kind of adventures that we love to see and hear and read about. In many of our favorite stories, there is a character who serves as a great teacher or mentor. Dumbledore in *Harry Potter*, Gandalf in *The Lord of the Rings*, Yoda or Obi-Wan in *Star Wars*—you name it. These are the ones who offer us the wisdom we need to make the journey.

Where can we find the wisdom that we need to make our journey to happiness and making the most of our lives? Who can help us deal with the kind of temptations that the ring represented to Frodo so we won't get sidetracked? How can we learn to defend ourselves against, in the language of Harry Potter, the "dark arts" of our own cognitive biases? Couldn't psychology offer us at least a few simple Jedi mind tricks for the stormtroopers that we may face? Where can we find that mother Mary that Paul McCartney writes about in the *Beatle's* song *Let It Be,* who whispers the words of wisdom when we need them?

For many centuries, we humans have turned to various sources for the words of wisdom that help us make the most of our lives. Philosophy and religion have often tried to address some of the most challenging questions that we have faced as a species. History and literature have had much to say about how we can learn from our mistakes and use our imaginations to try to find the way to a better life. For many of us rely primarily on the knowledge and experience of our family members and friends to help us negotiate the twists, turns, and forks in the roads of our lives.

As we discovered in the last chapter, only recently has science begun to be fully applied to some of our most important questions about how to live a better life. The positive psychology movement that began in 1998 is a new and concerted effort to use the scientific method to enable us to live our lives with greater joy, happiness, meaning, and fulfillment. When applied to this goal, science may be a rich new source of wisdom, because it enables us to test and refine our ideas and theories about how to find happiness and best live our lives.

In this chapter, I will go into depth about how the positive psychology movement has evolved, expand on the definition of positive psychology as being distinct from the movement itself, and clarify what positive psychology is not in order to avoid the most common problems in studying it. My goal is to demonstrate how positive psychology may become a rich new source of the kind of wisdom we all seek and need. While we may never meet people who are exactly like the wisest teachers and mentors we learn about in our favorite stories, positive psychology may bring us closer to some of their wisdom and what they might have to say to us.

Background of the Positive Psychology Movement

I will return to pick up with the story of Martin Seligman and the beginning of the positive psychology movement in 1998, but first I want to set the context to help you to understand those who helped to lay the groundwork during the century before. At that time, there were a few rare psychologists who were interested in the best that was possible for human beings, but most were primarily concerned with how we go wrong and assumed that simply removing it would make everything right.

Even the *National Institute of Mental Health* was funding much more research on treating mental illness than finding ways to promote and enhance mental health and well-being. Some have joked that it might have been more appropriately named the *National Institutes of Mental Illness*. There was a *Diagnostic and Statistical Manual of Mental Disorders* that described all the ways that we can be mentally ill, but no comparable manual to describe mental health or all the things that can go right with us.

Most researchers who sought to study human beings at their best were like "voices crying in the wilderness" with little funding or support. Abraham Maslow was an outstanding exception with his focus on peak experiences and self-actualization.[2] Carl Rogers was another exception from the humanistic psychology movement who believed in the inherent potential of human beings to grow towards becoming what he called a "fully-functioning person."[3] Finally, even though she was originally trained in the Freudian tradition, Karen Horney wrote about the human striving to be an authentic person with great potential for growth and happiness.[4]

Although all psychological schools and theories probably have something to say about what could bring us a better life, the humanistic and existential traditions seemed to say the most that was relevant for the new positive psychology movement. Humanistic psychology had focused on the inherent growth potential of human beings towards an authentic and fulfilling life. Existential psychology had emphasized the importance of a sense of meaning in life and the value of confronting ultimate questions of life and death. However, both of these traditions had not consistently emphasized scientific research enough to influence the development of psychology as a whole.

However, by the end of the 20th century, there were many who began to do rigorous research on questions that were directly related to human happiness and optimal functioning. Ed Diener had studied happiness as what he called "subjective well-being."[5] Carol Ryff had developed a measure of psychological well-being that included a variety of components of positive psychological functioning.[6] Mihaly Csikszentmihalyi had done research identifying an experience that he called "flow," which occurs when people are absorbed in a challenging task.[7] Albert Bandura had identified what he called "self-efficacy," which he defined as the belief that you can accomplish a specific goal.[8]

There were also those whose work expanded beyond the simple idea that humans' only goals are to seek pleasure and avoid pain. From an existential perspective, Viktor Frankl wrote about the human tendency to seek meaning and developed a therapy to help people do it.[9] Ken Pargament used the latest research methods to study religion and spirituality as ways to seek what is most sacred and significant in life.[10] Jon Kabat-Zinn developed an intervention that uses the ancient practice of mindfulness to bring healing to people who could not find help with Western medicine.[11]

One of the critical theoretical advances that laid the foundation for the positive psychology movement was making a distinction between positive and negative emotions. David Watson helped to show that rather than being opposite sides of the same coin, positive emotions such as joy and happiness may exist on a separate continuum from negative emotions such as fear and sadness.[12] Thus, having few bad feelings may not mean that you are having lots of good feelings. In other words, it is possible that you may not be anxious or depressed but that you still may not experience much joy, happiness, meaning, or fulfillment in your life.

It might also mean that even if you are experiencing some anxiety and depression, that doesn't necessarily mean you won't also be able to experience some meaning and joy. This can be true of some of the greatest challenges and stresses that we face in life such as going to college, being in a long-term relationship, or having a child. Both may sometimes bring feelings of fear or sadness. At the same time, they may also bring us some of the greatest and most lasting feelings of joy and satisfaction and the sense that life is worth living. While psychology had primarily focused on reducing negative emotions, there had been very little emphasis on how to increase positive emotions.

Founding of the Positive Psychology Movement

All of this was background for when Martin Seligman was elected president of the American Psychological Association in 1998. Aside from the rare exceptions noted above, the primary focus in psychology had been on removing the negative and getting rid of what might be wrong with us. This had even been true in Seligman's career as he had focused on understanding and treating depression. He had studied "learned helplessness" in dogs as a model for understanding how human beings may get and stay depressed.[13] He did experiments where dogs could not get food after repeatedly trying and would end up looking and acting much like depressed humans.

So by the time Seligman was elected president, he was trying to think about what to emphasize and focus on during his tenure. He decided on what he called "positive psychology" to balance the tendency in psychology to focus so much on the negative. In 2000, he wrote an article in the *American Psychologist* with Mihaly Csikszentmihalyi that was titled *Positive Psychology: An Introduction*. In this article, he told the story of the event that may have had the strongest influence in getting him to switch his focus from the negative to the positive:

> The moment took place in my garden while I was weeding with my five-year-old daughter, Nikki. I

have to confess that even though I write books about children, I'm really not all that good with children. I am goal oriented and time urgent, and when I'm weeding in the garden, I'm actually trying to get the weeding done. Nikki, however, was throwing weeds into the air, singing, and dancing around. I yelled at her. She walked away, then came back and said, 'Daddy, I want to talk to you.' 'Yes, Nikki?' 'Daddy, do you remember before my fifth birthday? From the time I was three to the time I was five, I was a whiner. I whined every day. When I turned five, I decided not to whine anymore. That was the hardest thing I've ever done. And if I can stop whining, you can stop being such a grouch (p. 5-6)'.[14]

Whisper words of wisdom—right out of the mouths of babes! After this, Seligman admitted to himself that he had been a grouch and a dark cloud in a house full of sunshine. He resolved to change. But most important for psychology, he noticed that Nikki was able to correct what was wrong herself and that he had missed the beautiful strengths that he now resolved to nurture. He decided to use the influence of his presidency to begin what became the positive psychology movement.

In his later book, *Flourish*, Seligman tells the story of the initial funding he received to do the kind of positive psychology research that he envisioned.[15] As the story is told, he began receiving checks from an anonymous foundation who had heard of his renown and wanted him to do research that made some kind of a positive difference. And, as if it was from a spy novel, the lawyers of the foundation said that if he revealed the identity of the foundation then he would no longer get any funding from them.

After receiving an additional check for $120,000, he mentioned to them that he had an idea to use the money for something that he was starting to call "positive psychology." After explaining what he meant and writing a three-page proposal, he soon received a check for $1.5 million! In the absence of money from large illness-focused funders such as the *National Institute of Mental Health*, this funding helped the positive psychology movement get off to a good start in supporting some of his own research. He also made some of these initial funds available to other promising researchers.

Evolution of the Positive Psychology Movement

During the early years of the positive psychology movement, Seligman used his influence and funding to bring together a growing group of well-established and promising new psychology researchers. These included those who had already been doing research on happiness such as Ed Diener,[16] optimal functioning such as Mihaly Csikszentmiyali,[17] and hope such as Rick Snyder.[18] He also recruited Christopher Peterson to spearhead a large project to identify the kind of human virtues and strengths that may increase happiness and well-being.

Peterson worked together with a large group of social scientists to develop what became known by some as the "Un-DSM." DSM stands for the *Diagnostic and Statistical Manual of Mental Disorders* which has long been the standard for abnormal psychology and psychiatry. The Un-DSM was published in 2004 and titled *Character Strengths and Virtues: A Handbook and Classification* with Peterson and Seligman as the editors.[19] It included chapters on 24 human strengths grouped under the six virtues of wisdom, courage, humanity, justice, temperance, and transcendence. This became the definitive description of human strengths and what can go right with people and enable them to function at their best.

Seligman and this growing group of senior psychologists and social scientists also used their funding to attract and reward young researchers. Barbara Fredrickson and Sonja Lyubomirsky were two of these early recruits who have become significant leaders in the positive psychology movement. Fredrickson has developed an influential new theory about why humans evolved to have positive emotions and the functions that positive emotions may serve.[20] Lyubomirsky has identified a variety of ways to increase happiness and begun to determine how their effects may vary for different kinds of people.[21]

Others who had already been doing work relevant for understanding what makes life worth living began to join the movement. Robert Emmons had pioneered the study of the familiar but taken for granted human quality of gratitude. He developed and tested various ways to increase gratitude and studied their effects.[22] Michael McCullough began to study the effects of forgiveness and to find ways to increase it in those who had been hurt by other people.[23] Both gratitude and forgiveness were human strengths that had been frequently emphasized in religion, philosophy, and literature, but largely neglected in psychology.

Along with this growing community of researchers, there have been a number of accomplishments marking the growth and success of the positive psychology movement. First, several new scientific journals were begun that focused on happiness and well-being including *The Journal of Positive Psychology*. Second, many of the most prominent researchers in the positive psychology movement wrote books to make their research more accessible to the general public. Third, several national and international associations, including the *International Positive Psychology Association* (IPPA), were created to foster the sharing of positive psychology research, theory, and applications.

In addition to building an international community of researchers, the positive psychology movement has found many applications with counselors, health practitioners, education, sports, business, and government. The movement has begun to provide some of the much needed science for the growing profession of personal coaching. Positive psychology has found a natural place in organizational settings because of its goal of enabling people to function at their best. Positive psychology has also played a role in getting some local and national governments to focus more on increasing happiness rather than monetary growth alone.

Along with this progress in the development of the positive psychology movement, there have been several who have cautioned against the dangers of a superficial focus on the positive and neglecting the negative. Paul Wong called for a *Positive Psychology 2.0* which would focus more on meaning than happiness and do a better job of balancing an understanding of positive and negative emotions and experiences.[24] Itai Ivtzan is the lead author on a book titled *Second Wave Positive Psychology* which argues for a greater emphasis on how difficult and painful experiences may play a role in human transformation and fulfillment.[25]

Since the birth of the positive psychology movement, there have also been many parallel developments that mirror the goals of the positive psychology movement, even if they have not been directly tied to it. One of the most important examples is the growth of interest and research into mindfulness as written about and taught by Jon Kabat-Zinn.[26] Both the ability to be mindful as he defines it, and the Mindfulness-Based Stress Reduction (MBSR) intervention he developed, have had strong implications for enabling people to live with greater joy, meaning, and fulfillment.

Other parallel developments include the growing interest in lovingkindness and compassion meditations and what has often been referred to as mindfulness- and acceptance-based psychological interventions. The *Greater Good Science Center* in

Berkeley, California is an example of a research center devoted to the study of compassion and altruistic behavior. Mindfulness- and acceptance-based therapies such as Mindfulness-Based Cognitive Therapy, Dialectical Behavioral Therapy, and Acceptance and Commitment Therapy balance the Western emphasis on control with a more Eastern focus on acceptance, and all have potential for increasing meaning and fulfillment.

Since Martin Seligman first challenged psychology to focus on what it had long neglected, the positive psychology movement has begun to accomplish many of its goals. First, it has refined the definition of what human beings value as not just avoiding pain and suffering, but as also seeking joy, happiness, meaning, and fulfillment. Second, it has provided a new language for identifying and studying the human qualities and strengths that can help us all move forward towards to better lives. Third, and most important, it has made it much more acceptable to bring the full power of science to answer the kind of questions that may be important for living life to the fullest.

Finally, there have been a couple of persistent questions about the future of the positive psychology movement. First, how well has the positive psychology movement served its purpose in bringing the rest of psychology to focus on human beings at their best? Second, will the movement continue to exist as a separate entity or subarea within psychology, or will it fade away as it is integrated into the rest of psychology? One thing is very likely: the kinds of questions about what makes life worth living will probably continue to be asked by people all over the world and by people like you and me.

Beyond the Positive Psychology Movement

Now that we have a better idea of the background and evolution of the positive psychology movement, I want to define what I will mean by positive psychology as distinct from the positive psychology movement. Chris Peterson wrote a book called

Pursuing the Good Life filled with reflections on positive psychology.[27] In it, there is a chapter titled: *"Is Positive Psychology Bullshit?"* His answer is particularly useful in distinguishing between positive psychology and the positive psychology movement—as well as with popular psychology and self-help:

> Positive psychology is an umbrella term that organizes the work of those of us who have heeded the recommendation to study scientifically what makes life worth living. Specific examples of positive psychology theory, research, and practice can be good or bad or ugly, just like anything else. The umbrella cannot be bullshit (p. 23).[28]

He goes on to say that someone who identifies as a positive psychologist could be "full of it" because what they say may be based on bullshit and not good scientific theory or research.

Peterson's words point to the necessity of making a distinction between two primary ways that people talk about positive psychology. First, the term "positive psychology" was originally intended to be just such an umbrella term to include all of the attempts to scientifically study what brings us joy, happiness, meaning, and fulfillment—or in Peterson's words "what makes life worth living." Second, people often use the term "positive psychology" to refer to people who identify with the positive psychology movement or specific writing or research findings by people who are a part of the movement. I will continue to use the term "positive psychology" to refer to the first and the term "positive psychology movement" to refer to specific people and research associated with the movement.

The confusion between these two meanings of positive psychology is very common in the media and has been the source of countless arguments and misunderstandings. Many people criticize "positive psychology" because they associate it with positive thinking, unrealistic optimism, or those who smile all the time and may annoy others by being ungodly cheerful early in the morning. There have been researchers associated with the positive psychology movement who have presented findings about the need to experience a certain ratio of positive to negative emotions which were later challenged as using poor research methods. Positive psychology, in the primary sense that I am using it, is not a statement of beliefs about what should make us happy, it is the application of the best methods of modern science to discover what actually does make us happy.

The Full Definition of Positive Psychology

Now that I have tried to make a distinction between positive psychology and the positive psychology movement, I want to expand on the definition that I gave in the last chapter. There I wrote that positive psychology is the application of the scientific method to enable us to make the most of our lives and live them to the fullest. This definition is an attempt to integrate the full range of definitions that different people both within and outside of the positive psychology movement have offered.

These have included things like "positive psychology is the science of happiness," "the science of what makes life worth living," and "the science of optimal human functioning." This includes a focus on the subjective experience of feeling pleasure or being happy, the meaningful experiences of helping others and trying to be a good person, and the ability to function at the highest level that is possible for us.

The common thread among most definitions of positive psychology has been using the scientific method to enable all human beings to better live the kind of life that they most desire and that may be best for them. This includes bringing us the things that we most seek for their own sake, such as happiness, joy, meaning, good relationships, and fulfillment. When I use the phrase "to make the most of our lives and live them to the fullest", I am trying to capture all of the things that express what it is that we most seek in our lives and what are our greatest and most authentic and enduring longings and desires.

With this all in mind as a background, I would like to offer the expanded and full definition of positive psychology that I am using and focusing on in this book:

> Positive psychology is the application of the scientific method to enable us to make the most of our lives and live them to the fullest. This means to move towards the kind of things that we seek most for their own sake such as joy, happiness, meaning, and fulfillment. This also includes experiencing happiness, being a good person in relation to others, and functioning or being at our best.

While the positive psychology movement includes all of the efforts of people to do this in response to Seligman's call in 1998, positive psychology itself is—as Chris Peterson wrote—the umbrella or overarching term for all of the efforts to do this both before and after the movement began.

What Positive Psychology Is Not

The final thing I want to do in this chapter is to be clear about what positive psychology is not. I do this in order to help avoid some of the most common problems and misunderstandings in learning and talking about positive psychology.

1. *Positive psychology is not the avoidance of the negative.*

One of the greatest causes for confusion in understanding positive psychology may be simply due to the use of the word "positive." Martin Seligman and others have struggled with whether it is best word to use and have largely decided to keep it because its advantages may outweigh its disadvantages, and no one has yet been able to find a better alternative. The word "positive" has had the advantage of getting psychology to focus more on the positive emotions and experiences that have been neglected in light of the strong focus on negative emotions and experience. However, the word positive was not intended to mean that psychology should focus only on the positive at the expense of the negative.

During one my classes, I asked a former student to suddenly appear in class dressed as Darth Vader to question whether positive psychology meant the denial of everything bad, harmful, or negative in life. The word positive is not meant to imply the avoidance of the negative, but to be sure to bring science to the task of enabling people to move in a positive or beneficial direction. As I saw in the first positive psychology class I taught and have seen in every subsequent class, the efforts of science to enable us to live with the greatest joy, meaning, and fulfillment often mean confronting the stresses and traumas that we face—which is anything but avoidance or denial.

2. *Positive psychology is not just about superficial happiness.*

Another danger of learning about positive psychology is that it may be equated with what has been called "happiology," or which refers to only seeking pleasure or superficial forms of happiness. The explosion of books about happiness since the dawn of the positive psychology movement has made it difficult to prevent this from happening. The temptation is to only focus on things like pleasure and positive emotions rather than meaning, purpose, and making life worth living.

Martin Seligman himself has tried to counter this by continuing to develop a theory of the good life as not just involving pleasure but also other things such as engagement, good relationships, meaning, and accomplishment. The development of the classification of character strengths and virtues by Peterson and Seligman has also helped because it emphasizes human strengths that not only make people happy but also benefit others and improve community life.

3. *Positive psychology is not just common sense.*

Because common sense often addresses questions related to happiness and well-being, it may be easy to mistake positive psychology for just plain common sense or what we learned in kindergarten or Sunday school. When it focuses on everyday human thought and behavior, all of psychology is in danger of doing research that could all too easily be published in the *"Journal of Completely Obvious Results."* It is true that some of the consistent findings from positive psychology research have supported the benefits of commonly valued attitudes and behaviors such as kindness, gratitude, humor, and forgiveness. However, it is also true that much of the common sense we take for granted is confusing and contradictory and its effectiveness depends on personal and situational factors that we do not understand very well.

One of the most common and dangerous cognitive biases we fall into is something called "selective exposure." This is where we only expose ourselves to the people and beliefs that are comfortable and familiar and are not even aware how much we avoid different points of view. For example, Western culture is pervaded with the idea that money can buy happiness and people who question this may be met with great disbelief or even avoided. Using the language of the *Harry Potter* books, the "defense against the dark art" of selective exposure is choosing to expose ourselves to people and beliefs that we are not comfortable or familiar with. The use of the scientific method in positive psychology is a wonderful tool for doing this as it enables us to put our cherished beliefs to the test against ideas we may have been much less aware of or open to.

4. *Positive psychology is not only for those already doing well.*

Because positive psychology focuses on making the most of our lives, some have assumed that it is only for certain kinds of people—those who are already happy, rich, talented, or functioning at a high level. Shawn Achor gives a humorous and insightful TED Talk about positive psychology where he presents the bell curve as representing a full range of human happiness and success.[29] The bell curve is sometimes used by positive psychology teachers to illustrate how psychology had previously only focused on the middle or left of the curve and neglected the right side, which is the side that represents the people who are happiest or functioning at their best.

It is, however, critical to understand that positive psychology does not just focus on people who are already near or at the top of their game. It is just as important for those who are poor, struggling, sick, or stressed out because for them happiness is often an even greater challenge. Many times in teaching positive psychology, I have seen the greatest benefits for students who were struggling with an illness, a loss, or other major life crisis. So, when picturing a bell curve, think about it representing all the possibilities of your own behavior with positive psychology as having the goal of enabling you to move toward the end that represents you at your best.

5. *Positive psychology is not only for optimists.*

In the 1999 movie *South Park: Bigger, Longer, and Uncut*, there is a little French boy who embodies the stereotype of the gloomy existentialist who is cynical and pessimistic about everything in life. Despite this exaggerated character, there are many who take great comfort in never expecting or being open to anything really good happening. For many, it is much easier to be the critic who puts down the attempts of others to be happy rather than be willing to take a chance and see if something new works for them. "Defensive pessimism" is the name for when people choose to have low expectations about the future because it prevents them from having to be disappointed. But while it may prevent disappointment, it may also keep them from taking a risk and doing something that might bring lasting happiness and well-being.

I have come across many students who have been wary of positive psychology because they thought they may be rejected by their more pessimistic and cynical friends and family members. Being open to positive psychology requires a special kind of courage and willingness to seem uncool to those who are cynical and doubt the possibility of a better life. The TV show *Breaking Bad* is one example of how it may in some ways seem cool in our culture to be bad and rather uncool to be good. While there are many examples of breaking bad in our culture, many of the founders and people who have benefited the most from positive psychology have been anything but naïve optimists and have pointed the way to a whole new form of cool.

Positive Psychology as a Way Forward

I began this chapter by asking how we might respond to the new call to adventure presented to us by positive psychology. I mentioned the kind of teachers and mentors in our stories that often share the words of wisdom that our favorite characters need in order to move forward in their challenging journey.

In this chapter, I tried to present the story of a new movement within psychology for using what may be the most powerful method we have for addressing the most important questions we face. I talked about how the positive psychology movement evolved out of some voices crying in the wilderness into a growing community of researchers who have been trying to help us find our way to a life of greater happiness. Finally, I talked about how the aim of positive psychology transcends the movement and provided some defenses against common misunderstandings about it.

What is positive psychology? It is science's answer to the question of how to make the most of our lives and live them to the fullest. It may be our best hope for finding the kind of wisdom embodied in the Yodas and Dumbledores of our greatest stories. Where psychology was once so stuck on fixing what was wrong with a small minority of us, it is now poised to help us all on our journey towards whatever may be our own unique "holy grail." My goal of the next two chapters is to help you begin to understand and identify for yourself just what that may be.

Chapter 3

The Scientific Pursuit of Happiness

Happiness is not out there for us to find.
The reason that it's not out there is that it's inside us.

—Sonja Lyubomirsky[1]

Before there was the offbeat movie *Monty Python and the Holy Grail*, there was the legend of the Holy Grail. The Holy Grail was the cup used by Jesus at the Last Supper and the quests to find it by medieval knights are the stuff of Arthurian tales. Over time, the "holy grail" became a symbol for that one thing that is most sincerely and intensely pursued. It is something that you want very much but is very hard to get.

Sonja Lyubomirsky is one of the leaders of the positive psychology movement who has done pioneering research on the study of happiness and written books including *The How of Happiness* and *The Myths of Happiness*. In the introduction to former, she writes about happiness and the Holy Grail:

> Happiness, in my humble opinion, is the Holy Grail, 'the meaning and purpose of life,' as Aristotle famously said, 'the whole aim and end of human existence' (p. 2).[2]

But just what is happiness and is it the same for everyone? And perhaps most important, what are the things that make us happy and how much is it possible to find, achieve, or increase them?

What Is Happiness?

One way to begin to answer this question is to think of the things that bring us happiness. Take a minute and try to answer this question for yourself. You might think of a time or place in your life when you were particularly happy. You might think of some of the best times you have had with some of your favorite people or when you have accomplished something important to you. You might think of eating at your favorite restaurant or enjoying your favorite music or when you were doing something that you love. What was it about these things that led you to say that you were happy?

Ed Diener has been nicknamed "Dr. Happiness" because of all the research he has done to understand happiness around the world and the factors related to it. Diener calls happiness "subjective well-being" which he views as a person's cognitive and affective evaluations of their lives.[3] He thinks that subjective well-being involves three different things: relatively high levels of positive or pleasurable emotions, relatively low levels of negative or painful emotions, and the judgment that one is satisfied with their life. Were these some of the kinds of things you were experiencing when doing the things that made you happy?

If you thought about experiencing pleasure and other positive emotions such as joy, love, interest, and contentment, then you are not alone. The association of positive emotions with what we mean by happiness is probably the strongest and most common component of most definitions of happiness. Yet before the positive psychology movement, positive emotions were much less studied and well understood than the negative emotion component that Diener thinks is also an important part of happiness. Part of the reason for this is probably that people assumed that positive emotions were just the lack of negative emotions but part of it may also be the way we evolved to pay more attention to all things negative.

What Is the Negativity Bias?

Just after the dawn of the positive psychology movement, Roy Baumeister and his colleagues published a review paper titled *Bad is Stronger than Good* where they presented evidence that humans have evolved to have what they called a "negativity bias."[4] This is the idea that negative thoughts, emotions, and experiences have a stronger effect on us than neutral or positive things. We may have evolved to pay more attention to negative emotions and experiences because they may signal threats to our lives. If we don't pay attention to something positive we may get another chance, but if we don't see the tiger or snake in the grass we may not.

We can see this negativity bias expressed in many different area of our lives. If we see ten faces in a crowd and all but one angry face is smiling at us, it is no surprise which one we will pay the most attention to. Research with couples has shown that it may be important to have many more positive interactions to offset the potential damage done by one negative interaction. Research on decision-making has shown that potential costs are more heavily weighed than potential benefits. The news media may get more attention and higher ratings if they do stories about the worst things that people do rather than the best. Psychology researchers may pay much more attention to avoiding mental illness than enabling people to experience mental health and live their lives to the fullest.

Robert Sapolsky wrote a book with the creative title *Why Zebras Don't Get Ulcers* that sheds light on why this negatively bias is a problem.[5] In short, the reason that zebras don't get ulcers is that their stress response systems have evolved to deal with the stressors that they still experience—like running away from lions! The reason that we humans do get ulcers is that our stress response systems overreact to small things that are not life threatening and our negativity bias exaggerates this response. The initial "fight-or-flight" response that we can have to a traffic jam or computer crash can provoke the same physiological response as that zebra getting ready to run away from a lion. When the negativity bias combines with our tendency to react physically to small stuff that goes wrong, this produces the wear and tear on our bodies that causes chronic illness and can lead to an early death.

The other reason that the negativity bias can be such a problem is that it keeps us from seeing and experiencing so much of what could make us happy. One of the main reasons that people may get depressed is that they focus too much on what is wrong with their lives and the potential consequences. The cognitive therapies developed by Aaron Beck and Albert Ellis are designed to enable people to see their lives as a more realistic and rational balance between the positive and negative.[6-7] The movie *It's a Wonderful Life* is not so much about a change in circumstances as it is about the changed perspective that enables George Bailey to see that, despite the negative around him, he really does have a wonderful life.

The human tendency to pay more attention to the negative can also help us understand why it was so important for Martin Seligman to start a positive psychology movement. And, as you will see, one goal of the movement has been to find simple and effective ways to counter this bias by increasing our focus on positive emotions and experiences. Seligman experienced this himself the day he was confronted by his young daughter in their garden. All it took was for her to tell him to stop being such a grouch and he knew then and there that he needed to change.

There are many who are beginning to write books that are shedding new light on the effects of our negativity bias and the potential ways we may overcome it. Steven Pinker wrote a comprehensive review of the history of human violence providing evidence that it is has greatly *declined* over the past several hundred years.[8] He titled the book *The Better Angels of Our Nature* after the words Abraham Lincoln used to help reunite his country. Cultivating these angels could be thought of as a primary goal of positive psychology. In support of the notion of a negativity bias, Pinker argues that one reason we may not see this reduction is the tendency of the news media to only report the worst.

Rick Hanson has written a useful book that both acknowledges the destructive effects of the negativity bias and also provides practical ways to reduce it.[9] He expresses this bias in saying that our brains are like Velcro for negative experiences and like Teflon for positive ones. The book is titled *Hardwiring Happiness* because he is trying to help us break some of our hardwired bias to the negative with a new openness to and embrace of positive experiences and emotions. He uses the simple acronym HEAL to encourage people to do this by Having positive experiences, Enriching them, Absorbing them, and then Linking positive and negative material.

What Good Are Positive Emotions?

Now that we have a better idea of why we have focused so little on the positive emotions that are at the core of what most of us define as happiness, it is time to understand why they may be important. Did you ever think about why we may have evolved to have emotions like joy, love, interest, and contentment? It may be easier to understand how many of our negative emotions, such as anger, fear, and sadness, may have enabled us to survive long enough to pass on our genes. Anger empowers us to fight and reach our goals. Fear helps us react to a threat or motivate us to avoid it. Sadness can show others we are hurting or give us the time we need to rest and heal. But why do we have positive emotions?

The most influential and well-supported answer to this question arose directly from one of the early leaders of the positive psychology movement. Barbara Fredrickson had worked with some of the top emotion researchers in the world including Robert Levenson, Richard Lazarus, and Paul Ekman. Among Ekman's many accomplishments, he did cross-cultural research demonstrating that people around the world can recognize the facial expression of six basic emotions of anger, disgust, fear, happiness, sadness, and surprise. Notice that only four are clearly negative and only one is clearly positive—again reflecting a negativity bias in human evolution or at least in psychological research.

Out of her early experience with these top researchers and curiosity about why we have positive emotions, Fredrickson developed what she called the "broaden-and-build theory" about the evolution and function of positive emotions.[10] While negative emotions serve the more immediate survival need of dealing with a threat, she has argued that positive emotions may, over a longer period of time, broaden and build the kinds of skills and resources that may enhance our survival. Whereas negative emotions narrow our thoughts and actions to dealing with one specific immediate threat, positive emotions increase the adaptive thoughts and actions that can come to mind during a future threat.

The broaden hypothesis specifically states that one function of positive emotions is to widen the selection of possible thoughts and actions that spontaneously come to mind when faced with a challenge in the future. Both Fredrickson and Alice Isen have presented a variety of experimental evidence supporting this hypothesis. Isen's research consistently shows that people think in more flexible and creative ways after being induced to experience positive emotions.[11] Fredrickson and Christine Branigan have shown research participants short clips to induce either positive or negative emotions and found that those induced to have positive emotions thought of more things to do than those induced to have negative emotions.[12]

The build hypothesis specifically states that the function of positive emotions is to spur the development of resources that can be used in the future and that can place people in positive trajectories of growth. Fredrickson and Shelly Gable have provided much evidence to support this hypothesis. Gable found that positive emotional exchanges between partners within close relationships predicted an increase in resources for better relationships.[13] In addition, Fredrickson found that the daily experiences of positive emotions predicted increases in resilience which in turn were related to greater satisfaction with life.[14]

Fredrickson also writes about how some of the primary positive emotions such as joy, interest, love, and contentment may have this effect.[15] You can probably think of ways that these emotions may help you learn to better deal with challenges in the future. Joy creates the urge to play, be creative, and push the limits. Interest initiates the urge to explore, try new things, and take in new information. Contentment moves us to sit back and savor which makes it possible for us to integrate what has been learned and experienced. Love, when experienced in a healthy relationship, motivate us to play, explore, and learn how to relate to others.

One common example of how these positive emotions may help us broaden and build our resources is through playing team sports. Being a part of a baseball, soccer, basketball, or football team as a child may help us build resources for coping with some of the stresses and challenges we may face in our adult life. Joy might motivate us to practice and play. Interest may drive us to learn all about the rules and possible ways to win. Contentment with having performed well might give us the time we need to savor our successes, recover our strength, and reflect on what we learned. Finally, having a positive connection and love for our teammates may enable us to learn and work together in ways that may help us win and be successful.

Does Happiness Cause Success?

The idea that positive emotions may broaden and build our resources for functioning better in the future raises questions about whether happiness may play a role in success. When thinking about the relationship between success and happiness, it is probably more common to think about success causing happiness rather than happiness causing success. We might think that the effects of winning a race on feeling joy might be greater than the effect of joy in enabling us to win a race. Established theories about goals and emotions propose that the emotion of happiness is a result of having reached a desired goal, which suggests that success would lead to happiness.

But what about the other way around? Do you think that being happy encourages us to relax and stop trying or that happiness is a motivator for trying harder and greater success in the future? The result of a 2005 review of 225 studies by Sonja Lyubomirsky, Ed Diener, and Laura King provides strong evidence that happiness frequently leads to success.[16] They focused on the relationship between happiness, especially measures of positive emotion, and a full range of indicators of success. They reviewed cross-sectional, longitudinal, and experimental studies showing that happy people were more likely to have good marriages and better relationships, higher incomes, better work performance, more community involvement, better health, and a longer life.

Why do you think that being happy may lead to success in all of these domains? The authors conclude that the most important reason may have been that they were higher in positive emotion and on the kinds of personal characteristics that it may promote. Further, they suggested that happiness may lead to a greater likelihood of approaching possibilities for success in the future and better reactions to negative emotions when they occur. Positive emotions may not only broaden and build resources for dealing with threats but also help us deal with a full range of challenges that increase the likelihood of success. Thus, while happiness may be an end goal and reward in itself, it may also be a means to the end of successfully accomplishing our goals.

What Makes Us Happy?

If happiness not only feels good but also leads to success in the future, then what causes it and what can we do to make ourselves happy? How much is happiness something we are born with and determined by our genes? How much is it related to our environment and what happens around us? And how much is it something that we have control over and can change?

Sonja Lyubomirsky, Kennon Sheldon, and David Schkade wrote a review in 2005 called *Pursuing Happiness: The Architecture of Sustainable Change* where they addressed each of these questions by reviewing all of the past research on happiness and well-being.[17] They came up with estimates of how important three of the major determinants of happiness are, which has been sometimes referred to as the "happiness formula." The formula has been written as $H = S + C + V$ where H equals our enduring level of happiness, S equals our biological set point, C equals the conditions of our life, and V equals our voluntary activities. Thus, the idea is that our enduring level of happiness is generally determined by the combination of our biological set point, the conditions of our life, and voluntary activities over which we have control.

In addition, Lyubomirsky and her colleagues wanted to understand how important each of these three factors are, based on previous research, and tried to determine what percent of the total variation of our happiness may be accounted for by each. They estimated that our biological set point probably accounts for about 50% based on longitudinal twin studies of the stability of personality characteristics related to happiness. They estimated that the conditions of our life account for only about 10% when they considered studies of life circumstances such as age, gender, ethnicity, marital status, income, where we live, and our history of various life events. They estimated that the remaining 40% may be due to the voluntary and intentional activities that we engage in that can affect our happiness.

While Lyubomirsky undertook the valuable task of determining the relative importance of what makes us happy, these percentages are only general estimates that can be criticized on several grounds. First, the 50% for the genetic set point may be too large because it was determined by examining personality characteristics which are, by nature, stable over time. They may not have fully taken into account that our happiness levels may not be as stable as our personalities even if they are somewhat related. Second, the 10% for the conditions of our lives has been strongly criticized as being too little because it may not account for the greater variation of conditions that may be found when people with very poor social, economic, and health conditions are better represented in research. Third, these percentages are just general estimates and the actual percentage for individuals like you or I may be very different. For example, people who know more about voluntary activities that could change their level of happiness may have more control over it.

What Are the Factors Related to Happiness?

The *World Happiness Report* may be a good place to start in trying to understand this question.[18] It is a survey of global happiness published every year that ranks 155 countries by happiness levels and reports on factors related to happiness. In 2017, the top three countries were Norway, Denmark, and Iceland while the United States ranked 14th. On a ten point happiness scale, there was a difference of four points between the most and the least happy countries. Three quarters of the differences between these countries are accounted for by differences in gross domestic product per capita, healthy years of life expectancy, social support (having someone to count on in times of trouble), trust (in government and business), perceived freedom to make life decisions, and generosity (as measured by recent donations).

The United States and several other countries were studied to determine the importance of a similar group of factors in predicting life satisfaction. They examined the relative value of seven variables: income, gender, years of educations, employment, having a partner, physical illness, and mental illness. A partial correlation coefficient between 0.00 and 1.00 indicated the strength of the relationship when controlling for the other factors. A positive correlation meant that the factor was related to more life satisfaction and a negative correlation meant that it was related to less. They found that the factors having the strongest relationship with life satisfaction were having a partner (.34), not having a mental illness (-.21), and income (.16). There were much weaker correlations for female gender (.08), not having a physical illness (-.05), employment (.05), and years of education (.05).

This is consistent with research by Ed Diener and others over the past 25 years showing that although income is related to happiness, social relationships and mental health may be even more important. Both Diener and Chris Peterson have written about the fundamental role that close interpersonal relationships may play in happiness. In addition, Diener has argued that money may have a different relationship with life satisfaction (your judgment about how satisfied you are with your life) and the experience of positive emotions (how much you experience joy, love, interest, and contentment).[19] Although life satisfaction continues to increase from low to middle to high income, positive emotions increase from low to middle income but are about the same at high income as they are for people of middle income.

The other fascinating finding about the potential effect of money on happiness suggest that it may depend on how you spend it—in at least a couple of ways. First, the research of Ryan Howell suggests that you may get more happiness from your money by spending it on experiences, such as taking classes, going to concerts or movies, and traveling, rather than on buying possessions such as clothing, furniture, or a car.[20] The reasons may be that (1) we feel more alive after spending our money on experiences than on possessions, (2) experiences continue to provide happy memories while the value of possessions fade over time, and (3) experiences may serve to connect us more with other people than do possessions.

Second, the research of Elizabeth Dunn suggests that money may bring more happiness if you spend it on someone else rather than yourself.[21] First, she did a survey and found that the amount given to others was positively correlated with happiness. Next, she studied people at work and found that receiving bonuses did not predict later happiness unless part of the bonus was spent on someone else. Finally, she randomized people to either spend money on themselves or on another person. She found that spending money on others made them happier even though they predicted that spending money on themselves would make them happier.

The final issue that needs to be addressed in citing all of these statistics is the danger of generalization and the myths that it may create. The great majority of the research on happiness could be called nomothetic which involves trying to establish general relationships between variables by averaging across large samples of people. In contrast, what has been called an idiographic approach to research focuses more on the study of unique individuals and how a collection of influences may work together to produce each person's experience of happiness.

Focusing on specific individuals rather than averaging across everyone is particularly important in positive psychology because it aims to understand the best of what is possible for each of us rather than just determining the average.

Thus, we need to be careful that a small correlation based on a large sample will not be generalized to create hard and fast rules about what is necessary for happiness. For example, just because there may be a correlation between happiness and having a partner, it does not mean that you have to have a partner in order to be happy. Sonja Lyubomirsky tackles this kind of trap in her book *The Myths of Happiness*.[22] She presents evidence against common misconceptions that happiness requires finding the right partner, right job, or having money, and that you can't be happy if you lose your relationship, your health, or "never play shortstop for the New York Yankees." However life has treated you, it is important to see happiness research as a guide to identifying what may makes us happy, rather than the last word on whether or not we can be happy.

What Is the Hedonic Treadmill?

That being said, there is still one potential challenge to greater happiness that I have not yet identified. Regardless of how much the conditions of our lives may have to do with our happiness, they raise the same issue as does the idea of a biological set point: How much control do we have over whether we are happy or not? If at least part of the aim of positive psychology is to use the scientific method to enable us to be happier, then how much progress can we expect? We have seen that the happiness formula includes conditions over which we may have little control and a biological set point over which we may have even less control.

Our potential lack of control over our happiness has been highlighted in a challenging problem that was identified nearly 50 years ago. In 1971, Philip Brickman and Donald Campbell described what has come to be known as the "hedonic treadmill."[23] The hedonic treadmill is the idea that our level of happiness returns to a pre-established set point after we rise or fall in our accomplishments or possessions, or after we experience other positive or negative events. The idea is that after having something good happen, such as getting a raise, we will be happier for a few months but will soon return to our happiness set point where we were before we got the raise. Similarly, after having something bad happen such as a stock market crash, we may be less happy for a while but will soon return to our previous level of happiness.

In 1978, Brickman and his colleagues Dan Coates and Ronnie Janoff-Bulman presented evidence to support this theory.[24] They found that, over time, lottery winners were not happier than non-winners and that people with paraplegia (who have lost the feeling and use of their legs) were not much less happy than people who could walk. The lottery winners also took significantly less pleasure from common everyday events than non-winners. Other researchers have found that good and bad life events generally only affect happiness if they occurred in the past few months and that even the most negative emotional reactions usually subside with time.

In 2006, Ed Diener, Richard Lucas, and Christie Scollon wrote a review for the *American Psychologist* titled *Beyond the Hedonic Treadmill: Revising the Adaptation Theory of Well-Being.*[25] They presented a variety of evidence from recent, larger, and well-designed studies which demonstrate that individuals may vary in their own set points and levels of adaptation. They also argued that the adaptation that occurs is most often in the positive direction after a negative event because people generally report themselves to be happy. Most important for positive psychology, they argued that we can change our previous level of happiness by engaging in the "voluntary and intentional activities" that are highlighted in the happiness formula.

How Can We Beat the Hedonic Treadmill?

What are the things we can do to raise our biological set point and counter the effects of negative conditions and circumstances? What can we do to beat the hedonic treadmill and raise our happiness to a higher level? One of the best answers I have seen to this question was presented by another young leader of the positive psychology movement. Jonathan Haidt (pronounced "height") won an early career award for studying a neglected positive emotion called "elevation," that I will discuss in the next chapter. He also wrote one of the best books that I have read on what psychology has to offer us all. In *The Happiness Hypothesis*, Haidt identifies three things that may help us beat the hedonic treadmill.[26]

The first thing may not come as a surprise if you were born in the past 30 years, but for many it has seemed like no less than a life-changing miracle. This is the development of a new class of psychiatric medications that have relatively few side effects and may result in long-term changes in happiness. These began with the introduction of *Prozac* in 1986 and continued with other selective serotonin reuptake inhibitors (SSRI) such as *Paxil, Zoloft,* and *Celexa* and grew to include serotonin-norepinephrine reuptake inhibitors (SNRI) such as *Effexor* and *Cymbalta*. In good positive psychology fashion, for many these medications have not only reduced depression but also enabled them to consistently experience more of the positive emotions that are at the core of what many define as happiness.

The second thing that Haidt mentions is something that psychologists spend more time practicing and studying. There is evidence that certain kinds of psychotherapy may also have long-term effects on happiness. There is the strongest and most consistent support for cognitive-behavioral therapy (CBT), which may result in long-term increases in happiness because it enables people to see and respond to the world in a better way.

Other interventions, including mindfulness- and acceptance-based approaches, are increasingly being studied and may have similar long-term effects. Finally, while medications such as SSRIs and SNRIs may boost happiness while people continue to take them, there is evidence that the effects of psychotherapy may last long after end the treatment.

The third possible way to beat the hedonic treadmill that Haidt mentions is meditation. Neuroscience researchers have discovered what they call "neuroplasticity," which is the ability of the brain to change and create new connections between brain cells across the life span. The persistent effort to focus the attention of the mind in meditation may result in changes in both brain structure and function that bring greater happiness. Research on the effects of mindfulness meditation suggest that it produces lasting changes in the brain consistent with experiencing more positive emotions and fewer negative emotions. For example, Richard Davidson and his colleagues have studied long-term meditators and found exceptionally high levels of brain activity associated with positive emotion.[27]

Although Haidt mentions medication, psychotherapy, and meditation, these are broad categories of change agents. There is certainly much more to be discovered about what may enable us to move to a consistently higher level of happiness. While medication represents a direct attempt to alter our biochemical make-up to experience more happiness, both psychotherapy and meditation involve the voluntary and intentional behaviors that Lyubomirsky and others think may account for a good portion of our happiness. Although people like Ed Diener have provided evidence for the strong influence of personal relationships and rewarding employment on happiness, there is still much to be learned about how changes in our relationships, social network, and work life may enable us to rise to new levels of happiness.[28]

Finally, it has become a primary goal of the positive psychology movement to enable us to find the most effective and efficient ways to beat the hedonic treadmill and raise our happiness. Sonja Lyubomirsky and Acacia Parks have made this a part of their long-term research programs. Lyubomirsky's book *The How of Happiness* presents much of what she and others have learned about what voluntary and intentional activities may be catalysts for moving to and staying at higher levels of happiness.[29] Acacia Parks edited a comprehensive volume titled *Positive Psychological Interventions* which presents some of the most effective and promising interventions for increasing happiness.[30] Variations of many of the best of these activities are in Appendix D and will be expanded upon in much of the rest of this book.

They include a variety of effective and rewarding ways to change our perspective, behavior, relationships, and world. Changing our perspective involves seeing and appreciating more of the good that we may have been missing around us. Changing our behavior involves identifying our strengths and learning to use them in new ways to reach our goals. Changing our relationships involves finding new ways to respond to and cultivate what is best in others. Finally, changing our world involves the simple and profound ways these changes may ripple beyond the small things we do to influence others and impact the world around us.

Beyond the Holy Grail of Happiness

I'll never forget what my sister-in-law said when she was asked what she wanted for her three children: "I just want them to be happy." On the one hand, it is such a simple answer. On the other, it can be so hard for us to achieve—or even know what it means to be happy. Many of us may agree with Sonja Lyubomirsky that our holy grail is simply to be happy. In this chapter, we saw that psychologists have most often defined happiness in the same way that many of us would: having less pain, being satisfied with our lives, and experiencing more positive emotions like joy, love, interest, and contentment.

We have also seen that our happiness is affected by at least three major things: biological factors over which we have little control, the conditions of our lives over which we may have some control, and finally by our own intentional and voluntary efforts to be happy—over which we may have a great deal of control. In addition, we learned about two of the greatest challenges we face on our quest for greater happiness: the negativity bias and the hedonic treadmill. In *Harry Potter* language, they may be two of the greatest "dark arts" against which we most need a defense and the kind of guidance we see in Dumbledore and the mentors we see in our favorite stories.

While happiness may seem like such a supreme and simple goal, in the next chapter we will consider the full range of things that we love and seek. Although many of them are related to the kind of happiness we talked about in this chapter, they also go beyond simply feeling good and avoiding feeling bad. In fact, some of them are so important to us that we may be willing to sacrifice a great deal and put up with long periods of pain and feeling bad in order to have hope of finding them. It is in the next chapter that we will begin to focus on the kind of things that may embody an even more wonderful holy grail than many of us have ever imagined.

Chapter 4

The Good Life and Human Well-Being

Happiness is not a goal...
it's a by-product of a life well lived.

—*Eleanor Roosevelt*[1]

Several years ago, I had the chance to go to a beautiful resort near Cancun, Mexico. I went with a beautiful woman and we paid a very reasonable price to have all the best food and drink. There were beautiful people and dancing and swimming pools and beaches galore. The sun was shining and the cool ocean breeze was blowing. It was supposed to be paradise and a mountaintop experience. But I was not happy in the relationship, I felt guilty and sad for the local people who had to serve us, and I got one of the worst sunburns that I have ever had the first time I went out on the beach. I look back on it now as one of the most miserable experiences of my life.

Have you ever had an experience like that? You thought that something would make you happy and it had the complete opposite effect. You thought it was all about experiencing the immediate pleasure of food, "sex, drugs, and rock and roll," and it left you feeling empty and alone. Or you thought that something you were sure would make you happy fell short and left you wondering what happened—and whether there really was any more to life. This chapter is about that "something more" that we may doubt but no less dream about. It is portrayed as a variety of things in great stories—Frodo and Sam coming home to the Shire, Harry Potter finding out who he was, or Dorothy realizing she had what she needed within herself.

With the pressure to publish or perish in academic psychology and the ever-present cynicism toward people trying to study what may be good about life, it can be hard enough to build a career doing research on something that sounds as soft and fluffy as happiness. How much harder it can be to go beyond the simple experience of immediate pleasure to understanding the larger and more complex things that may bring us the greatest joy and fulfillment. Until recently, psychology had not provided much help. However, the positive psychology movement is providing new hope for understanding the question of what makes life worth living and for appreciating the breadth and the depth of the kind of answers that we can discover. I hope that you will take this chapter as both an encouragement and a challenge to be open to this question and to begin to answer it for yourself.

Hedonic and Eudaimonic Well-Being

Martin Seligman has talked about two different ways that people go about seeking happiness.[2] First is the hedonic approach, which originated with the Greek philosopher Aristippus, and the second is the eudaimonic approach, that was offered by Aristotle as an alternative path. Hedonia is the ability to experience pleasure and eudaimonia is the ability to be true to your inner self. The primary goal of the hedonic approach is to seek as much pleasure as possible while avoiding painful experiences. This might involve things like putting all of your free time into going to bars, restaurants, or resorts to feel good right now. The primary goal of the eudaimonic approach is to seek personal fulfillment and the realization of your own unique potential. This might involve taking classes, discovering your gifts and talents, expressing who you are, or doing something meaningful that makes a difference for other people.

Another related contrast is the difference that Seligman draws between pleasure and gratification in his book *Authentic*

Happiness.[3] The raw feeling of pleasure is a primary goal of the hedonic life while the deeper and more lasting experience of gratification is a primary goal of the eudaimonic life. Seligman gives examples of the raw feeling of pleasure including great food, a back rub, perfume, or a hot shower. In contrast, he describes gratification as being totally absorbed or immersed in what one is doing—something which doesn't necessarily involve money at all. He further defines gratification as what occurs when we are doing what we are good at in using our own personal strengths.

This distinction between hedonic and eudaimonic approaches to happiness is closely related to the distinction that many have made between seeking pleasure and seeking meaning. The value of having a sense of meaning was beautifully described in Viktor Frankl's classic book *Man's Search for Meaning.*[4] He believed our need for meaning is a fundamental part of being human and that it is at least as important as our desire for pleasure. He had an all too real and challenging opportunity to put his theory to the test when he was taken to a concentration camp during World War II. *Man's Search for Meaning* is the story of Frankl's experience in the concentration camp and how he came to believe that maintaining a sense of meaning and purpose was the main reason he survived.

Frankl's work has had a lasting effect on the positive psychology movement in getting researchers to ask whether meaning may sometimes be even more important than pleasure. Can you think of a time you did something that involved less pleasure and more pain because it helped you meet a goal that was meaningful to you? This could be going to college, having a child, or making sacrifices to become better at a sport or some other activity you love. Martin Luther King Jr. wrote about how his sense of purpose about what he was doing was stronger than his fear and anxiety about the bomb threats he was receiving. William Wallace was the Scottish knight who led the resistance against the English occupation. The movie *Braveheart* shows how he knowingly risked his life for a higher cause even though he must have known it meant a loss of worldly pleasures and possibly a very painful death.

Roy Baumeister and his colleagues examined the difference between what they called a happy life and a meaningful life.[5] They did a large survey examining what things they were each related to. They used statements like "in general I consider myself happy" to measure happiness and "in general I consider my life to be meaningful" to measure meaningfulness. They found that being happy and finding life meaningful overlapped but that there were also important differences. Happiness was seen as fleeting while meaning was seen as lasting longer. Happiness was also related to being a taker rather than a giver, while meaningfulness was associated with being a giver rather than a taker. Meaning was associated with stress and challenge and self-expression while happiness was not.

Understanding Psychological Well-Being

The distinction between hedonic and eudaimonic well-being has often been part of a larger distinction made between happiness and well-being. While happiness has been defined as more positive emotions, fewer negative emotions, and high life satisfaction; well-being has been thought of as something more. You might seek the pleasure of eating chocolate or taking a hot bath, but you might also seek the meaning of raising a child or giving to a homeless person, or the sense of accomplishment that comes from doing well in a hard class or climbing to the top of a mountain.

The term "well-being" implies living well in a holistic sense that does not just involve immediate pleasure. The distinction between intrinsic and extrinsic motivation may help us understand well-being and how something other than pleasure may be important in its own right. Intrinsic motivation is the motivation to seek something for no other reason than to have or experience the thing itself. The thing sought is an end in itself and is its own reward because it is good, enjoyable, or the right thing to do. Extrinsic motivation is the motivation to do something because it is a means toward some other end. You might be extrinsically motivated to do well at a job because you want to make money. You might be intrinsically motivated to volunteer for a job because you enjoy it for its own sake even if you do not make any money.

I have talked about the idea of the "holy grail" as a symbol of something that is sincerely and intensely pursued. Pleasure and meaning are at least two of the things that human beings may intensely pursue. What else is there that we may be intrinsically motivated to seek and which may be an inherent part of being and living well? What else might make our lives worth living and be an inherent part of well-being? I want to take you on a journey to see the other things that have been identified in psychology. I also want you to think about how important each of these is to you and whether you think anything is missing. The two people who are pioneers on this journey are Martin Seligman, and psychologist Carol Ryff, whose earlier work helped lay the foundation for the positive psychology movement.

Ryff's Components of Well-Being

Back in 1989, Carol Ryff published an article with a title that that is particularly fitting for this chapter: *Happiness is Everything, or Is It? Explorations on the Meaning of Psychological Well-Being.*[6] Ryff challenged the prevailing assumption that we should only focus on being free of anxiety, depression, and other forms of psychopathology. She also noted that current researchers were not considering previous theories about positive psychological functioning. She reviewed the rich history of theories related to psychological well-being developed by people like Carl Jung,

Gordon Allport, Erik Erikson, and Carl Rogers. Based on her review and integration of these theories, she came up with a model of psychological well-being that included six different components. The questionnaire that she developed to assess them is still frequently used as a measure of eudaimonic well-being.

The six components that Ryff identified have much to say about what may be a "holy grail" or primary aim in life for many of us. First, she identified a component that she called a sense of Purpose in Life, which is very close to the idea of meaning that we discussed above and that Viktor Frankl has written about. Ryff defined Purpose in Life as having life goals and a sense of directedness, feeling that there is meaning in life, and holding beliefs that give life purpose. She derived this component from life span developmental theories such as Erik Erikson's stages of psychosocial development that refer to changing purposes and goals in life. Ryff affirmed the value of having a sense of meaning and purpose as intrinsic to our lives and involving something more than merely trying to seek pleasure and avoid pain.

Second, she identified another component that she called Environmental Mastery, which she defined as having a sense of mastery and competence in managing the environment, making effective use of surrounding opportunities, and being able to choose and create contexts that match personal needs and values. The way that human beings have come to dominate life on earth may have negative implications for other life forms and the environment, but it is also a supreme indication of the success with which humans have come to gain mastery over their environment. Psychology has a long history of studying the value of both perceived and actual self-control, but here Ryff identifies mastery of the world around us as having inherent value and being a goal in itself.

Third, she identified something that may be more emphasized in Western than Eastern cultures, but nonetheless is probably important for everyone. Ryff identified Autonomy as an essential component of well-being and defined it as being self-determining and independent, being able to resist social pressures to think and act in certain ways, and regulating and evaluating one's behavior from within by personal standards. Here she drew on the work of people like Carl Jung who wrote about individuation and Carl Rogers who wrote about the fully functioning person having an internal locus of evaluation. Unlike other components of well-being, the goal of autonomy is often lifted up as an ideal in many modern movies and television shows, even if many in Western culture often lose their autonomy by falling into the latest fads.

Fourth, Ryff identifies something else that is equally challenging and revered in popular culture and has also been an important focus in the newly developed mindfulness- and acceptance-based therapies. She identified Self-acceptance as another component of well-being that is also tied to the work of Carl Rogers and more recent research on self-esteem. She defined it as having a positive attitude toward the self, acknowledging and accepting both good and bad aspects of the self, and feeling positive about your past life. Her definition highlights some of the challenges about understanding and defining self-acceptance. What is a positive attitude towards ourselves and how might it translate into dealing with negative or harmful parts of ourselves? Is it possible to fully accept ourselves today even if we wish we would have behaved differently in the past?

Fifth, Ryff identifies the same thing that we already heard was a strong focus in the thought and work of Ed Diener and Chris Peterson. Diener once said that he had rarely ever seen anyone who said that they were happy if they didn't have good, close relationships. Peterson often repeated the phrase "other people matter" in his positive psychology lectures and talked about how it was a good summary of what positive psychology research has demonstrated about the "good life." The fifth aspect of well-being that Ryff identified was Positive Relations with Others, which she defined as having warm, satisfying, trusting relationships with others, being concerned about the welfare of others, and being capable of empathy, affection, and intimacy, and understanding give and take in relationships.

Finally, Ryff identified a component that was easily left out of the older emphasis in psychology on just getting rid of bad things, like anxiety and depression. Ryff dared to assert the value of something often at the center of the kind of hero's journey we will introduce in the next chapter, but that has so often been neglected or avoided in mainstream academic psychology. The sixth component of well-being for Ryff is Personal Growth, which she defined as a feeling of continued development, seeing the self as growing and expanding, and having the sense of realizing one's potential. Here she again drew on the visions of some of the luminaries of the past century, such as Carl Jung, Carl Rogers, and Abraham Maslow. In many ways, personal growth, in the fullest, deepest, and richest sense, is a primary goal of positive psychology.

So here it was, nearly 10 years before the birth of the positive psychology movement—we had something of a voice crying in the wilderness asserting that there may be something more to life than only what psychology had been focusing on. Also, the idea that we may be intrinsically motivated to seek these six things cannot be stressed enough. Think about your own life. Have there been times when you found that mastering something around you was rewarding even if you didn't feel pleasure at the time? Have there been times when you had to be true to yourself even when your best friends and family members were telling you to do otherwise? Were there times when you sacrificed immediate pleasure for growing as a person by taking a class, going to a religious service, or doing something to benefit someone else?

The PERMA Theory of Well-Being

In his 2011 book, *Flourish,* Martin Seligman presented his own theory of well-being.[7] He had the work of Carol Ryff and others to draw on and wanted to develop a theory that went beyond what he called "happiology" and the traditional idea of happiness as only involving emotions and life satisfaction. Before the positive psychology movement, so much psychology research had focused on reducing negative emotions. Even the recent emphasis on happiness only added a focus on positive emotion and life satisfaction. He argued that measures of life satisfaction may only indicate how cheerful people are feeling when they fill out a questionnaire. He thought it was all just too mood and emotion centered, which left little room for what well-being might mean for those who are not predisposed to experience lots of positive emotion.

In his 2002 book *Authentic Happiness,* Seligman began to build a theory of well-being that not only included positive emotions but also included meaning and something he was starting to call engagement.[8] By 2011, he was ready to add two more elements that he thought were an inherent part of human well-being. He used the acronym PERMA which stands for what he theorized were the five basic elements of well-being: (1) Positive Emotion, (2) Engagement, (3) Relationships, (4) Meaning, and (5) Accomplishment.[9] He argued that each of these five elements met the three basic criteria he set in that (1) it contributes to well-being, (2) many people pursue it for its own sake, not merely to get any of the other elements, and (3) it is defined independently of the other elements. Seligman presented the following five elements as an overarching framework for understanding human well-being and what makes life worth living:

1. *Positive Emotion*

The first element in the acronym PERMA is what Seligman calls Positive Emotion, which for him also means "the pleasant life." But whereas this element was the primary goal and cornerstone of the previous notions of hedonic happiness, it is now just one element of many in a more comprehensive theory of eudaimonic well-being.

Based on all that we have already discussed with regard to happiness and positive emotions, it is not hard to understand why this element needed to be included. In general, positive emotions such as joy, love, interest, and contentment are some of the clearest and most straightforward things that we often seek. We have already seen how Barbara Fredrickson's broaden-and-build theory addresses the evolutionary significance and function of positive emotions as enabling us to better cope with future problems and adversity.[10] But who can deny that we seek to experience these emotions for their own sake—just because they feel good—and would do it even if they were not a means to some other end.

Another thing to point out about the element of Positive Emotion is that our understanding of it has grown greatly in the past 20 years. Whereas before, we had identified and studied a range of negative emotions, since the dawn of the positive psychology movement we have begun to greatly increase our understanding of positive emotions. There are several positive emotions that not only have become a new focus of study but also have the potential for enriching our experience of what it means to be human. For example, "inspiration" has been studied as an emotion that can stimulate us to do something creative or good, as has "awe," an emotion which may motivate us to appreciate and learn from what is vast and beautiful.

The emotion that is now called "elevation" deserves special attention.[11] I already mentioned that Jonathan Haidt was one of the young leaders of the positive psychology movement. He received an award from the Templeton Foundation for his research on the emotion that he named "elevation." Haidt had joined the psychology faculty at the University of Virginia near where Thomas Jefferson lived at Monticello. He had been studying the ways that people experience the emotion of disgust when they see someone else behaving badly. He began to wonder if there was an opposite emotion that people experienced when they saw someone do something good. He soon discovered that not only did Jefferson write about "the pursuit of happiness" but also that he had actually described the physical feelings and motivation to do good that people experience when they see others doing good things.

Over the next few years, Haidt began to study this emotional response using the same scientific methods he had used to study negative emotions like disgust. He defined elevation as a warm or glowing feeling in the chest that motivates people to better themselves morally. He said it was triggered by witnessing acts of human moral beauty or virtue. As he and others have studied elevation, they found that it may increase the desire to help others and involve the release of the hormone oxytocin, which has been associated with social bonding. In one experiment, they induced elevation by showing a video of the life of Mother Teresa vs. a neutral or funny clip for a control group. They found that those who watched the Mother Teresa clip were more likely to experience a warm, pleasant, or "tingling" feeling; and report wanting to help others and become better people.

The study of elevation and related positive emotions such as awe and inspiration cast a new light on the potential place of positive emotions in overall well-being. These emotions may not only involve immediate pleasure, but also the broadening and building of resources that benefit the individual in the future. They may also have a positive impact on others and our communal life. In terms of Martin Seligman's theory of well-being, they may affect other elements such as increasing meaning in life or the building of better relationships. As Dacher Keltner has written about in *The Compassionate Instinct*, human beings may have evolved with emotional responses that promote the survival of others as much as the survival of the individual.[12] The human capacity to be inspired and experience elevation may be part of what Lincoln called "the better angels of our nature," which may give us hope for working together in dealing with our greatest problems.

2. *Engagement*

The second element in the acronym PERMA is what Seligman calls Engagement, which refers to the experience of being absorbed, interested, and involved in an activity. The idea that engagement may be an inherent part of well-being means that whether or not you are aware of any positive or negative emotions, it can be intrinsically rewarding to be fully absorbed in a task just for the sake of the experience. This element represents a unique addition to the work of Carol Ryff in painting a fuller picture of human well-being.

The person most responsible for identifying the inherent value of engagement is probably Mihaly Csikszentmihalyi (pronounced "cheeks sent me high"). He was studying the experience of artists who seemed to get lost in their work and identified what he called "flow."[13] He later came to see that this same flow state is something that people can experience during all kinds of human activities. Csikszentmihalyi and his colleague Jeanne Nakamura identified six factors involved in flow:[14]

1. Intense and focused concentration on the present moment.

2. Merging of action and awareness.

3. A loss of reflective self-consciousness.

4. A sense of personal control or agency over the situation or activity.

5. A distortion of temporal experience, one's subjective experience of time is altered.

6. Experience of the activity as intrinsically rewarding.

Try to think of times when you were completely involved in an activity and may have been experiencing many or all of these things. The activity could be almost anything but is usually something moderately challenging where you are free to continue to fully focus on the task at hand. It could be doing something artistic like painting, drawing, singing, or playing a musical instrument. It could be doing something very physical such as hiking, running, rock climbing, dancing, yoga, or martial arts. It could be something that might be considered work such as cooking, cleaning, fixing a car, or building a house. Did you lose track of time? Did you have a hard time stopping? What did you experience during the time you were fully engaged and how did you feel afterwards?

Although a flow state can be entered with many kinds of activities, Csikszentmihalyi thinks that three conditions are necessary:[15]

1. You must be clear about the goals of the activity and what would be considered progress.

2. The task must have clear and immediate feedback for you. This makes it possible for you to adjust your effort to maintain the flow state.

3. There must be a good balance between the perceived challenges of tasks and your perceived skills.

For example, if you are downhill skiing or snow-boarding, your clear goal may be negotiating the twists and turns and getting safely to the bottom of the mountain. You are receiving the immediate feedback of the wind on your face, the changing view of the slope as you descend, and the shifting feeling of the snow on the ground as you move down the mountain. Perhaps most important, the path and the slope you are descending is not too easy and not too hard but a challenging match for your skills.

One of the amazing and ironic things about the flow state is that while you are in it you are so focused on what you are doing that you are not usually aware of what you are thinking or feeling. Even though you may only intermittently be aware of positive emotions such as joy and excitement, for the most part you only think about how much of a great time you had after you stop doing the activity. Even though you may not be thinking about it much, you are intrinsically motivated to stay engaged during the activity so you can continue to have the experience. The potential negative consequences of your temptation to stay in the activity too long may include things like frostbite in the case of downhill skiing or frustration in your friends and family members when they wonder if they will ever see you again.

There is a wonderful example of flow in the movie that won the Academy Award for the best picture in 1981; *Chariots of Fire* is the true story of two runners from Great Britain who competed in the 1924 Olympics. One of the runners was Harold Abrams who ran because he felt that he had to prove that he was the best. The other runner was Eric Liddell who had nothing to prove but just loved to run. Liddell had a strong religious faith and said, "When I run, I feel God's pleasure." Abrams was extrinsically motivated to run and probably did not often experience flow. Liddell was intrinsically motivated to run and may be a prime example of flow. While both men won Olympic gold medals, Abrams was depressed afterwards because he no longer had a reason for living, but Liddell was happy because he still had what gave his life meaning and could continue to experience the joy of running.

The possibilities that flow offer for a better life and world have not escaped Martin Seligman and Csikszentmihalyi himself. Seligman has linked the experience of flow to the use of our greatest gifts and talents or what he calls our "signature strengths."[16] Seligman has argued that finding new ways to use these top strengths is an excellent way to put ourselves in flow. For example, if one of your top strengths is the appreciation of beauty and excellence, then painting or photography may be great opportunities for experiencing flow. If one of your top strengths is kindness, then finding creative new ways to give thoughtful gifts to others may help put you in flow.

There are a couple of other important benefits of knowing that flow and engagement may be an inherent part of well-being. First, no matter how much your biology or the conditions of your life reduce the possibility of pleasure or positive emotions, the opportunity to experience the flow state may only be limited by finding a goal-directed activity that is a good fit for your skills. Second, think of what may be possible if more people had jobs that matched their strengths and gave them more opportunities to experience flow. Not only might job satisfaction go up, but the ability to get much more done might increase as people focus better and work longer at tasks they find intrinsically satisfying and rewarding. Some of the exercises in Appendix D are designed to help you find more ways to experience flow by helping you identify your strengths, use them in new ways, and intentionally doing things that may put you in a flow state.

3. *Relationships*

The third element in the acronym PERMA is what Seligman calls Relationships and is essentially the same as what

Carol Ryff calls Positive Relations with Others. Although it is only called Relationships to fit the PERMA acronym, it really means positive or healthy relationships that involve feeling loved, supported, and valued by others. There is no denying that sometimes human relationships can be very harmful, abusive, destructive, and anything but positive.

There are several points that can be made about why positive relationships may be an essential element of well-being, which are often sought for their own sake and may even be the most important thing in someone's life. First, many happiness researchers, such as Ed Diener, have found that when people are asked to describe the happiest times in their lives, they frequently involve sharing good times with friends or family members. There may be times that we experience certain immediate physical pleasures alone such as taking a hot bath after a long day or enjoying our favorite dessert. But most of the best times that people remember about their lives involve interacting with and being around other people.

Second, think of the all the ways that people are willing to sacrifice and experience pain for the sake of those they care about and love. Although the sexual act itself can certainly be a powerful motivator for bringing children into the world, it probably takes much more to motivate people to put in all the effort and care parents take to raise children and adolescents. In addition, there are countless other caregivers who have continued to sacrifice so much of their time and energy to alleviate the suffering of their good friends and family members.

Third, the sometimes extremely faint hope of having a positive relationship with a partner or spouse has kept many in an abusive relationship long after it took a tremendous toll on their happiness and ability to experience other kinds of well-being. Similarly, there is evidence that being neglected or left alone as a child is worse than some of the kinds of active emotional or physical abuse that children sometimes experience.

This is consistent with the research showing that loneliness is detrimental and that social support is good for both our mental and physical health.

Finally, there is evidence that one of the most important reasons that humans have such large brains is to relate to other humans. The size of the social network is one of the few things that correlates with brain size for different kinds of primates. The research of anthropologist Robin Dunbar suggests that the reason human brains have evolved to be so large is that it gives us the capacity to have a larger social circle.[17] It is difficult to imagine anything more complex than the human brain or that anything that could replace the challenge and stimulation of relating to other human beings.

4. *Meaning*

The fourth element in the acronym PERMA is what Seligman calls Meaning, which is essentially the same as what Carol Ryff calls Purpose in Life. It refers to having a sense of purpose in life, a direction where life is going, or feeling that life is valuable and worth living. I have already talked about the value of Meaning as part of eudaimonia and Ryff's understanding of psychological well-being. However, there are a couple additional things that Seligman stresses about Meaning that may have implications beyond the individual and may be important to add here.

First, Seligman does more to emphasize that having a sense of meaning and purpose involves "belonging to and serving something that is bigger than the self" (p. 17).[18] Thus, the definition given for the element of Meaning in the questionnaire developed to assess PERMA by Margaret Butler and Peggy Kern includes "connecting to something greater than ourselves, such as religious faith, a charity or a personally meaningful goal."[19] Psychology has traditionally been hesitant to address what may be beyond the realm of individuals, and especially topics that involve religion and spirituality. However, for many people, religion, spirituality, and other pursuits that are greater than the self may be the closest things they experience and think about as their own holy grail of well-being.

Second, Seligman writes that while the element of Positive Emotion can be judged solely by subjective experience, the element of Meaning typically involves a more objective validation outside of one's self. He gives the example of a person feeling like they are having a meaningful conversation when they smoked marijuana and stayed up all night in college, but later come to realize that it was only "adolescent gibberish."[20] He also provides the example of Abraham Lincoln whose tendency towards depression often caused him to feel that his life was meaningless even through history would judge otherwise. Thus, leading a meaningful life may both involve our own subjective judgment that we are doing something meaningful and also the perhaps more objective validation of others and the larger human community.

5. *Accomplishment*

The fifth and final element in the acronym PERMA is what Seligman calls Accomplishment, which has also been referred to as Achievement and is roughly related to Ryff's component of Environmental Mastery. While she defined Environmental Mastery as having a sense of mastery in managing the environment, making use of surrounding opportunities, and finding contexts that suite personal needs and values; Seligman's element of Accomplishment has been defined as making progress towards and achieving goals and keeping up with daily responsibilities. Both involve the subjective perception of mastery over larger and smaller life matters and the kind of achievements or accomplishments that can be verified by others.

The key in appreciating Accomplishment as a separate and distinct element of well-being is understanding that some people seek it for its own sake. It is easy to see how our achievements may produce other benefits such as the positive emotions of joy and contentment or a sense of meaningfulness when we contribute to the well-being of others. But to add it as an element of well-being, Seligman believes that a primary motivator for many people is just the sense of mastery in doing or accomplishing something. For Seligman, playing bridge is an example of something that he does primarily for achievement's sake. For many, it may be mastering a sport or hobby that might not even make them feel a lot of positive emotions, that may be difficult to experience flow in, and that may be an isolated activity that does not connect them with others or serve a greater purpose.

The strong inherent value of accomplishment and environmental mastery in human well-being has a foundation in the work of psychologist Robert White.[21] In the 1950s, his research supported a phenomenon called "effectance motivation," which is the tendency to explore and influence the environment and involves "competence," which is the ability to interact effectively with the environment. The idea of effectance motivation ran contrary to the dominant theory of the day, supported by research with rats, which was that our primary motivation is to reduce biological needs such as hunger, thirst, and sleep. The implication of White's theory is that our desire to master our environment is a motivation that is intrinsic and inherent to being human. Thus, Ryff and Seligman both included this as primary aspect of human well-being.

The Big Picture of Happiness and Well-Being

Positive psychology is the application of the scientific method to making the most of our lives and living them to the fullest. In the last two chapters, I have tried to introduce you to what this may look like and the kinds of things it may involve. These are things that many of us seek for their own sake and may be fundamental elements of human happiness and well-being. In many ways, they are the holy grails that we value more than anything else and seek with the greatest effort, passion, and intensity. Here are the ten building blocks or elements of human happiness and well-being that we have discussed:

1. *Low Negative Emotion*—having few feelings of anger, fear, and sadness.

2. *Life Satisfaction*—having a high sense of satisfaction with your life.

3. *Positive Emotion*—feelings of joy, love, interest, contentment, awe, inspiration, and elevation.

4. *Engagement*—being engaged with life and experiencing flow in work and play.

5. *Relationships*—being loved and having good interpersonal relationships.

6. *Meaning*—having a sense of meaning, purpose, and direction in life.

7. *Accomplishment*—achieving important goals and mastering the world around you.

8. *Self-acceptance*—having a positive attitude toward yourself and fully accepting yourself.

9. *Autonomy*—being independent, self-determining, and true to who you are.

10. *Personal Growth*—continuing to grow as a person and realizing your full potential.

The first is having Low Negative Emotions such as anger, fear, and sadness, which was the focus of psychology before the dawn of the positive psychology movement. The second and third are having high Life Satisfaction and Positive Emotion which were added to having Low Negative Emotion in the definition of happiness by Ed Diener.[22] The next four are Engagement, Relationships, Meaning, and Accomplishment which are elements of eudaimonic well-being added to positive emotion by Seligman to complete his PERMA theory of well-being. As noted above, Seligman's elements of Relationships, Meaning, and Accomplishment are similar to Ryff's components of Positive Relations with Others, Purpose in Life, and Environmental Mastery, respectively. The final three building block are Self-acceptance, Autonomy, and Personal Growth, which were three additional components identified by Ryff.

One key point about everything after the first three, that make up the conventional definition of happiness, is that we may not be limited by the same kind of happiness formula that credited so much to things that we may not have control over. Even if the antidotes to the hedonic treadmill that we presented did not greatly add to what we could do to increase our happiness, Seligman and others thought that we may have much more control over things like whether we live a meaningful life, create satisfying relationships, frequently engage in flow, or accomplish something with our lives. This broader and more comprehensive framework for what makes life worth living can provide a powerful new hope and incentive for making the most and best of whoever we are and wherever we find ourselves.

Finally, rather than seeing any of these ten elements or building blocks as set in stone or having the same value for all of us, I would encourage you to use your own imagination and creativity to do two things. First, think about whether anything is missing from this list. Think about your life and the lives of those who are most important to you. Is there anything else that they or you have devoted yourself to for its own sake? If so, add it to the list. Second, and most important, think of these elements as colors on a palette that you can use to paint a picture of the kind of life that you most want for yourself. You could even rank which are most important to you and which you would most like to work on. In the next chapter, I will show you how you can begin to do this by making a challenging, exciting, and rewarding new journey.

Chapter 5

The Hero's Journey in Positive Psychology

Follow your bliss and don't be afraid,
and doors will open where you didn't
know they were going to be.

—Joseph Campbell[1]

The problem with reading about science and even psychology in academic journals is that it can be so dull and boring. When I was in graduate school, we used to joke that some of the best psychologists seemed to be using their high IQs in a punishingly creative and cruel way. We wondered if they were trying to make something as inherently and intrinsically interesting as human behavior into what in an article could sometimes induce a mild coma or at least very deep sleep. One of my colleagues shared his complaint about reading psychology journals by telling me about a book titled *Learn to Write Badly: How to Succeed in the Social Sciences* by Michael Billig.[2] It seems that all too many psychologists in academia may have read it.

The repeated attempts to reduce the most fascinating aspects of human behavior to the official writing style of the *American Psychological Association* (APA) cannot fail to dampen our enthusiasm for psychology. The excessive use of psychological jargon for the small number of people who read academic journal articles made us wonder if psychology had lost touch with real people and everyday life. Because human beings are the subject matter of psychology and humans can be so fascinating, my friends and I thought that many psychologists must be using their creativity and intelligence primarily to find ways to put us to sleep.

Maybe I've gone a bit too far and maybe I shouldn't be one to talk. I wouldn't be surprised if you have started to nod off as I have gone through some of the theory and research in the past few chapters. But I am trying to make a point about why it can sometimes be so hard to learn about and digest something that science has discovered. It is probably not the subject matter of psychology that leaves us longing for a nap. Part of it may be that there is often little effort to relate it to something that really matters to us. It may have even more to do with the fact that psychologist research is sometimes presented like a computer program for machines that never need to sleep or struggle with maintaining their attention.

The Value of the Human Story

What I really want to do in this chapter is to build a bridge with something we have a much better chance of staying awake for and understanding—a human story. Do you remember what I said in the first sentence of the preface of this book? I said that, "This book grew out of what may be the happiest and most fulfilling experiences of my life." As an illustration of what we discussed in the last chapter, teaching the class wasn't always as pleasurable as a hot bath or as much fun as snowboarding, but there was a deep sense of fulfillment and meaning, which included getting to know the students and seeing how they benefited. It was the whole experience of teaching with a focus on the stories of real people who I came to really care about.

Ever since I began teaching positive psychology, I have been struck with the way that it has engaged students like no other course that I have taught in my many years of working in academia. In the preface, I also talked about the young man who shared the courage it took for him to be a soldier, the young woman who bounced back and grew after she had to leave New

Orleans because of Hurricane Katrina, and the other young man who I was afraid would harass me but instead gave a moving personal testimony of the power of forgiveness. Every time I have taught positive psychology, I have tried to learn the names of all of the students. I do this not just because it means something to them, but also because it gives me the opportunity to better learn and remember their stories, which have come to mean so much to me.

Positive psychology lends itself so well to telling human stories because it is through them that we can truly understand what it means to be at our best and have a life worth living. Usually during the second class, I show pictures of sports heroes and famous people most students are likely to know and ask them what they think enabled them to do the great things they have done. During the semester, we have movie nights where I show movies that I have learned over the years can have profound effects in inspiring happiness, hope, and the desire to be a better person. They are often true stories of people like Nelson Mandela in the movie *Invictus* who brought hope and healing to South Africa, Prince Albert the future king in *The King's Speech* who brought courage to England in the face of Hitler, and Erin Gruwell the high school teacher in *Freedom Writers* who enabled her students to believe in themselves by encouraging them to write about their own stories.

Narrative Psychology and the Benefits of Writing

Although it is easy to miss in mainstream psychology with its emphasis on quantitative research, there is another kind of research more common in other social sciences that places greater value on stories. In quantitative research, the data are in the form of numbers usually collected from a relatively large group of people to test preconceived hypotheses. In qualitative research, the data are in the form of words—or stories—usually collected from a smaller number of people, often to develop new theories. Thus, qualitative researchers may have a greater appreciation not only for the words that people use but for how they put them together into stories to form a narrative. Narrative psychology focuses on how people create meaning from their life experiences by thinking about themselves as part of a story.

Just as there were fewer psychologists focusing on increasing happiness than decreasing anxiety and depression before the birth of the positive psychology movement, there are fewer narrative psychologists who focus on the stories that people tell. One exception is Jerome Bruner who wrote about how human beings often understand and construct reality in terms of narratives.[3] The lack of stories may help explain why those journal articles written in logical propositions and APA style may be harder to read and remember. While an article may tell us that optimism and happiness are significantly related with a correlation coefficient of .35, the way that many of us best remember and make sense of this kind of relationship is to think of how optimism and happiness may be expressed together in the story of someone we know and care about.

Dan McAdams, who wrote *The Stories We Live By*,[4] is one of the most articulate proponents of the value of a narrative approach to understanding human beings. He has done creative and intriguing research using both quantitative and qualitative methods to understand personality and how we come to see and understand our "self." He has developed a three level model of personality that includes (1) the kind of broad personality characteristics studied in quantitative research such as the "Big Five" personality characteristics that include neuroticism, extraversion, openness to experience, agreeableness, and conscientiousness, (2) the characteristic ways that we adapt to our lives including our coping mechanisms, desires, and beliefs, and (3) the life stories that give us a unique sense of meaning and purpose or what he calls our "narrative identity."

McAdams developed a way to study this narrative identity and writes about how it may be important for each of us as individuals and even for communities in forming a collective identity. In examining the personal stories provided by research participants, he has looked for the differences in structure and content that may be related to psychological well-being. He argues that one of the most important aspects of a story is "narrative coherence" or how well the story fits together into a unified whole. He also contends that some of the most important aspects of content have to do with how much a person is able to "make meaning" from their story, whether there is a coherent positive resolution, and whether the narrator transitions from a negative to a positive state which he identifies as a "redemption" narrative

Interestingly, the work of McAdams and others in narrative psychology has been useful in understanding the beneficial effects of writing about stressful events. James Pennebaker has asked people to write about the most stressful experience of their lives and found that it may have a variety of health benefits.[5] Whereas he first thought these benefits may be due to the expression of their emotions, he later found that it may have more to do with the ways that people come to better understand and make sense of their experiences. With this as a background, he began to think that writing about stressful events may be most beneficial when people write in a way that enables them to construct a coherent narrative.

Joshua Smyth put this theory to the test by actually asking two groups of college students to write about their most stressful experience and a third group to write about mundane topics.[6] The first group writing about stressful experiences was instructed to use a narrative format that involved having a clear beginning, middle, and end and making their writing "story-like." The second group writing about stressful experiences was asked to write in the format of a bullet list that followed no particular temporal order. Smyth found that the only group showing signs of improvement relative to the control group was the one that used the narrative format. The bullet list group did not do any better than the group assigned to write about mundane topics.

Timothy Wilson added another twist to understanding the benefits of thinking about our lives as a narrative. Whereas McAdams identified a coherent positive resolution and the transition from a negative to a positive state in a narrative as beneficial, Wilson writes in his book *Redirect: Changing the Stories We Live By* about how it may be beneficial to actively reframe and rewrite parts of our own stories.[7] He draws on Pennebaker and others who have adapted his writing intervention but also takes it a step beyond in encouraging people to revise their narratives in ways that give them hope, meaning, and purpose. This technique has been used in the treatment of veterans to help create ways to find meaning in their experience.

Laura King is another person who has adapted Pennebaker's writing technique in a way that fits particularly well with positive psychology. Rather than ask people to write about their most stressful experiences, she has asked them to write about their "best possible self" that they can imagine in the future. She found that people experience many of the same benefits as writing about stressful experiences but without experiencing as many negative emotions while writing.[8] Rather than just reframing your current story, this technique can also include imagining future steps in your current story, thinking about how you can make a better future happen, and may make it more likely it will happen by giving you a plan to follow.

The Hero's Journey as a Guide for Our Story

Despite the focus on numbers and APA style in psychology journals, there is good reason to think that focusing on stories may add something important for positive psychology. Humans live their lives in a sequence of events across time and may most often try to make sense of the meaning and significance of their lives in personal stories. The challenge of making the most of our lives and living them to the fullest is something that unfolds over time and not at the instant we discover that something is statistically significant. Narrative psychology has highlighted the value of stories and shown how constructing a narrative can be beneficial for coping with the worst and envisioning a better life. But what can guide us in constructing this narrative? What can enable us to make sense of our challenges and stresses and redirect our life in a way that makes the most of our lives?

When I was thinking about this question back in 2006, I came across an old book I had never read before. It was written by someone who is not a psychologist, although he was very familiar with the work of Carl Jung. He studied stories for a living and was a professor of mythology. But he talked about myth in a way many had not thought about before. First, for him a myth was not what has been defined as a widely held false belief or idea or story that was not true. For him a myth was a story that had been passed down over time and preserved because it spoke to some of the very deepest and most important challenges that people faced. Second, he expanded upon an idea that the novelist James Joyce called the "monomyth," which is the idea that many of our greatest myths and stories contain strikingly similar themes and stages and may often be viewed as essential one overarching story.

The name of the person in question is Joseph Campbell. He found evidence of a monomyth in the stories of many cultures. He wrote about this in a book he published in 1949 called *The Hero with a Thousand Faces*.[9] The idea of the monomyth soon became known as "the hero's journey" where the story of the hero has a similar pattern in very different stories. But Campbell's contribution was not just that many of the great stories might be understood as a common story, he also tied this story to you and me and to every living human being. He contended that the reason these stories evolved and were preserved is that they continued to speak to so many people with profound wisdom. Moreover, the reason that many of us cannot put down a book or stop binge watching a TV drama may be that it deeply resonates with our own story. We are the heroes— or at least we can be the heroes.

The Stages of the Hero's Journey

But just what is the hero's journey? It is a common pattern of stages through which the character of a story passes on the way to reaching a larger goal. Many of these stages can be clearly seen in both ancient and modern stories and have been at the heart of some of our favorite and most popular movies. Before going through the stages, let me say a little about how the hero's journey came to be at the heart of one of our most popular movie franchises.

After having completed the original *Star Wars* trilogy, George Lucas invited Joseph Campbell to his Skywalker Ranch to see all three movies in one day.[10] Lucas had read Campbell's *The Hero with a Thousand Faces* and intentionally based the *Star Wars* movies on the hero's journey that Campbell described. Even though Campbell had read myths and stories from hundreds of years ago and from many cultures, he was not much of a movie-goer and had never seen a *Star Wars* movie. With Lucas, Campbell watched *Star Wars* (later titled *A New Hope*) in the morning, *The Empire Strikes Back* in the afternoon, and *Return of the Jedi* during the evening. At the end of the day, Campbell was impressed with Lucas' artistic imagination in recreating the hero's journey in outer space and clearly recognized the stages of the hero's journey.

The actual stages of the hero's journey have been presented in many different ways. Campbell identified 17 stages frequently included in the older myths and stories that he studied which have a few stages that are not as common in modern stories. The Disney story analyst Chris Vogler wrote *A Practical Guide Joseph Campbell's The Hero with a Thousand Faces*, which became very popular with Hollywood screenwriters and influenced the creation of several movies including *Aladdin* (1991) and *The Lion King* (1994).[11] In Vogler's guide and book called *The Writer's Journey: Mythic Structure for Writers*, he outlined 12 stages that may be best suited for our modern journey and for positive psychology.[12] I'll walk you through them with examples from the first *Star Wars* movie and the kind of hero's journey involved in putting positive psychology into practice.

1. *The Ordinary World*

The hero is in an uneasy or uncomfortable home or place where there is a limited awareness of a problem. In *Star Wars*, Luke Skywalker is restless and bored in living with his aunt and uncle and farming on the desert planet Tatooine. The Ordinary World for us may involve a vague sense that something may be missing from our lives and beginning to wonder if there is something more. It could mean solely focusing on increasing pleasure and reducing pain without realizing there may be other elements of well-being that can bring us joy and fulfillment.

2. *The Call to Adventure*

Remember this from the first chapter? The call to adventure is the increased awareness that there is a problem or a chance for change and movement towards something new. Luke finds a holographic message from Princess Leia stored in R2-D2 that calls him to a higher purpose. The Call to Adventure for us may involve thinking about leaving a job or a relationship, going to therapy, quitting smoking, or deciding to go back to school, traveling to a new place, or trying some of the positive psychology exercises that may bring greater happiness.

3. *Refusal of the Call*

This is the reluctance or resistance to change. It is the hesitation, fear, or ambivalence that we often feel and experience before we make a big change. Luke doubts his ability to make a difference and refuses to join the rebellion even after meeting Obi-Wan. He uses the excuse that he still has work to do on Tatooine. The Refusal of the Call for us could be to doubt that it is possible to change or find anything better in life. In the context of what happened in psychology, it was falling into the negativity bias by only focusing on removing bad things.

4. *Meeting the Mentor*

This involves meeting someone with the wisdom and experience to guide us and enable us to build the confidence and courage we need to make the journey. Although Luke originally refused to work with Obi-Wan, he finally allowed him to begin to teach him about the Jedi and the ways of the Force. Meeting the Mentor in our lives may mean finding a teacher, therapist, or friend who is further along the path that we want to walk. With positive psychology, it may mean to be open to what science can teach us about how to live our lives to the fullest.

5. *Crossing the Threshold*

This is committing to leaving the Ordinary World and doing something that puts us in a new place that is not as comfortable and familiar. Luke leaves his home planet and the strange people that he sees in the Cantina are clear evidence he has crossed the threshold. For us, Crossing the Threshold could mean leaving an abusive relationship, beginning treatment for substance abuse, beginning a new diet or exercise program, or identifying our strengths and trying to find new ways to use them on the way to a better life.

6. *Tests, Allies, Enemies*

This is a kind of catch-all stage that stands for the smaller trials and tribulations that may arise, the making of friends who can support us in our journey, and the challenges of dealing with those who present obstacles on our journey. Luke experiences several minor ups and downs, meets new allies in Han Solo and Chewbacca, and begins to face the stormtroopers. For us, this could mean dealing with the little set-backs that discourage us along the way, finding new ways to enlist the support of others, and having to deal with difficult people.

7. *Approach and Preparation*

The hero and the new found allies prepare for and approach the greatest challenges of the journey. Luke practices using a lightsaber with Obi-Wan and approaches the Death Star with his allies. The scene where they are almost swallowed by the trash compactor parallels many old stories, such as Jonah being in the belly of a whale in the Bible. For us, this could be preparing to take the most challenging step in reaching a goal, such as practicing for a marathon, studying for a big exam, or learning to use mindfulness to deal with a trauma or loss.

8. *The Ordeal*

This is where the hero actually faces or confronts their biggest fear which often feels like a life or death experience. In *Star Wars*, after Obi-Wan turns off the tractor beam and is killed by Darth Vader, Luke faces his own death in an ultimate challenge when he rescues Princess Leia. For us, this could be actually running a marathon, taking a big exam, interviewing for a big job, confronting a person who hurt us, or trying to use everything we learn from positive psychology to cope with a great loss or taking a big risk in doing what may make us happy.

9. *The Reward*

The hero takes possession of the treasure that was won in undergoing the ordeal and what may feel like surviving death. This is also sometimes called "stealing the sword" where a sword symbolizes the hero owning their new found power. Luke takes possession of the new power that he has found in trusting the Force. For us, this could be accepting the benefits of having passed the test, enjoying the satisfaction and confidence that comes in having completed a marathon, or knowing that we can make the best of our lives even if we had to face the worst.

10. *The Road Back*

The hero is driven to complete the adventure and cross a threshold from the Special World back to what becomes their new home. For Luke, this does not mean heading back to his old life at Tatooine but that he joins the overall offensive to destroy the Death Star. For us, this could mean taking our hard won rewards of having faced the worst to the realm of our new life. For someone who has learned something valuable from positive psychology, it could mean beginning to think about how to apply and use what was learned to face future challenges.

11. *The Resurrection*

This is the climax of the hero's journey where the hero who has faced death and received a reward now comes back as a transformed person. Luke takes what he has learned to become the calm and confident pilot who uses the Force to destroy the Death Star. In *The Lord of the Rings*, Gandalf the Grey comes back as Gandalf the White after defeating the Balrog. In positive psychology terms, the hero might have moved from living a rather dull, boring, and meaningless existence to becoming an example of what it means to live life to the fullest.

12. *Return with the Elixir*

The hero has returned home and discovers ways to be his transformed self with others and share his reward to make a difference for the larger community. In many old stories, the elixir is a magic potion. In *Star Wars*, it is represented in how Luke is now on the path to becoming a Jedi knight and is using the ways of the Force for the good of others. For us, this could be becoming a mentor to others who have faced similar trials and ordeals or using what we have learned through positive psychology to find new ways to bring happiness and well-being to others.

Now that we have gone through all of the stages, it is important to remember that they won't necessarily always occur or happen in the same order in all great myths or stories. It might also help to think of the journey as four larger movements that occur in myths and stories that lead to the positive resolution and redemption described by McAdams.[13] These movements include (1) leaving a comfort zone to face new challenges, (2) learning about how to deal with them, (3) facing the challenges directly with all that has been learned, and (4) taking what is gained from the experience to create a better life for ourselves and others.

The Hero's Journey and Positive Psychology

Now we come to the heart of the matter. How is the idea of the hero's journey relevant for learning about positive psychology? How can it help us make our most challenging and important life journeys? How can we use this idea to be happy and make the most of our lives? While I have already provided several clues, I will conclude this chapter by highlighting six ways the idea of a hero's journey may be relevant for positive psychology in helping us make the most of our lives and live them to the fullest.

1. *The hero's journey can help us follow the path of science.*

The opening sequence of the original television version of Star Trek used the phrase "to boldly go where no man has gone before." The Star Trek television shows and movies are a vision of the kinds of things that might be possible if we continue to follow the path of modern science. Whether or not we ever invent a transporter beam, the modern iPhone is in many ways more advanced than the communication devices used on the original Enterprise.

Science indeed can be a bold adventure. The use of the scientific method is in many ways comparable to the movements and stages of the hero's journey. It involves challenging what may be most comfortable and traveling into what may be completely unfamiliar territory. In psychology, it means putting our most cherished and deeply held beliefs about our world to the test and being willing to be proved wrong.

Think of some of what the greatest scientists have faced and endured and the price they have often paid for their hard-won discoveries. Galileo has been considered the father of the scientific method and was locked up for heresy because he dared to question the orthodoxy of the day that the sun revolved around the earth. Darwin created a revolution of thought with his theory of evolution that still stirs resistance and controversy to this day.

In the same way, the scientific endeavor to understand human happiness and well-being has met with great misunderstanding and resistance both within and outside of academic psychology. The hero's journey in positive psychology involves facing the death of our old views about what makes our lives worth living and being willing to find something new that, like penicillin or *Prozac*, could serve as a new elixir and boon for humankind.

2. *The hero's journey can help us understand what it means to be our best.*

If positive psychology is the use of the scientific method to make the most of our lives and live them to the fullest, then each of our individual paths to that goal is a hero's journey. We can think of the full range of possibilities for our life as points on a bell curve. The left part of the curve represents the small chance of making the worst of our lives, the middle part is the most likely chance of living an average and mediocre life, and the right part is the small chance of becoming our best. Positive psychology is about what we can do to make that chance of becoming our best a reality.

As we continue through this book, you will see many examples of people who have realized their potential. There may be few better than Nick Vujicic who was born with tetra-amelia syndrome, a rare disorder characterized by the absence of arms and legs. After he was born, his mother refused to hold or nurse him and he was later bullied as an adolescent. But after hearing the story of another young man with a severe disability, he dedicated himself to moving to the right end of his own bell curve. He developed a supreme sense of confidence that enabled him to inspire others as a motivational speaker and founded the non-profit organization *Life Without Limbs*. In his videos, he demonstrates all he can do without his limbs and comforts others who suffer from problems that may seem small in comparison.

Nick Vujicic is a prime example of how the path to making the most of what you are given can be one of the greatest kinds of hero's journeys. This journey is not easy and certainly not for the faint of heart. As with the journey that Campbell saw in the stories of Jesus, the Buddha, and so many others, it involves leaving your comfort zone for a special world that includes unexpected friends and wise mentors as well as the modern-day equivalent of medieval dragons. In stories old and new, it means daring to believe that there is a land like Narnia described by C.S. Lewis where we have the opportunity to face challenges and become more than we ever could have imagined.

3. *The hero's journey can help us see the value of our life.*

In asserting that the greatest hero's journey stories are really about us, Joseph Campbell was implying that there is great value in our own lives. In the *Harry Potter* series, the characters called dementors are dark, mysterious creatures who suck the life out of us and make everything cold. J.K. Rowling's inspiration for creating the dementors was the depression that she experienced when she was broke and homeless before she became famous.[14] What Harry Potter faced in fighting the dementors is essentially the same challenge that Rowling faced in fighting depression and that each of us may face in fighting our own "dementors."

To know that we are a part of the same kind of hero's journey as Harry Potter or Hermione in the *Harry Potter* books or Luke or Leia in *Star Wars* is to know that our journey can be just as challenging and inspiring. The sense of joy that Harry Potter felt when he realized that it was within him to fight off the dementors is the same joy that we can experience when we make a choice to fight off the discouraging thoughts and feelings that sometimes threaten us. The reason that we may love some of our favorite stories so much is because they are really about us. Seeing that character endure their trials, deal with their enemies, and face and triumph through their Ordeal is to experience the possibility of following the same path.

In thinking about our lives as a hero's journey, even the smallest choices that we make can have the greatest value. The effects of even the simple things that occur in the context of our journey is made clear in this famous quote attributed to Mahatma Gandhi:

> Your beliefs become your thoughts,
> Your thoughts become your words,

Your words become your actions,
Your actions become your habits,
Your habits become your values,
Your values become your destiny.[15]

The idea of a hero's journey gives us the overall framework for understanding how this can be and shows us the path to a life of great meaning and value.

4. *The hero's journey can inspire and motivate us to be our best.*

One of the reasons that we love stories about successful hero's journeys is that we admire and can identify with the heroes. The followers of most of the great world religions have often been motivated by the desire to follow one of their most admired leaders. Having the example of someone that you can relate to such as Nick Vujicic, Harry Potter, or J.K. Rowling can be a wonderful motivator for doing something difficult. The idea of a hero's journey opens the door for all of us to begin to look for the characters in our favorite stories that we most admire and love and use them as an alter ego to inspire and motivate us to achieve our goals. As we do this, we can rest assured that our own journey may ultimately be no less meaningful, satisfying, and significant.

For many, Nelson Mandela has been a great example for motivating them to face great difficulties and do the right thing. As you may know, Mandela was imprisoned for many years for speaking out against the apartheid in South Africa that involved so much racial discrimination and injustice. Amazingly, after Mandela was released, he was elected president of South Africa and chose to unite the country and forgive his captors rather than retaliate against them. Many have used the hero's journey of Mandela as a way to motivate them to endure similar injustice and suffering and find a way to forgive and work for reconciliation rather than retaliation and revenge. For many, there may be no better motivator for being at their best than the story of someone they admire and love who does the right thing.

5. *The hero's journey can help us face and benefit from the worst.*

Piers Worth wrote a chapter entitled *The Hero's Journey* in the book *Second Wave Positive Psychology: Embracing the Dark Side.*[16] The chapter elaborates on how the idea of a hero's journey provides an antidote to the easy assumption that positive psychology is all about sunshine and roses and never addresses the dark things that scare us. The hero's journey contains a strange new world, many trials and enemies along the way, and the kind of ordeal that makes us fear losing our lives as we know it. This makes it very hard for us to avoid and deny the reality of suffering, illness, and death that role models like the Buddha faced on his journey.

But at the same time, the hero's journey is also about the very real possibility of the rewards and new life that facing and coming to terms with our greatest challenges may offer to us. Like the Biblical story of Jacob wrestling with the mysterious being at night, even though he is injured, he doesn't let his visitor go until he receives a blessing. The hero's journey carries with it that supreme human opportunity for creativity whereby we may find a way to learn, grow, and benefit from even the worst things that happen in our lives. This can mean finding new pathways to well-being such as becoming close to others, a greater appreciation of life, and discovering a new sense of meaning and purpose.

Most important, the hero's journey presents the possibility of that ultimate reward or boon that becomes an elixir bringing hope and healing to the rest of the world. One familiar example is the person with an alcohol or substance abuse problem who faces their own abyss and comes out on the other side to help others with the same problem. Another example is the person who was physically and sexually abused as a child and faces their abuser in a way that breaks the cycle and offers a new story of healing and transformation for others who suffer in the same way. The story arc of the hero's journey points the way for bringing positive psychology to the places and times where we need it the most.

6. *The hero's journey can connect us with all of humanity.*

When I was planning to write this book, I thought about how much of a central role the idea of a hero's journey should have in it. One day, I was on my way to the store *Bed Bath & Beyond* to buy something as ordinary and every day as a throw rug. They didn't have anything that I was looking for, but I ended up getting something much better. I ran into a student that I had the year before in my positive psychology class.

As many students who recognize a former professor might do, she took a moment to say that she really enjoyed the class. But it was the next thing she said that really made me forget about throw rugs. She told me that the one thing that had meant the most to her in the class was the idea that we are all on a hero's journey. She said that this has continued to help her appreciate all of her own struggles and how we are all in it together.

There is a wonderful quote of uncertain origin that says, "Be kind, for everyone you meet is fighting a great battle."[17] In the same way, the idea of the hero's journey not only means we have the chance to be on a great path, but that being on this path may be one of the most important things we share with other people. The great battles that we fight may seem very different on the surface, but they are all part of a quest to make the most of what we have been given.

The hero's journey to make the most of our lives despite our trials and ordeals beckons in the same way to us all. We all have a choice between spending our lives in a boredom-induced stupor and responding to the same call that Harry, Hermione,

J.K., Nick, and Nelson responded to. There are many paths that we can take in life that will separate and divide us and get us into wars and conflicts. The hero's journey that positive psychology calls us to is one with the potential of uniting us all.

The Hero's Journey to a Life Worth Living

Positive psychology presents all of us with the opportunity to make the hero's journey to making the best of the life that we have. In this chapter, we saw that we may think and act in the context of stories and that it may matter how we think about and live our stories. While science may help us understand what it takes for us to make the journey, the hero's journey as highlighted by Joseph Campbell may help show us the way.

Before I move on to the next chapter, I would like for you to go back and think about the elements of human happiness and well-being that may be most important to you. Try to think of the picture that I asked you to paint from the palette of different colors that these elements represent. Which ones might be the most important goals for your hero's journey? Then begin to imagine your life as part of a journey in moving towards those goals. Undoubtedly, this will continue to evolve as you think about it in the chapters to come.

As you read on, try to hold this evolving picture as a goal for you, just as the heroes in your favorite stories had their great challenges and goals. The challenges that you face may be no less important than the challenges that they faced. The joy that you feel when you achieve your goals may be no less than the joy that they felt when they achieved theirs. Remember that their stories are really our stories—and that the purpose of positive psychology is to help all of us complete our common hero's journey. Your journey can be the story of a new hero that you write by living it every day.

Chapter 6

Preparing for Your Hero's Journey

What lies behind us and what lies before us
are tiny matters compared to what lies within us.

—*Ralph Waldo Emerson*[1]

The hero's journey in many of our favorite stories is about both reaching an external goal and an internal transformation. In the same way, the hero's journey in positive psychology is about reaching the things that bring us the most happiness and well-being and becoming the best that we can be. This chapter is designed to help prepare you for this journey by introducing you to what may help you on your way. It will prepare you for the coming chapters where you will discover much more about specific tools and resources.

I will begin by presenting a couple of ways to think about the road to human change and transformation. Next, I will talk about three change processes that have been at the heart of the effectiveness of modern psychotherapy and psychological interventions. Finally, I will introduce a new framework for learning about what may help us most in our journey. This will lay the groundwork for you to cross the threshold to a new adventure toward the kind of life that you seek.

The Stages of Change

While we have already outlined the stages of the hero's journey we find in stories, I would now like to introduce you to a couple of other models of change that have been used by therapists, clinicians, and health professionals. The first is called the transtheoretical model of change developed by James Prochaska and Carlo DiClemente.[2] The transtheoretical model is also known by the term "stages of change" because it includes the stages that people often go through in making successful changes in behaviors related to their health. The targets for change have included a variety of behaviors including quitting smoking, reducing alcohol use, exercising more, managing stress better, and preventing depression. They could also include increasing happiness and well-being.

The model presents six stages of change that are thought to help the people trying to make changes and their health providers understand the process of change and also help them see how their needs may be different at each stage. Although not everyone will go through all the stages in the same order, the order of the stages is (1) Precontemplation, (2) Contemplation, (3) Preparation, (4) Action, (5) Maintenance, and finally (6) Termination. Precontemplation is when you are not aware of the need to change, Contemplation is when you are starting to think that a change may be beneficial, Preparation is getting ready to take action in the next 30 days, Action is following through on a plan for change, Maintenance is when you have sustained a change for at least six months, and Termination is when the change becomes a habit and you no longer need to make an effort to maintain the change.

How might this be relevant for the hero's journey in positive psychology with a person trying to increase their happiness and well-being? Precontemplation may be similar to the Ordinary World in the hero's journey where you have only a limited awareness that there may be something better. Contemplation could mean becoming aware of a Call to Adventure to a Special World where there are greater possibilities for joy, meaning, and fulfillment. Preparation may involve meeting and learning from a Mentor and Allies and practicing to face the biggest challenges. Action may mean putting into practice what you are learning with the smaller Trials and greater Ordeals that may arise. Maintenance may involve embracing the newfound well-being and making it sustainable in your ongoing daily life. Termination may mean reaching a new equilibrium and set point where little effort is required to maintain your newfound happiness and well-being.

The PATH Process

The second model of change is called the PATH process and was introduced to me by a graduate student who taught it to many of my positive psychology students. PATH is an acronym that stands for Planning Alternative Tomorrows with Hope and it involves a planning process developed in the 1990s by Jack Pearpoint, John O'Brien, and Marsha Forrest.[3] While the stages of change model helps us understand the typical process of successful change, the PATH process provides a series of steps that can be proactively taken to make positive change happen. The process is very flexible and can be used with groups and organizations as well as individuals.

The PATH process uses a visual or "graphic" approach with a series of steps to help you make a long-term plan to reach your most important life goals. The process involves creating a map of these steps on a large sheet of poster paper and writing down what will help you reach your goals. The process may be best led by a trained facilitator, but individuals can also learn to do it themselves by reading about it. Either way, it is a wonderful way to get "unstuck" and start a new process of positive change in your life. When completed, you will have the poster as a practical reminder and guide to help you move towards your most important goals.

The process involves eight steps that usually take two to three hours to complete. Although you can go through the steps alone, it is best to gather together a "dream team" of other people who are willing to support you in the process. The eight steps in the PATH process are very well-suited for positive psychology and the idea of making a hero's journey. PATH is also a good match for the hope theory developed by Rick Snyder and that will be discussed in Chapter 13. When you are done, you will have a visual representation of your "best possible self" and a plan for making it happen.

The first step is called Touching the Dream and involves envisioning a "north star" that represents what you want most in life. This "north star" will orient and guide you in the rest of the process and be the starting point for breaking your dream down into realistic goals. This can be a direct way to imagine and bring to life the ten elements of well-being listed at the end of Chapter 4. The second step is called Sensing the Goal and it involves identifying "positive and possible" goals for the future and a timeframe for reaching these goals. If you had a dream of increasing the meaning and purpose in your life by helping troubled adolescents, for example, then this step might involve the more specific goal of starting a non-profit organization for them.

While the first two steps are focused on the best possible future, the third step is called Ground in the Now and involves identifying where you are now in relation to reaching your goals. If your goal is to start a non-profit to help adolescents, then focusing on the now can help you see how far you are from it and just what you need to do to begin to reach your goal.

The fourth step is called Invite Enrollment and involves identifying and inviting people who are in a good position to provide support to help you reach your goal. This might include the people on your "dream team" or other people you know who may have similar interests and could help you in the process of developing your non-profit. This step fits nicely with Meeting the Mentor and finding Allies in the hero's journey and with the value placed on human relationships in positive psychology.

The fifth step is called Building Strength and it involves recognizing ways to build strengths and acquire new skills and talents. This step reflects the primary emphasis in positive psychology on identifying and using strengths. It also supports the kind of training we see in the hero's journey where characters like Luke get trained in the ways of the Force and Harry Potter goes to school at *Hogwarts*.

The final three steps include making a plan to bridge the gap between the now and reaching the vision and goals described in the first two steps. The goals identified in these steps should follow the guidelines of the SMART acronym in that they are: (1) Specific, (2) Measurable, (3) Achievable, (4) Relevant, and (5) Time-bound.[4] The sixth step is to Identify Bold Steps to achieve longer-term goals for the next several months, the seventh step is Organizing the Month's Work by being specific about who will do what and when in the next month, and the eighth and final step is simply Committing to the First Step which means doing one thing to get started.

Whether or not you go through the PATH process with a trained facilitator, the process can be a wonderful tool for being more proactive in your own journey to whatever makes you most happy. Visualizing what you most want in your life may free you from the limitations of language. Furthermore, starting with imagining the best possible future before coming back to the now can counter the negativity bias that keeps you from believing your life can get better. Finally, enlisting people to support you may be a great way to begin and focusing on your strengths may give you an empowering new vision of yourself.

The Processes of Change in Psychotherapy

Now that we have an understanding of the typical stages of positive change and a framework for breaking down the changes we want to make, what processes enable us to change? I want to present three that have played a fundamental role in the effectiveness of modern psychotherapy. Even though they were primarily developed to reduce negative things such as anxiety and depression, they may also be critical for the hero's journey to a better life. The following processes represent the ordinary magic that can enable us to do something truly extraordinary.

1. *Cognitive Reappraisal*

The first process is called cognitive reappraisal and it is our ability to change the way we think about things. Cognitive reappraisal is a focus in the cognitive therapies developed by Aaron Beck and Albert Ellis.[5-6] Cognitive therapy is a fundamental component of cognitive-behavioral therapy which has received strong and consistent support for treating a variety of mental health and stress-related disorders. Near the end of Chapter 3, I indicated that cognitive-behavioral therapy may be one of the best tools for raising our enduring level of happiness.

The idea behind cognitive therapy is that the way that we think about our lives can influence how we behave and feel. If we think that a rejection by another person is the end of the world, then we are more likely to become withdrawn and feel depressed. If we think that a rejection by another person is an opportunity to learn something valuable about ourselves, then we are less likely to withdraw and get depressed. Thus, cognitive therapy research has tried to identify the kinds of thoughts that may cause us to become anxious or depressed and help us find ways to reappraise what happens to us so that we will behave and feel better.

The ability to think about the same things in different ways has even been studied using modern neuroimaging. Researchers have put people into MRI scanners and asked them to think about pictures in ways that make them feel better or worse.[7] They have found that thinking about these pictures in different ways actually influences the activity in parts of the brain that support emotion, such as the amygdala. For example, when participants think of a picture of a woman crying at a church as a wedding rather than a funeral, they might have less activity in the amygdala indicating that they may be experiencing less negative emotion.

The book *Feeling Good* by David Burns is an excellent resource for people who want to learn about the benefits of a cognitive approach to depression.[8] Burns presents ten distorted thinking patterns that can lead to depression and several of them reflect the negativity bias. For example, Mental Filter is where you pick out a single negative detail and dwell on it so much that your vision of reality becomes darkened. Overgeneralization is where you see a single negative event as a never-ending pattern of defeat. Disqualifying the Positive is insisting that positive experiences don't count as much as negative experiences. The goal of cognitive therapy is to challenge this distorted thinking and replace it with a more realistic view that can also see and appreciate the positive.

Thus, cognitive reappraisal may be a useful tool for enabling us to counteract our negativity bias in the way that we see the world. In *Harry Potter*, as I already noted, the dementors were characters that represent J.W. Rowling's earlier experience with depression. When the students began their classes at *Hogwarts*, they were taught to deal with their fears of what would bring them down by thinking about them in a ridiculous way and by conjuring up a powerful memory of something good. Part of the "magic" in *Harry Potter* may be none other than the remarkable human ability to change the way that we think about something. This is similar to the movie *The Sound of Music* when Maria teaches the children to counter feeling bad during a thunderstorm by thinking of their "favorite things."

The ability to use the ordinary magic of cognitive reappraisal in our own journey is a potentially powerful "force" we can use in so many different ways. Researchers in the positive psychology movement have been very creative in finding new ways to apply it. Bob Emmons, Martin Seligman, and others have developed interventions focusing on things that we are grateful for and noticing the good things that happen during the day.[9] Thinking about the things we are grateful for in the past is very similar to conjuring up the "patronus" in *Harry Potter* and noting good things that happen during the day is a way of developing an ever-growing list of "my favorite things." The ability to think about our lives in the context of a hero's journey towards a best possible self, as studied by Laura King, may be one of the most powerful applications of cognitive reappraisal.[10]

2. *Behavioral Activation*

The second fundamental process used in many effective psychotherapies and that may also be a powerful force for the hero's journey in positive psychology is behavioral activation. Neil Jacobsen was the lead author on a study published in 1996 showing that behavioral activation was the key component in the cognitive-behavioral treatment of depression.[11] Behavioral activation involves encouraging people to identify activities that they find the most intrinsically rewarding and reinforcing and then incorporating them into their lives. It is rooted in the earlier work of Peter Lewinsohn who gave depressed people a list of pleasant events or activities and "prescribed" that they go out and regularly do them.[12]

Behavioral activation is a major weapon against depression because depression not only involves more negative emotions such as sadness, but also fewer positive emotions and the inability to experience pleasure. Behavioral activation may be a way of jump starting what has been called approach motivation or the reward systems in our brains. A common misunderstanding of behavioral activation is that it is simply getting people to do things that most people might think feel good. The challenge facing therapists using behavioral activation is to find those very unique activities that are most rewarding and reinforcing for a particular person.

Although it has primarily been used to treat mental disorders such as depression, behavioral activation also has clear and direct applications for positive psychology. First, it focuses on activating the positive emotions that Barbara Fredrickson has found to be important for broadening and building future resources.[13] Second, some of the newly identified positive emotions such as elevation and inspiration may play a strong role in behavioral activation. Rather than just focusing on activities that bring immediate pleasure, a person could identify different kinds of activities that may increase meaning and positive relationships or provide additional opportunities to experience flow.

Behavioral activation can also be thought of as a primary motivator for making the hero's journey towards a better life. The final goal that is imagined in the PATH process can be so enticing that it may be very difficult *not* to go on the journey. The basic idea behind behavioral activation is also expressed in the work of Joseph Campbell when he talks about "following your bliss." For Campbell, bliss is not the name of a chocolate bar or about fleeting physical pleasures. For him, following your bliss means "the deepest sense of being in form and going where your body and soul want to go."[14] Following your bliss is part of a eudaimonic journey where you move towards a greater level of authentic self-realization in living your life to the fullest.

As with cognitive reappraisal, behavioral activation has also been a potent "force" in the development of new interventions in the positive psychology movement. The most obvious is helping people identify their own unique strengths, helping them come up with a variety of ways to use them, and encouraging them to use them in as many new ways as possible. In trying to raise children to behave better, researchers have found that it may be more effective to help them see themselves as the kind of people who do good things rather than reward them for each little good thing that they do. In the same way, a positive psychology focus on the kind of people we are rather than what we do may have a more meaningful and enduring effect on our lives.

3. *Exposure Therapy*

The third fundamental process in effective psychotherapy that we can use in our hero's journey was developed in the treatment of anxiety disorders. Exposure therapy is the process of exposing a person to the things that make them anxious or fearful until they no longer experience as much distress.[15] Exposure therapy makes use of the extinction process which has been studied and well-documented by behavioral psychologists in research with rodents.

In exposure therapy, the therapist works with a person to help them identify the things that make them feel anxious. These might be spiders and snakes in treating phobias, memories of traumatic events in treating posttraumatic stress disorder (PTSD), or things that trigger obsessive thoughts or compulsive behaviors in obsessive-compulsive disorder (OCD). The therapist develops a plan for exposing the person to the things that make them anxious, teaches them how to monitor their distress, and encourages them to expose themselves to the source of their anxiety until their distress reaction is naturally reduced.

There are at least three types of exposure procedures. The first is called "in vivo" exposure which means "real life" where the person is exposed to an actual fear-inducing situation. The second is called "imaginal" exposure where the person is asked to imagine a situation that makes them anxious. The third is called "interoceptive" exposure where the person is asked to expose themselves to bodily sensations linked to the source of their anxiety.

Exposure therapy is a process of change that may not have as obvious a place in positive psychology as cognitive reappraisal or behavioral activation. In the context of treating anxiety disorders, exposure therapy has generally been thought of as being about getting rid of something bad, whereas positive psychology is often thought of as moving towards something good. But in reality the two go hand-in-hand just as our bodies include both approach systems involved in positive emotions and avoidance systems involved in negative emotions.

One danger in the positive psychology movement is that in appreciating the value of positive emotions and the approach systems, the value of negative emotions and the avoidance systems may be underestimated or forgotten. Negative emotions evolved for the very important reason of helping us avoid things that will hurt us. However, they sometimes become so strong in response to things that are not very dangerous that they prevent us from reaching our goals and doing what it takes to be happy. For example, the anxiety that some people experience in social situations may keep them from meeting others, making friends, and eventually finding a good life partner.

If your only goal is to increase the pleasure in your life, then it might be easy to miss the value of exposure therapy. But if you are on a journey where you want to get the most out of your life and live it to the fullest, then you are bound to have to confront a range of very real fears. The idea of answering a Call to Adventure and Crossing a Threshold from an Ordinary to a new Special World carries with it the inevitable anxiety that we experience in a challenging and unfamiliar place. The Trials and Enemies represent the ongoing fears that we must confront and the Ordeal stands for the thing that we fear the most—often to the point of death.

In being relegated to journals about treating anxiety disorders, we are in danger of forgetting about the ordinary magic of exposure therapy. For the principle behind it provides a basis for developing the courage to face some of our greatest trials and challenges. Rather than just confronting spiders and riding elevators, it may mean taking risks in following in the footsteps of people like Nelson Mandela, Martin Luther King, Jr., Joan of Arc, and all those who have faced down their fears to do something great with their lives.

One of the best examples of how the principle of exposure therapy can enable us to go on a truly heroic journey is that of prolonged exposure for veterans and victims of sexual assault. Like Harry Potter, they are asked to face the Voldemort of their nightmares in exposing themselves again and again to the fear and horror that they experienced during some of the worst moments of their lives. Rather than try to avoid this, as would be natural for most of us, they are asked to march right into that darkest cave where the greatest dragon lives and confront it until they prevail.

Exposure therapy may be a great secret weapon to help us overcome the tendency both in and outside of positive psychology to try to avoid or escape the darkness. It is the possibility that we can actually face and do what we fear, and in the process experience the kind of Reward and Resurrection to which the hero's journey points. It is the great potion against the temptation to take the easy way out and avoid that place where spiders and snakes may lurk—but where we also might find our holy grail.

While the applications to positive psychology may be less obvious, the process of exposure therapy goes hand-in-hand with cognitive reappraisal and behavioral activation. Why should we expose ourselves to our fears? Why should we put ourselves through the modern form of torture that some experience when they begin to think about dating? Why not just stay home and call it a day? Because through cognitive reappraisal, we can begin to imagine a better future that may get us out of bed. Because through behavioral activation, we can build the motivation to do the tough and scary things we need to do to in order to gain or reach some of the things that will really make us happy.

Do you remember Bethany Hamilton? She was the young girl who had her left arm bitten off by a shark while surfing when she was 13 years old. I'm not sure that I would want to get back in the water after that. I didn't even want to take a shower after I saw the movie *Jaws*. But in Joseph Campbell's terms, "following your bliss" meant surfing for Bethany Hamilton. She was back in the ocean surfing after one month. Surfing was the best form of behavioral activation for Bethany and it motivated her to expose herself to her fear until it melted away into her greatest joy. The power of reappraisal helped her see surfing again with one arm as a challenge that she could overcome rather than the end of being able to do what she loved.

Discovering the Better Angels of Our Nature

While these three fundamental processes of change were developed before the dawn of the positive psychology movement, those in the movement have continued to make new contributions directly relevant for making the most of our lives. I have already talked about much of what they have done to help us gain a better understanding of happiness, well-being, and what we can aim for in our hero's journey to our best life. Now, I want to talk about what may be the most helpful and hopeful development in the movement.

The artist M.C. Escher has a circular drawing called *Angel-Devil* that is covered with both angels and devils that I suggest you look for on the Internet.[16] Depending on how you look at the drawing, you might see only angels or only devils. As we have already learned, Abraham Lincoln used the phrase "the better angels of our nature" to call out the best in people to begin to heal what had been a divided country.[17] Before the positive psychology movement, much of psychology had come to focus on what could go wrong with people. If the angels in

Escher's drawing represented "the better angels of our nature" and the devils the things that drag us down, then modern psychology had primarily focused on the devils.

The *Diagnostic and Statistical Manual* (DSM) became both the vocabulary of pathology and the lens through which much of modern psychiatry and psychology came to perceive what it means to be human. Mental health was the absence of mental illness. Just as there were so many more words to describe negative vs. positive emotions, so there were many more diagnoses and descriptions of what can go wrong with us rather than what can go right. This mirrored the negativity bias in the popular culture with an ever-growing number of movies and television shows depicting "breaking bad" whereas the few stories of "breaking good" were often lacking in depth and realism.

But the problem was not that there were no deeply moving and gripping true stories of breaking good. Although we take them for granted, they are all around us in the stories of Jesus, Buddha, Moses, Gandhi, Mother Teresa, Eleanor Roosevelt, and in many of our own mothers and fathers and other family members and friends. I have seen it time and time again in the lives of so many students who are just doing their best while fighting traffic, trying to find parking, working two jobs, or raising a child while going to school. The problem may not be that these stories do not exist, but that we have lost the ability to see them and allow them to come to life and shine into our own lives.

It is to this problem that the positive psychology movement may have provided one of its greatest contributions and most wonderful gifts. The movement gave us a new way of seeing ourselves. The development of what has been called the "Un-DSM" may be one of the most powerful tools we have for human change and transformation. It gives us a framework for viewing and understanding what can go right with us, what enables us to move to the good side of the bell curve, and what can help us make the most of our hero's journey. While much of previous psychology and the positive psychology movement itself represents more of an evolution of previous work, the introduction of a new way of seeing and understanding ourselves may be much more of a revolution.

The Classification of Virtues and Strengths

In Chapter 2, I introduced the "Un-DSM" as a book published in 2004 titled *Character Strengths and Virtues: A Handbook and Classification* edited by Chris Peterson and Martin Seligman.[18] The classification system presented in this book includes 24 positive characteristics or human strengths that have been organized under six groups of overarching "virtues." Now I would like to tell you more about how this book came to be and how it can provide a firm and comprehensive foundation for making our hero's journey.

Shortly after the dawn of the positive psychology movement, Martin Seligman recruited Chris Peterson to spearhead the development of a new classification of human strengths. Peterson gathered a talented and diverse group of 55 social scientists who worked together for three years to identify what can be best in all of us. Their goal was to determine what qualities were most universally considered to indicate the strength of character. They used the term "character strengths" to indicate qualities that are not only good for the individual person, but also have positive implications for other people and the larger society and world.

They came up with ten criteria for a character strength and decided that a strength would need to meet most of them. I want to focus on four of the most important criteria. First, "a strength contributes to various fulfillments that constitute the good life, for oneself and for others" (p. 17).[19] The strength should provide a means to the end of a joyful, meaningful, and fulfilling life. Second, "although strengths can and do produce desirable outcomes, each strength is morally valued in its own right, even in the absence of obvious beneficial outcomes" (p. 19).[20] The strength can also be considered an end it itself. Third, "the display of a strength by one person does not diminish others in the vicinity" (p. 21).[21] Also, although a strength might be used to hurt other people, it is not necessarily so and is most often used to benefit others. Fourth, "a character strength is embodied in consensual paragons" (p. 24)[22] and conversely there may also be people who show a "total absence of a given strength" (p. 26).[23] This means that we should be able to find good examples of people who do and do not embody the character strength in their lives, in history, and in stories.

The result of three years of the intense collaborative effort of Peterson and the other social scientists was to come up with what has been called the *Values in Action Classification of Human Strengths and Virtues* or VIA for short. The VIA consists of the six overarching categories of virtue that have been named Wisdom, Courage, Humanity, Justice, Temperance, and Transcendence. The following is a brief description of all six including the strengths associated with each:

1. *Wisdom*—cognitive strengths that entail the acquisition and use of knowledge including creativity, curiosity, open-mindedness, love of learning, and perspective.

2. *Courage*—emotional strengths that involve the exercise of will to accomplish goals in the face of opposition, external or internal including bravery, persistence, integrity, and vitality.

3. *Humanity*—interpersonal strengths that involve tending and befriending others including love, kindness, and social intelligence.

4. *Justice*—civic strengths that underlie healthy community life including fairness, citizenship, and leadership.

5. *Temperance*—strengths that protect against excess including forgiveness and mercy, humility or modesty, prudence, and self-control.

6. *Transcendence*—strengths that forge connections to the larger universe and provide meaning including the appreciation of beauty and excellence, gratitude, optimism, hope, humor, and meaning, purpose, and spirituality.

These virtues and character strengths and the process of developing them were fully described in the *Character Strengths and Virtues: A Handbook and Classification* handbook by Peterson and Seligman in 2004.[24] There are chapters describing each of the strengths by experts, which include a definition of the strength, what may increase or hinder it, and what can be done to modify or increase it. Most important, the publication of the book spurred a great deal of new research into the character strengths, a survey that can be used in research and that allows anyone to get feedback on their top strengths, and a growing list of ways to use and build the strengths.

The survey and a list of ways to use the strengths are two of the most useful resources. The *Values in Action Survey (VIA Survey)* is currently a 120 item questionnaire that you can take online and receive an immediate ranking of your strengths from the 1st to the 24th.[25] There is also a youth version for those under 18 years of age. The *340 Ways to Use VIA Character Strengths* by Tayyab Rashid lists a dozen or more ways to use each of the strengths and is easily accessible online.[26] Ryan Niemiec of the *Values in Action Institute* has also written books illustrating the character strengths in movies called *Positive Psychology at the Movies* and a new book on ways to build strengths called *Character Strengths Inventions*.[27-28]

In thinking about how to use the character strengths, it is important to understand that strengths can be misused and use wisdom and social intelligence to find the best ways to balance our strengths in reaching our goals. For example, a strength like perseverance may be overused when someone keeps trying to make a relationship work when their partner is not willing to make an effort. The wisdom to know the difference between what you can and cannot change expressed in the *Serenity Prayer* may help to prevent too much perseverance. As another example, humor may be misused when it makes light of something that hurts another person's feelings. Social intelligence might also be important in helping us find the best balance in when and how to try to be funny.

Finally, while the VIA classification does represent a thorough and comprehensive attempt to classify what is best about us into six categories of virtues, there are some important human strengths that may not easily fit into these categories. There are four other strengths frequently mentioned in positive psychology articles and books which cut across these categories and may be relevant for them all. These four are also particularly relevant for any kind of a hero's journey and will be covered in the next chapter. The first two have to do with the time dimension of our lives and have been called mindfulness, which is the ability to pay attention to the present, and self-efficacy, which involves our ability to move towards a better future. The second two are critical for how we deal with stress and adversity. They are resilience, which is our ability to bounce back from stress, and stress-related growth, which is our ability to learn, grow, and benefit from stress and adversity.

Using Top Strengths vs. Building Lower Strengths

There is a wonderful metaphor that has been circulating around the positive psychology movement. It is called the "sailboat metaphor." The idea is that we are like a sailboat and that there are a couple of different things we can devote our attention to in trying to move forward. First, we can try to look for and fix the holes in our boat that might slow us down or cause us to sink. Second, we can simply raise the sails and let the wind effortlessly move us forward. Looking for and fixing the holes is like paying attention to our weaknesses—the strengths listed at the bottom of our profile results in VIA survey, for example. Raising our sails is like finding new ways to use our strengths—those listed at the top of our VIA profile results.

Let me give you an example of two famous people you may have heard of. Stevie Wonder is a supremely talented and creative musician who became blind shortly after he was born. There is a story that Stevie's love of sound and music was inspired when an elementary teacher asked him to use his hearing to find a mouse that was loose in their classroom. Stevie calmly found the mouse, felt pride in his gift of hearing, and learned to focus on what was one of his greatest strengths rather than his inability to see.

The other person is James Earl Jones. He is the man behind the booming, dark voice of Darth Vader that has frightened so many—both young and old. As a child, Jones had a speech impediment and other children often laughed at him. His felt so bad about his stutter that he barely spoke to anyone for eight years. However, he worked hard to overcome it through poetry, public speaking, and acting—and you might just say that he overcompensated. His Darth Vader voice probably frightened many who laughed at him as a child.

The focus in psychology before the positive psychology movement was almost solely on looking for and fixing the holes in our boats. Similarly, the negativity bias motivates us to think much more about our weaknesses than our strengths. In contrast, an important goal in positive psychology has been to encourage us to raise our sails and enjoy the wind at our backs. Several studies have shown that identifying and finding new ways to use our top strengths may be some of the best ways to increase our happiness and well-being.[29]

However, just as the Escher drawing has both angels and devils, so it is essential for us to see the value in both using our strengths and addressing our weaknesses. Teri Rust and her colleagues did a study showing that working on both strengths and weaknesses can be important.[30] If the holes get large enough in our boats, we won't go anywhere but to the bottom. But if we don't raise our sails, we will never get to where we really want to be. The bottom line is that both are important, but that we need to be sure to focus on using our strengths because they can be such a great source of happiness and well-being and because it is so easy to get lost in focusing only on our weaknesses.

Climbing the Gandhi Ladder

There is another metaphor about a ladder that may help us understand how we can build and increase our strengths. Do you remember the quote from the last chapter that was attributed to Mahatma Gandhi? It was about how there is a progression from our beliefs, to our thoughts, to our words, to our actions, to our habits, to our values, and then to our destiny. Psychology has focused on a similar range of things from our emotions, which can shift and change frequently throughout a single day, to things that are very stable, such as the Big Five personality characteristics.

The VIA strengths and other positive qualities such as mindfulness, self-efficacy, resilience, and stress-related growth can span the range of the Gandhi Ladder. They may be fleeting behaviors but through habit can become stable personal characteristics. For one person, courage may be just a fleeting thought or something that is only rarely seen in their outward behavior. For another, courage may be a very stable strength that manifests itself in many different contexts and life situations. The goal for a person trying to build a strength is to move it from the domain of a belief or a thought, to something they begin to practice, to something that becomes habit, and finally to a very stable and consistent part of who they are that helps determine their destiny.

The phrase "neuron's that fire together wire together" has been used to describe the connection between our every thought and action and the changing structure of our brains. The book *Hardwiring Happiness* by Rick Hanson presents what we can do to "rewire" our brains and raise our happiness to a higher level.[31] There is strong evidence that our brains are plastic and flexible enough to continue to change throughout our lives. One focus in positive psychology interventions has been to find ways to make the behaviors that express human strengths a larger and more consistent part of who we are. For example, trying to look for the good in others on a daily basis may eventually make us a person with a special gift for seeing the best in others.

Moving Forward in the Journey

In this chapter, I have tried to lay the groundwork for the hero's journey and everything else that will follow in the coming chapters. First, I presented the Stages of Change as a roadmap for positive change and the PATH process as a way to begin to plan your own journey. This can help you understand your hero's journey in psychological terms that are easy to relate to and give you some of the concrete steps you may need for completing your journey.

Second, I presented three fundamental processes of change that have stood the tests of research and time in psychotherapy and that are also directly relevant for making the most of our lives. These processes are some of the ordinary magic that will so often come to life and move us to the next step of our journeys. While we may often be unaware of them, I wanted to give you the eyes to see them and the opportunity to begin to use them more as you travel.

Finally, I have presented an overview of the kinds of human qualities that we embody at our best and that may do the most to help us move forward. These included the *VIA Classification of Human Strengths and Virtues* and the additional basic strengths of mindfulness, self-efficacy, resilience, and stress-related growth that transcend all categories. As you will see, finding ways to cultivate and use these strengths might be the closest thing we can find to going to *Hogwarts* or going to Jedi training for facing the challenges that we may encounter.

In the next chapter, my goal is to give you some basic training in the four strengths that are fundamental to the use of all the others. In the chapters that follow, I will walk you through some of the latest and best theories and research on each of the strengths and how to build and better use them in your life. My overarching goal is to give you what you may need to begin to sail with the wind at your back in your hero's journey.

Chapter 7

Basic Training in the Fundamental Strengths

Do or do not. There is no try.

—Yoda[1]

Before we proceed to learning about each of the VIA strengths, I would like to introduce four strengths that are fundamental for them all and for moving towards the kind of life you most want. The first two have strong parallels in Jedi training in the *Star Wars* saga and can undoubtedly be a powerful "force" in our lives. The other two are critical for surviving and thriving in the midst of the trials and ordeals that we experience every day on our own hero's journey.

Casey Kasem was the host of the long running *American Top 40* radio program who always ended his show with the saying: "Keep your feet on the ground and keep reaching for the stars."[2] The first two strengths are what enable us to do both. Mindfulness enables us to keep our feet on the ground and be present to the current reality and circumstances of our lives. Self-efficacy enables us to reach for the stars to make the most of our lives and live them to the fullest. In this chapter, you will discover what we are coming to know about the value of paying attention to the present and believing in your ability to create a better future.

The other two strengths are often vital to the heroes in many of our favorite movies and stories. Resilience is the ability to bounce back and recover from the bad things that happen to us and stress-related growth is the ability to learn, grow, and benefit from even the worst that happens to us. We can see these in so many fictional heroes such as Indiana Jones, Rocky, and Katniss in *The Hunger Games*, and in so many who may be real life heroes such Mother Teresa, Abraham Lincoln, and Oprah Winfrey. In this chapter, you will find some of what psychology and science has to offer in coping with and making the best of the stress that you may face on your journey.

7.1. Mindfulness

The word "mindfulness" has come to mean different things to different people and has become very popular during the past 20 years. The definition that we will focus on is the one developed and used by Jon Kabat-Zinn who is most responsible for bringing mindfulness to the attention of science and positive psychology. In 1979, he founded the Stress Reduction Clinic at the University of Massachusetts where he used Buddhist teachings about mindfulness to develop the Mindfulness-Based Stress Reduction (MBSR) program which has been adapted and studied extensively in the treatment of a variety of psychological and stress-related disorders.

What Is Mindfulness?

The most quoted definition of mindfulness by Kabat-Zinn is probably the one from his book titled *Wherever You Go, There You Are: Mindfulness Meditation in Everyday Life.* He says that mindfulness means "paying attention in a particular way: on purpose, in the present moment, and nonjudgmentally" (p. 4).[3] What is often not quoted are the following sentences which make clear just how relevant mindfulness is for the quest to live our lives to the fullest:

> This kind of attention nurtures greater awareness, clarity, and acceptance of present-moment reality. It wakes us up to the fact that our lives unfold only in moments. If we are not fully present for many of

those moments, we may not only miss what is
most valuable in our lives but also fail to realize
the richness and the depth of our possibilities
for growth and transformation (p. 4).[4]

For Kabat-Zinn, the ability to pay attention to the present moment in a non-judgmental way is the primary ingredient and first principle for living and experiencing our lives to the fullest.

In an attempt to be as clear as possible about what he and most psychologists mean by mindfulness, I will restate his definition as follows: mindfulness is being aware of and paying attention to whatever is occurring in the present moment without making judgments about it. First, mindfulness involves being aware of whatever is occurring including the thoughts, feelings, and bodily sensations within you and whatever comes from all of your senses about what is happening around you. Second, mindfulness involves focusing your ongoing attention on this in the present moment and continuing moment by moment. Third, mindfulness involves the open and accepting observation of what is occurring without any attempts to judge whether any of it is good or bad or right or wrong.

This might sound easy or like something we may naturally do most of the time. But there are as many things that can keep us from doing this as there are that might distract Luke from focusing on the Force. Two of the largest things have to do with time and the almost irresistible urge to judge everything. First, we cannot completely focus on what is happening now because we are either lost in thinking about what happened in the past or what may happen in the future. Second, we are constantly judging and evaluating whether what we are thinking and feeling is useful and good or whether what is happening around us bodes ill or well for us. The ability to practice mindfulness involves allowing ourselves to let go of these judgments.

Why Is Mindfulness Important?

Why might this ability to be aware of and focus on the present moment be so important? For part of the answer we can look to the ways that mindfulness is being applied to help people with different problems. For example, the MBSR intervention that Kabat-Zinn developed to deal with chronic pain and stress has been adapted to help with recurrent depression, anxiety, weight management, diabetes, traumatic stress, dyslexia, attention deficit disorder, and to prevent relapse for those with substance abuse problems. Mindfulness may help by promoting feelings of relaxation, improving our ability to prevent and reduce stress, and enabling us to be more aware of and make better use of the good things in our lives.

The practice of mindfulness has also been extended to people and vocations where optimal functioning is important. As with training in the martial arts and as it might appear to be in training to be a Jedi knight in *Star Wars*, the ability to pay full attention to the present may be a critical component for being at your best. Mindfulness interventions are being developed and tested for soldiers, police officers, firefighters, and other first responders with the goal of improving performance as well as reducing anxiety and stress. One of the most interesting applications of mindfulness to performance is presented in George Mumford's book *The Mindful Athlete*.[5] Mumford worked with basketball coach Phil Jackson and players including Michael Jordan and Kobe Bryant and talked about how mindfulness can help all of us be at the top of our game.

One of the biggest reasons why mindfulness is so important is that many of us have become so busy and pressed for time. The growing emphasis on mindfulness and the revival of contemplative traditions in world religions may in part be a response to this lack of time. The ability to practice mindfulness in the midst of a busy and demanding schedule may provide the balance so many need. But the most basic and important reason that mindfulness is important may simply be that the only time that we can really experience our lives is the present moment.

How Can We Increase Mindfulness?

What can we do to improve our ability to practice mindfulness? How can we move it from being just an occasional or fleeting effort to a habit and then to a more stable and consistent strength? There are a variety of practices in Buddhism and other established traditions that we have only begun to draw on. The Dalai Lama, the leader of Tibetan Buddhism, has supported the scientific study of practices that foster mindfulness. In addition, the Vietnamese monk Thich Nhat Hanh has written many helpful books about practicing mindfulness.[6]

Out of the rich history and confluence of these people and traditions has grown a surprisingly small number of simple practices to foster mindfulness. In this way, learning to practice mindfulness is very similar to learning to use the Force in Stars Wars—it is simple but not easy. In fact, it can sound so surprisingly simple—but be so surprisingly difficult when we actually try to practice it. How easy it is to think that we can pay attention to our thoughts until we try. Before we even realize it, we are off to the races with our favorite fantasy about the future or regret about the past. The impatience of Luke while trying to learn the ways of the Force from Yoda is familiar to so many who have tried to practice mindfulness.

The most common practices for learning mindfulness are (1) to focus on your breathing; (2) to slowly move your attention across your whole body; (3) to focus on whatever thoughts, feelings, or sensations come to mind; and (4) to extend your practice to other aspects of your everyday life. The most common way to begin practicing mindfulness is to close your eyes and focus on your breath because it is always something you can be aware of and is so basic to your life. Just focusing on your breath may have a relaxing effect because it slows your breathing and body down. The most common instruction is to focus on your breath as it goes in and out through your nose, in and out of your lungs, or as your abdomen rises and falls.

The most important instruction is probably what to do with the inevitable distracting thoughts, feelings, sensations, and sounds around you. Rather than try to stop them or not pay attention to them by the simple force of will, you are instructed to either just note them and/or to simply return to focusing on your breath. This is where the non-judgment part of mindfulness practice really becomes important. Rather than putting yourself down for not doing it right, you simply note whatever thought, feeling, sensation, or sound has arisen and return to your breath. You may begin practicing this for just a few minutes and gradually increase the time up to 20 minutes or more.

Practicing mindfulness has been likened to sitting on the edge of a river while boats with your thoughts, feelings, and sensations float by. Your goal is not to try to stop them but to just allow them to pass by and avoid jumping on board. What this simple breathing exercise can do after much practice is to increase your ability to focus on one thing that is happening right now—your breathing. As you do this you will get better at not jumping on the boats passing by and be more able to focus all of your awareness and attention on whatever is most important at the time. When it comes time to focus on making the jump shot or remembering what you learned for the test, you are more likely to be all there and all in.

What Kabat-Zinn has called the "body scan" is another exercise that is often useful when starting to practice mindfulness.[7] It may be helpful to begin with one of the many audio recordings that can slowly guide you through focusing on the different parts of your body. Normally, you would lie down and this might take 30 to 45 minutes. As with focusing on the breath, this is particularly useful because you can do it wherever you are and it has the added benefit of increasing body awareness in a way that can reduce stress and improve your health. For example, after practicing mindful awareness, people with chronic pain sometimes discover that they have been imagining their pain to be worse than it is actually feels when they allow themselves to fully experience it.

The next practice for many in learning mindfulness can also be harder than it sounds and is often called "choiceless awareness." This practice allows your attention and awareness to go wherever it is drawn. It may move from your breath to a sound around you to a sensation in your stomach and then to a thought or feeling you are having. The goal is both to fully focus on whatever is the object of your attention but also to be flexible in allowing it to shift from one thing to another. You can see how this could be critical in the martial arts or a light saber battle or in responding to a complex and fast changing situation. Luke did this before destroying the Death Star by turning off the distracting incoming information from his ship's computer and was then able to fully focus on hitting his target.

The last type of exercise for learning mindfulness involves finding ways to practice it during your daily life. The most common example is what is called "walking meditation" where you walk in a slow, deliberate, and rhythmic manner so you can pay full attention to what you are doing moment by moment. Thich Nhat Hanh suggests in his book, *The Miracle of Mindfulness*,[8] that beyond walking, you can practice mindfulness during a great variety of everyday activities such as washing dishes, brushing your teeth, or gardening. This could be extended to many things in your life such as being with friends and family, singing and dancing, and using your strengths.

There is even a new mindfulness intervention designed to help you learn to build and use your strengths. Ryan Niemiec is a psychologist at the VIA Institute which supports the use of

VIA Classification of Strengths and Virtues. He adapted Kabat-Zinn's MBSR intervention to create a "Mindfulness-Based Strength Practice" (MBSP). MBSP is presented in his book *Mindfulness & Character Strengths: A Practical Guide to Flourishing* and is directly relevant to the goal of using strengths to increase happiness and well-being.[9] Niemiec has done research showing that MBSP increased life satisfaction, engagement, and flourishing relative to a non-treatment control group.[10]

If you are interested in practicing mindfulness and making it a strength for you, there are a range of books, audios, videos, and interventions that can help. The best place to start is often taking the eight week MBSR course or reading one of Kabat-Zinn's books. In his book, *Full Catastrophe Living,* he presents the foundations of the MBSR intervention and in *Wherever You Go, There You Are* he presents a program for mindfulness in everyday life.[11-12] Both are available with CDs to help you practice. Thich Nhat Hahn has written many good books applying mindfulness to a variety of topics including dealing with anger and building bridges between Buddhism and Christianity. George Mumford's book *The Mindful Athlete* is a good starting point if you want to use mindfulness to perform better in sports or other domains of your life.[13]

7.2. Self-Efficacy

As I mentioned earlier, both mindfulness and self-efficacy have been associated with Jedi training in *Star Wars.* Although these two strengths complement each other, they are also very different. While it is easy to trace the practice of mindfulness to ancient traditions, the idea of self-efficacy is rooted in more recent psychology. Most important, while mindfulness is necessary to stay grounded in the present, self-efficacy is critical for meeting future goals.

What Is Self-Efficacy?

Simply put, self-efficacy is our belief in our ability to do what it takes to reach a specific goal. Albert Bandura is the pioneer of the study of self-efficacy and he defines it as "people's beliefs in their capabilities to produce desired effects by their own actions" (p. vii).[14] Bandura published a paper in 1977 showing that self-efficacy was related to how people with a snake phobia could benefit from exposure therapy.[15] Despite having studied a variety of psychological topics, he decided to devote much of the rest of his career to studying self-efficacy.

There are two important distinctions that need to be made about self-efficacy in order to avoid common misconceptions. First, self-efficacy is the *belief* in a person's ability and not their actual *ability*. If there are two runners who have an equal ability, the one with the greater belief in that same ability will win the race because of their greater self-efficacy and not because of their greater ability. Second, self-efficacy is about accomplishing a specific goal or task rather than a more general confidence that any goal or task can be accomplished. The amount of self-efficacy that we have for one task, such as doing well in a psychology class, may be very different from how much we have for another, such as playing soccer.

What Are the Effects of Self-Efficacy?

Self-efficacy has been applied to a wide variety of things including improving mental and physical health, performance in school, sports, and on the job, and even social relationships. Self-efficacy has been shown to decrease common mental health problems such as anxiety and depression. People generally experience less anxiety when they are more confident in their ability to do a difficult task and are less depressed when they believe they can do what it takes to reach the goals that will bring them a sense of reward and satisfaction.

Self-efficacy may play an important role in relation to physical health for a couple reasons. First, it may increase healthy behaviors and reduce harmful behaviors. Self-efficacy has often been a key component in theories of how people improve health behaviors involving diet, exercise, and alcohol and substance use. For example, self-efficacy is important for both attempting and sustaining the effort to quit smoking. Second, self-efficacy may reduce the negative effects of stress on the body. Having low self-efficacy for a challenging task may increase the body's stress response which over time can damage the cardiovascular and immune systems and lead to the development of chronic disease.

Self-efficacy is also an important factor for success in school and sports. Bandura did a study showing that the self-efficacy of children for doing school work was positively related to their academic performance. Others have shown that increasing self-efficacy may improve writing performance and that lower self-efficacy may help to explain why fewer women than men choose careers in math and science. There is also much evidence showing that self-efficacy predicts better athletic performance in a variety of sports. Sandra Moritz analyzed 45 studies and found that the average correlation between self-efficacy and sports performance was .38.[16]

Finally, self-efficacy appears to play an important role in our social relationships as well as our performance at work. Higher self-efficacy has been related to greater relationship satisfaction and to the behaviors that maintain a good relationship. Self-efficacy may affect the ability to make friends, pursue romantic relationships, and give and receive help. Self-efficacy has consistently been an important factor on the job. Alexander Stajkovic analyzed 114 studies of the relationship between self-efficacy and work performance and found the same .38 average correlation that was reported above for self-efficacy and sports performance.[17]

Why Is Self-Efficacy So Beneficial?

What might explain the positive effects of self-efficacy? First, people with greater self-efficacy are more likely to approach difficult tasks as challenges to be mastered rather than threats to be avoided. Having lower self-efficacy can make tasks seem too difficult which can lead to poorer preparation or practice. For example, people with higher self-efficacy for the challenging task of quitting smoking are less likely to even try in the first place.

Second, people with greater self-efficacy may set more challenging goals and maintain a stronger commitment when facing obstacles than those with lower self-efficacy. A high school student with higher self-efficacy for playing football may be more likely than one with lower self-efficacy to go out for the varsity as opposed to the junior varsity team. A college student with higher self-efficacy for studying may be more likely to apply to graduate school than a student with lower self-efficacy for doing schoolwork.

Third, people with greater self-efficacy are more successful because they take a wider view of the task resulting in better decisions while those lower in self-efficacy lose their perspective. The positive emotions that people experience when they believe in their ability to do something can broaden their perspective and allow them to think of and see more options. The negative emotions associated with low self-efficacy may mean getting lost in details or trivialities and losing the big picture.

Fourth, people with higher self-efficacy often recover more quickly and sustain their efforts in the face of set-backs. When trying to improve health behaviors such as reducing alcohol and substance abuse or improve one's diet, the ability to respond in a constructive way to a relapse or set-back is critical. People with high self-efficacy are more likely to attribute a set-back to external factors and things they can control than are those with low self-efficacy who tend to blame themselves and focus on things they cannot control.

Fifth, self-efficacy may reduce the stress and emotional distress experienced while engaging in a difficult task. The expression "don't ever let them see you sweat" carries the assumption that we have control over sweating. In the "heat" of the moment we may have little control over this, but self-efficacy may determine how much we feel anxious and end up sweating in the first place. The more self-efficacy we have for a task, the more likely we will be cool, calm, and collected.

How Can We Increase Self-Efficacy?

Because self-efficacy is so important, there has been a great deal of research on its sources and how to increase it. There are at least five primary ways. As I go through them, think about something you would like to do better and which one of these you might like to try in order to boost your self-efficacy for it.

1. *Performance Experiences*

For many, the best way to increase their confidence in a particularly task is simply to practice performing the task or something close to it. Even the smallest success on a similar task can increase self-efficacy. In the movie, *What about Bob?* the psychiatrist asked his patient, played by Bill Murray, to take "baby steps." In building your confidence to run a marathon, this could mean beginning with once around the track and gradually building up to a mile, and then three, and then five, and then 10 miles or more.

The other principle that can help in using performance experiences to build self-efficacy is to break the most complex and challenging tasks down into simpler things that can be learned one by one. If you want to become a great martial artist, you need to begin with the simplest tasks and earn your first belt before moving on to more complex tasks and eventually a black belt. If you want to try to make the most of your life, then you may need to break it down into smaller steps that allow you to learn and practice building and using the strengths you will need.

2. *Vicarious Experiences*

One of the wonderful gifts of being human is that we have such an incredible capacity to mirror the behavior of others. Neuroscientists have discovered "mirror neurons" in our brains that respond the same way when we watch someone else do something as when we do it ourselves.

The word "vicarious" means to experience something in our minds through the feelings or actions of another person. The ability to vicariously experience ourselves achieving a goal through the observation of another person is a powerful way to build self-efficacy. This observation can come through watching a good friend or family member, watching or reading about a sports hero or famous person, or even through fictional stories. One important point about vicarious experience is that the person performing the task and the task itself should be as similar as possible to you and what you want to do.

3. *Imaginal Experiences*

We also have the capacity to use our imaginations to boost our self-efficacy. But the distinction between doing what it takes to reach a goal and actually reaching that goal may be critical for our success. Shelley Taylor did research with college students comparing the effects of imagining what it would be like to get an A on an exam versus imagining studying for the exam in a way that would lead to an A.[18] The students who imagined studying began studying earlier, studied more hours, and did better on the exam than those who only imagined getting an A.

Using your imagination may be most helpful when you not only imagine your goal but also all of the kinds of things that you may need to do to reach it. We can illustrate this in relation to reaching the larger goal of living life to the fullest. In order to build your self-efficacy for reaching such a complex and challenging goal, it may be necessary to not just imagine your best possible self, but also to imagine all of the steps you may need to make by using something like the PATH process and see yourself using many of the other strengths we will discuss.

4. *Positive Feedback*

The first three ways to increase your self-efficacy are things you can do and include doing something yourself, watching others doing something, or imagining yourself doing what it takes to reach a goal. The fourth way to increase self-efficacy is not as directly under your control. It is the positive feedback and encouragement that you receive from others about your progress in reaching a goal.

There are a couple things that are important for positive feedback to have the maximum effect. First, the more specific the better. Rather than hearing that someone likes your new positive outlook, it would be more effective for them to say that they appreciated the way that you complimented them for being kind. Second, the effectiveness of their feedback will depend on how much you trust the person and see them as an expert in what you are doing.

While the encouragement of other people may not be as directly under your immediate control, there is much you can do to make that encouragement more likely. As illustrated in the PATH process, you can actively enlist people to support you in reaching a goal and tell them just what you would like from them in terms of specific feedback. Also, you can spend less time around people who might provide destructive feedback or prevent you from reaching your goal.

5. *Reducing Stress and Emotional Distress*

As with positive feedback, reducing stress and emotional distress may be a less direct way of increasing self-efficacy than the first three ways we discussed. Research has shown that people often interpret feeling anxious and stressed as an indication that they won't perform as well as they otherwise would. This is similar to the kind of distorted thinking that is identified in cognitive therapy as "emotional reasoning" where a person thinks they *are* bad because they *feel* bad.

While there are many ways that we can reduce stress and distress, there are at least two primary ways that have been used in psychology. The first is cognitive reappraisal where we come to think about our situation in a less threatening way. We might remember that it is normal to have feelings of anxiety when doing things that are challenging but having those feelings does not mean that we are not capable of doing them.

The other primary way to deal with the stress and distress that makes it hard to believe in ourselves, is related to what we have already talked about with mindfulness and what we will next be talking about with resilience and stress-related growth. Practicing mindfulness by paying attention to your breath can reduce stress but so can a whole host of other relaxation and stress reduction techniques.

7.3. Resilience

There are few things that are more admired in another person than resilience. There are so many examples. The story of Bethany Hamilton who returns to surf soon after she loses her arm to a shark is a wonderful example of resilience. The popularity of the Rocky movies speaks for our love of underdogs who come back to fight against all odds. The theme of the ruler or leader who falls and recovers to lead again is common in both ancient and modern stories. Because life is so full of stress and adversity, we love and admire those who show us that it is possible to bounce back and prevail.

What Is Resilience?

Resilience can be defined in both a specific and a more general way. The root word of "resilience" is the word "resil" which means to spring back to its original position. Thus, the most basic definition may be that resilience is the ability to bounce back or recover from stress.[19] However, the word resilience is also used in other more general ways that may be best captured by saying that resilience is positive adaptation to stress.

The study of resilience is one of the great shining lights in psychology before the dawn of the positive psychology movement. Resilience first came to the forefront in the 1970s when Emmy Werner used the term to describe some of the children she was studying in Hawaii.[20] The families of the children that Werner studied were poor and many of the parents were mentally ill, struggled with substance abuse, and/or were out of work. What struck Werner was that while two-thirds of the children were adversely affected by developing substance abuse problems or teenage pregnancies, the other one-third did not develop these problems, and Werner called these children "resilient." Thus, other researchers began to try to understand how and why some people can experience severe stress without being adversely affected.

During the past 40 years, resilience research has grown from studying children to adults and in trying to understand resilience in relation to a variety of stressful events. These have included traumatic events such as natural disasters, terrorist attacks, sexual assault, and military combat. In addition, they have included many of the major stressful events that are more common and less life-threatening such as divorce, bereavement, and chronic illness. Finally, they have also included the chronic stress of daily hassles that most of us experience such as interpersonal conflicts, financial strain, noise, traffic, and problems with computers and other technology.

The ways that we have evolved to respond to stress are also important for understanding resilience. Until recently, scientists focused primarily on the "fight-or-flight" response as our natural biological response to stressful events. This response occurs rapidly and involves the activation of the sympathetic nervous system to mobilize as much of the body's resources as possible for fighting or fleeing. Alternatively, our normal state when not facing an immediate stressor has been called the "rest-and-digest" state which involves the activation of the parasympathetic nervous system when there are no immediate threats.

In 2000, Shelley Taylor described another stress response rooted in human evolution that she called "tend-and-befriend."[21] This response does not occur as quickly after the onset of a stressor and may have evolved to enable us to tend or protect our offspring and befriend or enable us to reach out to others for mutual support. The tend-and-befriend response may involve the secretion of the hormone oxytocin which is associated with social bonding. The fight-or-flight and tend-and-befriend responses may both play an important role in resilience, but the key may be to learn to better control them and to know when it may be best to use each.

The study of resilience is a prime example of positive psychology's goal of understanding people at their best. The early research conducted by Martin Seligman focused on getting dogs to learn to be helpless as a model of how humans become depressed.[22] However, as with Werner's study of children in Hawaii, he found that there was a group of the dogs that could not be made to be helpless. This is similar to the more recent findings by George Bonanno that resilience is a surprisingly common response to major negative events and that only about 25% of those who experience a traumatic event actually develop posttraumatic stress disorder (PTSD).[23]

As with other aspects of positive psychology, the best research may involve both nomothetic attempts to study what is general for large groups of people and the idiographic approach which involves studying individuals who are particularly resilient. While studies of large groups of people may give us clues about the kinds of things that potentially help everyone be resilient, the study of exceptional individuals can help us understand how these factors may come together in a person's life. The study of resilient individuals is also in accord with our affinity for stories and can inspire and motivate positive emotions, such as elevation described by Jonathan Haidt.[24]

What Enables Us to Be Resilient?

What makes it possible for a person to bounce back and respond positively to a stressful event? There are a variety of things that have consistently been identified across different kinds of people and stressors. Two that are undoubtedly important are those we have already discussed in this chapter. Jon Kabat-Zinn developed mindfulness-based stress reduction (MBSR) because he thought it would effectively help people deal with stress.[25] Mindfulness helps us feel more relaxed, improve our ability to manage our emotions, and find better solutions to our problems. Also, as we learned above, self-efficacy may be critical for resilience because it enables us to deal more effectively with inevitable set-backs in trying to attain our goals.

The third factor that may increase resilience is taking an active rather than an avoidant approach to coping with stress. Active coping involves trying to fully understand a problem, considering a full array of possible responses, planning a constructive response, and then following through with active efforts to cope with it. The efforts can either be problem-focused, in that they aim at changing the source of the problem or stressor, or they can be emotion-focused, in that they aim at managing the emotional response to a problem or stressor that cannot be controlled. In contrast, avoidant coping involves things like denying that there is a problem, giving up on dealing with it, or turning to alcohol or substance abuse to try not to think about it.

The fourth factor that may increase resilience is social support, which involves having people in your life who can help you deal with a stressful situation. Just the perception that you have people there for you when you need them has consistently been shown to be a powerful weapon against some of the negative effects of stress on health. The value of social support is clearly demonstrated in the hero's journey, through mentors and friends. It is also echoed in the PATH process of actively trying to identify and enroll other people who can support you in trying to reach your goals. The opposite of feeling supported is a sense of loneliness, which has been shown to be destructive and harmful to health.

The fifth factor that can increase resilience is not important for everyone but may be particularly important for some people facing great stressors. While psychology and science had long neglected the study of spirituality and religion, Ken Pargament and others have pioneered the study of how people use their religious faith and spiritual practices to help them cope with stress.[26] They have found that religion and spirituality may help people cope with stress in a variety of ways. These include the comfort and strength that can come from believing in a higher power; the ways that practices such a meditation, prayer, and worship can reduce stress and provide perspective; and the social support that can come from a closely knit community with shared values and beliefs.

The sixth factor has become a special focus of the positive psychology movement. Barbara Fredrickson, Alex Zautra, and others have provided consistent evidence that positive emotions can be a powerful source of resilience. Fredrickson's broaden-and-build theory of positive emotions asserts that a variety of positive emotions such as joy, love, interest, and contentment can build resources for dealing with stress and adversity.[27] Her research has shown that people use positive emotions to bounce back from negative emotional experiences. Alex Zautra has shown that the ability to be aware of positive emotion in the midst of stressful experiences may be important for staying balanced and keeping perspective while feeling stressed and experiencing negative emotions.[28]

How Can We Increase Resilience?

We have seen that six primary sources of resilience are mindfulness, self-efficacy, active coping, social support, spirituality, and positive emotions. What can we do to make these more a part of our lives and use them to help us better respond to the stress and adversity we experience? Earlier in this chapter I went over ways to begin to practice mindfulness and what we can do to increase self-efficacy. For mindfulness, it may be particularly useful to learn to focus on the breath and body to be aware of our stress responses and to begin to slow them down. There are a host of other relaxation strategies and techniques that can also reduce the stress response, such as progressive relaxation, yoga, guided imagery, and other forms of meditation.

In using self-efficacy to increase resilience, the focus should be on increasing your belief that you can do what it takes to deal with whatever stressors you may face. You could practice in small ways with smaller stressors, you could observe and learn from others who are particularly good at dealing with stress, and you could imagine yourself using what you learned when you face a future stressor. There is a useful technique called Stress Inoculation Training where you clearly identify a problem or stressor, acquire the skills you need and rehearse them, and apply the skills you learned and rehearsed to cope with the stress when it arises.[29] This technique makes particularly creative use of both imagining what you will do to cope with a future stressor and role-playing to rehearse your response.

Both mindfulness and self-efficacy can be part of the active coping process that can also be a foundation for resilience. Mindfulness enables you to get the best read on the current situation and decide about the best strategy or course of action. Self-efficacy is the belief that you can do what it takes to cope in an active way that really makes a difference. Trying to first identify the best response, choosing the best one, and imaging and rehearsing it is a strong foundation for active coping. The other important thing to remember with active coping is called "coping flexibility," which is the ability to match a particular coping strategy with a specific problem or stressor. For example, active coping could mean trying to remove a stressor *or* it could mean changing your response to it depending on how much control you have over the source of stress.

The things that you can do to build the other three resilience resources will be a central focus in the coming chapters and occupy a primary place in the hero's journey in positive psychology. Increasing social support includes actively enlisting others as illustrated in the PATH process and using the strengths of love, kindness, and social intelligence that will be discussed as part of the virtue of Humanity. Increasing spirituality includes finding ways to identify sources of meaning and purpose that can put your stress into perspective and will be addressed as part of the virtue of Transcendence. Finally, increasing positive emotions involves all of our strengths and it will continue to be a primary focus as one of the most sought-after elements of happiness and well-being.

7.4. Stress-Related Growth

The final fundamental strength I will discuss in this chapter also has to do with our response to stress and adversity. But rather than just bouncing back or recovering from stress, stress-related growth uses stress as an occasion to take our lives to a whole new level. The ability to learn and grow from the stressful things that we experience is one of the most underappreciated, yet potentially fruitful human strengths. It is reflected directly in the later stages of the hero's journey as it involves finding a Reward in the Ordeal, experiencing the Resurrection to a new life, and Returning with an Elixir that brings healing and good news for others.

What Is Stress-Related Growth?

I will define stress-related growth as the ability to learn, grow, and find benefits in and through stressful events and experiences. Stress-related growth has also been referred to a "posttraumatic growth" or simply "finding benefits" in stressful events. The term "posttraumatic growth," as a positive or helpful experience is used in contrast to the more familiar term "posttraumatic stress," as a negative or harmful experience. I prefer to use the term stress-related growth because it implies the ability to grow through all kinds of stressful events and not just those involving trauma.

While the study of stress-related growth is relatively new to psychology and science, the idea of being able to learn, grow, and find benefits in even the most stressful experiences is at least as old as the stories of Buddha and Jesus. Buddha faced the demon Mara under the Bodhi tree, as well as suffering, illness, and death as part of his path to enlightenment. Jesus was mocked, beaten, and crucified on a cross before being resurrected with the gift of salvation for all. From the fictional realm of *The Lord of the Rings*, Gandalf the Grey was cast down towards hell in fighting the Balrog before being transformed into Gandalf the White.

The idea of benefiting from the negative things that happen to us is also communicated in common quotes and expressions. The saying "it was a blessing in disguise" carries with it the notion that good things can surprise us from places where we may least expect them. The expression "every cloud has a silver lining" communicates the idea that it is possible to find something good in anything no matter how bad. The saying "when life hands you a lemon, make lemonade" adds the notion that we have it within ourselves to create something good out of something that at first seems bad.

Ten years before the birth of the positive psychology movement, Richard Tedeschi and Lawrence Calhoun pioneered the study of what they first named "posttraumatic growth."[30] In the past 20 years, there have been an ever increasing number of studies examining stress-related growth, why it occurs, and how to foster it. The great majority of studies have focused on traumatic events or major life crises that might be considered something like the Ordeal in the hero's journey.

What Do We Know About Stress-Related Growth?

Across a full range of studies of people facing a host of negative and stressful events, Tedeschi, Calhoun, and others have found that people consistently report benefits and growth.[31] In fact, although some degree of psychological distress is common during or following highly negative events, the number of growth experiences after traumatic events may far outnumber the reports of psychiatric disorders. Although it varies with the type and severity of the event, usually 50% or more of those experiencing a major stressful event report some kind of benefit.

The types of benefits that people report generally fall into five major categories.[32] First, they report a change in perspective involving a greater appreciation of life as well as a change in priorities and what is important to them. Second, they report warmer and more intimate relationships with other people. Third, they report a greater sense of personal strength which often involves the kinds of strengths we are discussing in this and subsequent chapters. Fourth, they report a recognition of new possibilities or paths for one's life which often reflect a hero's journey. Finally, they report spiritual growth which may or may not be related to involvement with organized religion.

How Can We Increase Stress-Related Growth?

There are several things that foster stress-related growth including positive reappraisal, emotional self-disclosure, spirituality, and constructing a coherent narrative. Positive reappraisal is the ability to think about something in a more positive, beneficial, and constructive way. Positive reappraisal fosters stress-related growth by making it possible to see even the most stressful or negative event as offering something positive to learn and grow from. A person may think about the proverbial lemon in a different way and realize that they can use it to make lemonade.

Emotional disclosure involves telling the story of one's experience with trauma or stress in a way that all thoughts and feelings are freely disclosed. As we have seen, James Pennebaker and Joshua Smyth have demonstrated the positive effects of emotional disclosure on health.[33] The process of exposing yourself to all of the details of what happened by talking about it or writing it down may help you make sense of it and find benefits. Annette Stanton has done research using a variation of the Pennebaker writing exercise to foster finding benefits in the experience of having cancer.[34]

Spirituality can foster the belief in a higher power that can bring good out of whatever happens, the idea that there is a positive reason, meaning, or purpose for everything that happens, and the ability to draw on stories where good comes from the bad. Such is the Old Testament story where Joseph tells the brothers who tried to kill him: "you intended to harm me, but God intended it for good to accomplish what is now being done, the saving of many lives" (Genesis 50:20, *New*

International Version). Many religious and spiritual traditions have stories with themes of stress-related growth.

The final thing that may foster stress-related growth is the construction of a narrative in conjunction with using some of the above. This narrative may be most effective if it has the kind of positive resolution and redemption themes that Dan McAdams identified and is also an expression of the classic hero's journey.[35] For example, the person may have fully exposed themselves to a stressful or traumatic experience through emotional disclosure, reappraised the event as a meaningful event with a gift for others, and constructed a narrative with a positive resolution.

Graduating From Basic Training

The chapter has been about the fundamentals that we need in order to make our own hero's journey. Each of the four strengths that were presented can begin with the smallest and most fleeting thoughts. Then we can proceed up the Gandhi ladder to practice until it becomes a habit and finally an enduring and trustworthy strength.

The first two strengths we talked about are basic in that they enable us to stay fully present in our experience and also dare to reach for the kind of life we most want for ourselves in the future. Mindfulness enables us to recognize now as the only time that we can live our lives and it can be fostered by simple things such focusing on our breathing, scanning our body, following our awareness, and finding ways to practice in our daily activities. Self-efficacy is what enables us to use our other strengths and can be increased by taking small practice steps, observing others, using our imagination, surrounding ourselves with encouraging people, and reducing our stress when striving for our goals.

The other two strengths we discussed are basic for dealing with the inevitable trials and ordeals that we face all along our journey. Resilience is the ability to bounce back and positively adapt to stress and can be fostered by mindfulness and self-efficacy as well as an active approach to coping, social support, positive emotions, and spirituality. Stress-related growth is the ability to learn, grow, and benefit from stressful experiences and can be increased by fully processing the experience and thinking about it in ways that create a positive and coherent narrative such as the classic hero's journey.

Once we understand these four potentially powerful allies, we can recognize and learn about them in the stories of others and put them into practice in creating our own story. Examples of mindfulness and self-efficacy can be seen in many stories, such Jedi training in the ways of the Force in *Star Wars*. Examples of resilience and stress-related growth abound in ancient stories of Jesus and the Buddha, as well as fictional heroes such as Rocky, Wonder Woman, Indiana Jones, Black Panther, and Buffy the Vampire Slayer—and even the person down the street.

Now that we have completed basic training, it is on to more advanced training in the ways of the "force" of modern science and the ordinary magic we can call on to make our lives extraordinary. Now begins the master training that, until recently, had so often been ignored or forgotten in psychology and science. Now is the time to begin with the basic question of what is wisdom and, most importantly, where can we find it?

Chapter 8

The Wisdom to Find the Way

Happiness can be found, even in the darkest of times,
if one only remembers to turn on the light.

—Albus Dumbledore[1]

I remember times in my life when I was facing a fork in the road. The hardest were when I was trying to decide where to go to college and whether to take a job. For some of us, the toughest decisions might be who to date or whether to get married or whether to break up or get divorced. It may also be something truly heart wrenching like whether to continue fighting a life threatening illness or whether to let go and die with dignity. It might be trying to find the right words that allow us to be both kind and honest with someone who hurt us. It might be how to get over a loss or deal with depression or a substance abuse problem. In one way or another, we are asking the question at the heart of this book—how can we find lasting happiness in the face of all the adversity, stress, and darkness we often see around us?

Many of the toughest decisions that we will ever face are not taught about in school. It is for these decisions that we long for a mentor with something of the wisdom of Yoda in *Star Wars* or Gandalf in *The Lord of the Rings*. "When we find ourselves in times of trouble," as the *Beatles* song *Let It Be* goes, we may long for that "mother Mary" who whispers words of wisdom. Perhaps we turn to that parent or grandparent who just seems to understand everything better than most people. Perhaps we turn to that one friend we can confide in who is young but wise beyond their years. As Dumbledore said to the students at *Hogwarts*, "Happiness can be found, even in the darkest of times, if one only remembers to turn on the light." This sounds so simple, but how exactly do we do it? This is the focus of this chapter.

There are five strengths listed under the virtue of Wisdom and Knowledge in the VIA classification. The *VIA Institute on Character* defines these as cognitive strengths that involve the acquisition and use of knowledge. These strengths are wisdom itself, curiosity, judgment, love of learning, and creativity, and these are five of the lights we can turn on to find our way to happiness in the dark. We will talk about each of these in turn in this chapter but, in short, wisdom is practical knowledge and understanding, curiosity and love of learning are what motivate us to learn and become wise, open-mindedness is what enables us to see the whole picture, and creativity is that ordinary magic that enables us to face and overcome some of our greatest challenges.

8.1. Wisdom

The strength of wisdom is probably one of the most important for our happiness and well-being. The history of the study of wisdom in philosophy and religion and now psychology can offer us so much for our hero's journey.

What Is Wisdom?

Wisdom has been defined on *dictionary.com* as "knowledge of what is true or right coupled with just judgment as to action, sagacity, discernment, or insight."[2] The psychologist Paul Baltes defines wisdom as "an expert knowledge system concerning the fundamental pragmatics of life."[3] The *VIA Institute on Character* defines wisdom or "perspective" as "distinct from intelligence but represents a high level of knowledge, the capacity to give advice and to recognize and weigh multiple sides before making a decision."[4] In integrating the definitions of wisdom, I will define wisdom as the practical knowledge and understanding that enables us to achieve happiness and well-being.

There are several ways that wisdom can be different from intelligence and the kind of knowledge we often learn at school. First, wisdom is like "street smarts" in that it is applicable to our daily lives and the most challenging and difficult real-life decisions that we have to make. Second, wisdom does not often require a particularly high score on standardized intelligence tests, but does require the willingness to learn from daily life and experience. Third, wisdom involves the ability to weigh, balance, and integrate different kinds of knowledge from a variety of sources including formal education and reading, interpersonal relationships, and personal reflection. Fourth, wisdom is generally aimed at producing constructive and beneficial outcomes that foster happiness and well-being.

Although wisdom has long been a focus in philosophy and religion, it has only recently come under the full attention of psychology. The two psychologists who have made lasting contributions to understanding of wisdom have been Robert Sternberg and Paul Baltes. Sternberg has presented what he calls a "balance theory of wisdom" where he contends that the development of wisdom involves learning to balance the knowledge gained from multiple interests for the common good.[5] These interests include those of both oneself and others, and the common good includes enabling people to better adapt to and shape their current environment and to better select other or new environments. Thus, the acquisition of wisdom is a process that involves aiming for what is good for all people in the context of our daily lives and environment.

What Is the Berlin Wisdom Paradigm?

Paul Baltes has had a long career studying wisdom using what he calls the *Berlin Wisdom Paradigm*.[6] This paradigm is a way of doing research about wisdom that has been very useful in enabling us to study it and understand what it is. The purpose of this paradigm has been to understand how wisdom applies to planning future life goals, management of critical life problems, and making sense of past experiences. Baltes developed five criteria that further specify what he means in defining wisdom as "an expert knowledge system in the fundamental practicalities of life" (p. 122).[7]

The first is "factual knowledge about the fundamental pragmatics of life" which involves knowing values about a variety of things including human nature, interpersonal relationships, social norms, life-long development, and critical life events. The second is "procedural knowledge about the fundamental pragmatics of life" which involves strategies for dealing with the meaning and conduct of life. The third is "contextual knowledge," which involves knowing about how the social, historical, and cultural situation influences our lives. The fourth is "relativistic knowledge," which involves the understanding and tolerance of differences in values between individuals and society. The fifth involves the "recognition and management of uncertainty" based on the limitation of our thinking, only having access to certain parts of reality, and not being able to know the future.

After developing these criteria, Baltes and his colleagues did a series of studies where they presented people with short statements about fictional challenges or difficult situations. They then asked them to think out loud about what they believe a person should consider and do while they were being recorded. Here are a few examples of the challenging situations presented to the participants:[8-9]

1. Someone receives a telephone call from a good friend who says that he or she cannot go on like this and has decided to take his or her own life.

2. One is part of a dual-career couple who have to weigh the gains and losses involved if one partner accepts a job in a different state.

3. A 15-year-old girl wants to get married right away.

Finally, the researchers rate what the research participants say according to how much they demonstrate the five criteria for wisdom. Here are examples of what were rated low and high wisdom responses that were given when research participants were asked about the third situation above:

1. *Low wisdom-related score*—"A 15-year-old girls wants to get married. No, no way, marrying at age 15 would be utterly wrong. One has to tell the girl that marriage is not possible" (p. 333).[10]

2. *High wisdom-related score*—"Well, on the surface, this seems like an easy problem. On average marriage for a 15-year-old is not a good thing. But there are situations where the average case does not fit. Perhaps in this instance, special life circumstances are involved, such that the girl has a terminal illness. Or the girl has just lost her parents. And also, this girl may live in another culture or historical period. Perhaps she was raised with a value system different from our own. In addition, one has to think about adequate ways of talking with the girl and to consider her emotional state" (p. 333).[11]

The studies using these types of challenging scenarios also tried to determine what variables were the best predictors of who was wise. They showed that personal characteristics and life experiences were much more important than age and intelligence. The personal characteristics that were related to wisdom were creativity; social intelligence; flexible thinking that involves evaluation, comparison, moving beyond existing rules; and being tolerant of ambiguity. The life experiences related to wisdom were contact with excellent mentors and some exposure to structured and critical life experiences. The people higher in wisdom were more likely to value the welfare of other people more than their own happiness and were highly engaged in working for the well-being of others.

In addition to these findings, the Berlin Wisdom Paradigm and other recent studies of wisdom have shown us that we can take a scientific approach to studying wisdom. This may involve an ongoing back and forth between wise people, wise solutions to problems, and the criteria for wisdom itself. The process might be circular in that (1) people in different contexts and cultures could nominate wise people based on the best current criteria for wisdom, (2) this new group of wise people could work together to further refine and test these criteria on challenging situations, and (3) another diverse group could nominate other wisdom experts who begin the process again. The result could be an evolving better understanding of wisdom, and a growing group of people who can better deal with our most pressing problems.

Is Wisdom a Master Virtue?

Barry Schwarz and Kenneth Sharpe have written about wisdom in the context of the other virtues and strengths in the VIA classification. They argue that wisdom may be a "master virtue" that might guide us in the better practice of all the other virtues and strengths.[12] They believe that the strengths should not be treated in isolation but that it is important to think about how they can be balanced and integrated in dealing with different situations. They used the analogy of a bodybuilder to help make their point. Just as a bodybuilder who only develops the arms and chest and ignores the rest of the body might have trouble standing up straight, so only developing some strengths and ignoring others may lead to similar imbalances and deformities of behavior and character.

Schwartz and Sharpe think there may be at least three ways that wisdom can help a person best decide which strengths would be best in a given circumstance. The first is to enable a person to decide which strengths are most relevant for the current situation. For example, very different strengths might be called for in dealing with a suicidal friend versus passing an organic chemistry test. The second is to enable a person to decide how to specifically apply a relevant strength. If you decide you want to use love in helping your friend with a substance abuse problem, would you want to use a gentle or a more "tough" form of love? The third is to use wisdom to decide among strengths that may be in conflict with each other. If a particularly sensitive friend asks you how they look, would you want them to be more honest or kind?

What Are Maximizing and Satisficing?

In addition to arguing that wisdom may be a master virtue, Barry Schwartz has made a distinction between decision-making styles that may have important implications for both wisdom and happiness.[13] When you are shopping for a particular item, do you visit every possible website and store and try to find out as much as you can about all of the alternatives before making a final decision? Or do you just consider a few options and make a decision when you find one that you think is good enough? Schwartz gave the name "maximizers" to the first group of people who comprehensively consider every possible option with the final goal of selecting the very best one. He gave the name "satisficers" to the second group who consider a few possibilities until an option is found that is acceptable or good enough.

Many people might think that the most logical and rational approach might be to maximize, but in most situations the wise choice seems to be the satisficing strategy. Schwartz has found that people are usually happier, less disappointed, and experience less regret when they stop searching once they find something that is good enough. He suggests that, unless there are very good reasons for doing otherwise, satisficing is usually the wiser strategy and that after making the decision it is better to focus on the advantages of the choice rather than the disadvantages. Satisficing may be the better choice when there are many options, because all the time and energy that goes into weighing them all is usually not worth what may end up feeling like a very minor or insignificant difference in the long run.

What Can We Do to Increase Wisdom?

Although psychology has only recently begun to focus on wisdom, there are at least seven ways that have been identified to increase it.

1. *Learn from wise people that you know.*

This can involve either finding a mentor or just talking with other people about the best examples of wisdom. You can try to find a formal mentor through a mentorship program; a teacher, therapist, or clergyperson; or even a wise and experienced friend or family member. Whether or not they can meet with you regularly, you can interview them and ask them about what they think wisdom is and how they have made some of the most difficult decisions in their lives.

2. *Learn about wise people in history.*

Reading about and watching documentaries about people in the past or the present can be great ways to foster wisdom. Try to identify people who have experienced and successfully dealt with some of the same kinds of challenges that you have faced or may face in the future. Both autobiographies and biographies can be great ways to really understand how a person came to be wise. Look for the key decision points in their lives and pay specific attention to the reasons that they give for choosing the way they did.

3. *Have imaginary dialogues with a wise person.*

Try to identify someone you know, someone from history, or even a fictional character who represents wisdom to you. Try to imagine that they are there to answer your most challenging questions. Ask them the questions about your life that are most important to you and then imagine how they would respond to you. The best way to do this is to talk it out or even to write or type your answers because it forces you to be specific in what you say. As many have learned in doing this, some of the best answers to your questions may already be within you.

4. *Read wisdom literature and find relevant quotes.*

Many world religious and philosophical traditions have literature that directly addresses what wisdom is and provide short sayings or quotes that may express the wisdom you need. Find and go through lists of wise quotes or quotes from wise people and identify the ones that speak to you the most. Then talk with a friend or mentor about why they speak to you and write about what struck you and how you can use it in your life. Finally, build a collection of quotes over time and think about how they can balance and complement each other.

5. *Get to know people with different perspectives.*

I had a professor who once said that it is the people who are most different from us who may have the answer to our most difficult questions. When we only get to know and talk with people like us, we are limiting ourselves to the people who may have many of the same biases and blind spots. Try to find someone with a different background or from another culture and be open to what they have to say. As with the general process of becoming wise itself, this may be very confusing and disorienting at first, but over time can really open you up to new answers and more healthy and constructive perspective.

6. *Travel to unfamiliar places.*

Traveling to new and different places with unfamiliar cultures and languages may be one of the best ways to increase our perspective and wisdom. Go to places that are outside your comfort zone and pay attention to how things are similar to and different from what you are used to. You may not even have to go to another state or country to do this, but be sure it is a place you have never been before. One wisdom intervention showed that even taking an imaginary journey to very different countries such as Germany, Egypt, Italy, and China could boost wisdom.

7. *Become a mentor to someone else.*

I can certainly attest to the saying that one of the best ways to learn something is teach it. This may be doubly true for wisdom and mentoring which requires the ongoing openness to and engagement with people who are facing challenging questions. Whether you are a formal mentor or mentor others as a parent, teacher, coach, or even good friend; trying to help others find their path in life may be a great way to grow in wisdom yourself. Mentoring can keep us accountable for continuing to grow in wisdom and confidence when facing tough situations.

8.2. Curiosity

Can you think of a time when your curiosity got you in trouble? Perhaps you were so curious about something that you risked being hurt or losing time or money. I remember the scene in the movie *Silence of the Lambs* when Clarice Starling first met Hannibal Lector. Just like Clarice, your own curiosity in seeing a movie about such a frightening person might raise your anxiety and fear. At other times, curiosity may result in mostly positive emotions such as seeing your friend's new baby for the first time. Whatever the result, curiosity motivates us to explore and learn new things. Curiosity may have killed the cat, but it sure has played a big role in human evolution and it sure can play a big role in our happiness.

What Is Curiosity?

Dictionary.com defines curiosity as "inquisitiveness or the desire to learn or know about anything."[14] Todd Kashdan wrote the chapter on curiosity in the *Character Strengths and Virtues*[15] handbook and later wrote a book entitled, *Curious? Discover the Missing Ingredient to a Fulfilling Life.*[16] He defined curiosity as "the recognition, pursuit, and intense desire to explore novel, challenging, and uncertain events" (p. 125).[17] The *VIA Institute on Character* defines curiosity as "taking an interest in ongoing experience for its own sake; finding subjects and topics fascinating; exploring and discovering."[18] Thus, I will define curiosity simply as the desire to learn and know more about something.

Theories about curiosity have shifted from an emphasis on the negative alone to a better balance between the negative and the positive. The older theories viewed curiosity as a motivator for escaping danger and bad situations. We are curious about finding a way to prevent or cure a disease so that we do not have to suffer. The newer theories appreciate the fact that curiosity may sometimes be directed towards enabling us to gain and achieve things that are intrinsically rewarding, such as discovering our favorite wine or just learning about wine. Thus, curiosity may be a primary motivator in both avoiding the bad things that cause us to suffer and in approaching the good things that bring us positive emotions.

Todd Kashdan argues that curiosity may drive us from the simple pursuit of hedonic happiness to the richer pursuit of eudaimonic happiness.[19] If you remember, hedonia is primarily just about pleasure, whereas eudaimonia is much more about a meaningful and fulfilling life. Kashdan thinks that curiosity may be a mechanism that enables us to both create and discover meaning in our lives. Like Martin Seligman, he recognizes that the best way to find happiness may be not to seek it directly, but to find things that are meaningful and fulfilling. Curiosity may be both the spark and the engine that pulls us out of our comfort zones and drives us to explore and discover new things.

Charles Spielberger and Laura Starr developed a theory about the forces that determine whether or not we try to satisfy our curiosity.[20] The "optimal stimulation/dual process theory" predicts that exploratory behavior will depend on weighing the potential rewards versus the potential costs. Curiosity is fueled by the potential reward, whereas anxiety is fueled by the potential costs. If curiosity is stronger than anxiety, then a person will attempt to satisfy their curiosity by exploring the environment. If, on the other hand, anxiety is stronger than curiosity, then a person will not risk exploring the environment. But if history is any indication, sometimes human curiosity must have been extremely strong to counter the anxiety of doing things like exploring a jungle, crossing an ocean, or going to the moon.

How Can We Use Curiosity to Increase Happiness?

As Kashdan suggests, curiosity may enable us to get out of the rut of only trying to increase pleasure and decrease pain.[21] In paying attention to and cultivating curiosity we can discover what brings us a fuller and richer life and find the motivation to accomplish our goals in achieving it. As Joseph Campbell talked about finding and following our bliss, curiosity is one of our best tools for discovering what we are most passionate about and for giving us the energy and strength to continue to learn about it.[22] For Campbell, his early curiosity was about the stories that brought meaning to other people. For many of us, it may begin with a childhood hobby or sport or what we think is a minor or trivial interest that may carry with it a clue to something that we could love and enjoy for the rest of our lives.

These are several specific ways we can cultivate and increase our curiosity and allow it to guide us in our quest for a better life:

1. *Read and watch videos.*

Make a list of the things that you are most interested in. Choose the top ones and set aside time to surf the Internet to find out as much as possible about them. Look online for videos you can watch and books you can read to find out more.

2. *Take a class, workshop, or seminar.*

Go through lists of classes at schools and through newspapers and Internet postings of workshops and seminars. Identify the one that you find most interesting. Go to one of the classes and pay attention to what it feels like when you learn new things.

3. *Notice the new in the old.*

Try to find things that you have never noticed before in familiar people and places. For example, make a list of the things you never saw in what a good friend wears or in what you see along a familiar drive. See how many new things you can notice.

4. *See what makes you happy.*

Since being happy and experiencing positive emotions is a primary motivator for all of us, make a list of the simple things you can do that might make you happy. Some should be familiar and some should be completely new. See how much happiness each experience brings.

8.3. Open-mindedness

There is an old song from the 1960s that goes "What the world needs now is love, sweet love. It's the only thing that there's just too little of." Well, I am not here to argue that the world doesn't need love, and we will be focusing on love in a later chapter. But I do want to argue that the strength of open-mindedness, as defined in the VIA classification, may be even more rare and possibly even more needed in the world today.

What Is Open-mindedness?

Perhaps more than any of the 24 character strengths, one word does not convey the full meaning of this strength. The *Character Strengths and Virtues* handbook equates open-mindedness with judgment and critical thinking and defines it as "the willingness to search actively for evidence against one's favored beliefs, plans, or goals, and to weigh such evidence fairly when it is available" (p. 144).[23] The *VIA Institute on Character* now calls it Judgment and defines it as "thinking things through and examining them from all sides; not jumping to conclusions; being able to change one's mind in light of evidence; and weighing all evidence fairly."[24]

One of the best ways to understand this kind of open-mindedness is to consider its opposite. "Selective exposure" is the tendency to maintain our beliefs by exposing ourselves only to what we are comfortable and familiar with and what is likely to support what we already believe. This is similar to the "myside bias" which is when people evaluate evidence in a way that is biased towards their previous attitudes and opinions. The thing that makes selective exposure and the myside bias so dangerous is that we are usually not aware we are doing them. The kind of open-minded judgment and critical thinking that the VIA developers identified as a strength may be one of our greatest weapons against selective exposure and the myside bias.

The movie *12 Angry Men* is a prime example of these biases and how they might be overcome by open-mindedness. The movie takes place in a jury room where 12 men are there to decide the fate of an 18-year-old Hispanic man from a poor part of town, who allegedly stabbed his father to death. Though the evidence was weak and circumstantial, 11 men vote guilty and only one man votes not guilty in their initial vote. The rest of the movie is the story of how this one man becomes the catalyst for a process whereby everyone else reconsiders their votes, until finally they all vote not guilty. The movie is a study of the development of open-mindedness as each of the jurors confront their own prejudices in opening their minds to the truth.

Just as wisdom may represent balancing different perspectives, open-mindedness may often be the critical ingredient for wisdom in confronting our most deeply ingrained prejudices and biases. It is easy to see selective exposure and the myside bias in other people, but very difficult to see in ourselves. The most obvious places to look for it may be in controversial topics in politics and religion. For example, the conservative Republican who only exposes himself to Fox News or Rush Limbaugh and the liberal or progressive Democratic who only exposes herself to MSNBC or Rachel Maddow.

What Can We Do to Increase Open-mindedness?

Here the suggestions may sound simple and straightforward but can be some of the hardest things we will ever try to do:

1. *Talk to someone with an opposing point of view.*

Identify someone who is both thoughtful and respectful of other people, but who has a completely different viewpoint than you. Arrange a time to get together and simply focus on listening to them and trying to understand their perspective. Practice active listening which involves reflecting back to them what you think they are saying to make sure that you fully understand. If they want to hear your perspective, tell them that you would be glad to get together again in the future to tell them, but for now you just want to understand their point of view.

2. *Learn about a different point of view.*

Either read about or watch a thoughtful presentation of a point of view that is completely opposite or different from your own. The key here is to find someone who can present the different perspective in a thoughtful, articulate, and respectful way rather than someone who presents a poor argument or who is easy to discount. As you read or listen, try to write down what you think are their best arguments. After you are done, write down your best arguments for your perspective and compare the arguments on both sides.

3. *Play the devil's advocate with people who agree with you.*

Identify a person or group of people who are willing to allow you to take the opposite position on something important on which you agree. Tell them you want them to present their position first and then you would like to do your best to play devil's advocate. Afterwards, ask them how they felt and talk about how you felt. Next, switch roles and have one of your friends play devil's advocate. Again, when you are finished ask them how they felt and talk about how you felt.

4. *Make a new friend who has a different point of view but who you otherwise like very much.*

Psychologists such as Jonathan Haidt have argued that having a good relationship with someone with a different point of view may be a more powerful source of change than logical arguments alone.[25] The people you otherwise like and admire may be those who you are most willing and open to learn from about a different perspective. They may also be the most willing and able to learn from you. Try to understand how someone you otherwise like very much can have such a different point of view than you.

8.4. Love of Learning

The fourth strength under the virtue of wisdom is one that we can easily misunderstand and taken for granted. Love of learning is not only about how much we enjoy the subjects that are often required and taught in formal education; it is our desire to increase our knowledge and understanding regarding anything. The movie *Good Will Hunting* provides a powerful example of a person who loved to learn and excelled even if he did not have the opportunity for higher education. He loved to learn so much that he mastered math to the point where he could solve a problem that students at a prestigious university could not.

What Is Love of Learning?

The *Character Strengths and Virtues* handbook suggests that "when people have love of learning as a strength, they are cognitively engaged. They typically experience positive feelings in the process of acquiring skills, satisfying curiosity, building on existing knowledge, and/or learning something completely new" (p. 163).[26] The *VIA Institute on Character* defines love of learning as "mastering new skills, topics, and bodies of knowledge, whether on one's own or formally; obviously related to the strength of curiosity but goes beyond it to describe the tendency to add systematically to what one knows."[27]

Love of learning is rooted in curiosity and also provides a unique and powerful foundation for the development of wisdom and ultimately the pursuit of happiness and well-being. Even if love of learning is not one of our top strengths or does not generalize to everything we can learn about, almost all of us love to learn about the things that are most interesting to us or enable us to reach our goals. We may be endlessly fascinated with a hobby that seems to provide no help in reaching any other end in our lives. At the same time, we may be completely uninterested in sports until we realize it may be a way to attract a person that we really like.

There are several things that can nurture love of learning. The first is to focus on mastering a subject rather than performing well on a test. The emphasis in many schools on test performance may do more to motivate students to get a particular score rather than really learn the material. The second way to encourage students to develop love of learning is to praise them for their effort and not for their performance. Being rewarded for doing your best rather than winning is a way to reinforce the effort that leads to continuous improvement in the long run. The third way is to teach people to view their failures—to fail to get a good grade or pass a course, for example—as opportunities to learn from their mistakes rather than viewing them as the end of the world.

What Can We Do to Increase Love of Learning?

There are a range of specific things we can do to boost love of learning:

1. *Focus on what you are most interested in.*

You might remember that intrinsic motivation is the desire to seek something for no other reason than that it is an end in itself. Make a list of the things that you are most interested in. It may help to think about what you loved to do as a child or what you like to do whenever you have any free time. What are your favorite sports or hobbies? Give yourself permission to learn more about them. If there is a course you have to take that you are not very interested in, try to find at least one aspect of it that piques your interest and focus more on learning that.

2. *Learn about something you are good at.*

Begin with your top strengths or make a list of the things you are good at. As we begin to use our top strengths in new ways, we become even more motivated to learn about them and the best parts of ourselves. Even if they may not seem to be as interesting to you as your favorite sports or hobbies, the things you are good at often bring other important rewards such as money and the recognition of other people we care about. We often become more interested in doing what we are rewarded for and may begin enjoying it more for itself.

3. *Do what helps you reach goals.*

Try to identify the goals that are most important and meaningful to you. Then think about what kinds of things may enable you to reach these goals. You may come to see some activities for which you never had much interest in a new light when you see how they can help you achieve something really important. For example, many parents discover a new love of learning about child psychology and development when they have their first child.

4. *Identify one thing you think would make you most happy.*

Think about all of the elements of happiness and well-being that we have discussed. Try to identify one thing as a kind of "holy grail" that you would be willing to make a high priority in seeking. Take it upon yourself to design your own course to learn all you can about what it would take to find or achieve it. Remember all the effort you put into some of the classes and tests at school that you were much less interested in. Then put in at least as much effort while reminding yourself how much more of a reward that seeking to learn about this most important thing can bring.

8.5. Creativity

I still remember the excitement I felt when I watched the movie *Raiders of the Lost Ark* for the first time. Indiana Jones was trying to get the powerful lost ark before the Germans and Hitler could get it to use in War World II. The Germans had stolen the ark from Jones and left him tied up with Marion in an underground cavern filled with what he feared most—snakes! Somehow he was able to escape from the cave and discover that the Germans were hauling the ark away in a truck. With his typical way of "making it up as he went along," Jones was able to steal a horse, jump from the horse onto the truck, survive being thrown off the truck by pulling himself under it as it was moving, and finally throw the driver out to take possession of the truck and the ark.

Even though this was a typical action movie display of physical rough and tumble, it was also an outstanding example of what is one of our most amazing human strengths. Creativity is the strength that may have done the most to enable us to rise above other species, thrive and multiply, tame the atom, create the iPhone, and walk on the moon. Human creativity is what inspired Brian Swimme to say, "Four billion years ago planet Earth was molten rock and now it sings opera."[28] Creativity is the one strength that we may need the most in finding a way to turn the light on in the darkness. And though we might think it is a strength that we will never possess, there are ways to awaken it in all of us.

What Is Creativity?

The *Character Strengths and Virtues* handbook says that creativity involves producing original ideas and behaviors that are adaptive, making a positive contribution to self and/or others.[29] The *VIA Institute on Character* defines it as "thinking of novel and productive ways to conceptualize and do things; includes artistic achievement but is not limited to it" and also provides the synonyms of "originality" and "ingenuity."[30] But despite these longer definitions, creativity basically comes down to two things. First and most important, it is the production of something that is novel or original. Second, it is usually defined as something that is or can be adaptive and beneficial. Thus, my definition will simply be that creativity is adaptive originality—or coming up with something new that can be constructive or beneficial.

Creativity has also been broken down into different types that give hope to all of us mere mortals who won't be the next Albert Einstein or Pablo Picasso. First, there was a distinction between Big-C creativity as the rare and exceptional creativity of great scientists and artists and little-c creativity as the everyday creativity and ingenuity that we all can exercise in generating new solutions to the everyday problems we encounter. Second, James Kaufman and Ronald Beghetto added Pro-C creativity which is exhibited by people who are creative in their vocations, even if they are not famous, and mini-c creativity which involves the ability to experience transformative learning through personally meaningful interpretations of experiences, actions, and insights.[31]

The four C model shows us how creativity as adaptive originality can manifest itself in a variety of ways. Big-C is the traditional idea of creativity associated with people like Einstein and Picasso and that has a major impact on society, culture, or the world, and which many of us feel is completely out of reach for us. Little-c involves the kind of novel solutions that each of us comes up with to common problems like fitting everything into our schedule and making ends meet when we have a very small budget. Pro-C is the kind of creativity that we may be able to attain if we gain enough experience and expertise in our job to come up with new solutions to important problems. Finally, mini-c is precisely the kind of creativity this book calls for in taking the discoveries of positive psychology and weaving them into our life story in a way that enables us to make the most of our life and live it to the fullest.

The other important distinction to make about creativity is that it can be understood and studied in relation to creative people, creative products, or creative processes. All three approaches have their advantages and disadvantages and are necessary to fully understand creativity. First, the study of Big-C creative people such as Albert Einstein, Marie Curie, Leonardo Da Vinci, and Pablo Picasso can enable us to understand how many different factors can come together in a life story to make a creative person. Second, the study of creative products such as the atom bomb or the ceiling of the Sistine Chapel can help us understand what led to such an important jump in science or art. Third, the study of the creative process may be most useful to us all, as it can shed light on what we can do to become more creative.

What Factors Enhance the Creative Process?

Whether or not we ever embody Big-C or Pro-C, there are processes that we can cultivate that are common to all four types of creativity. The first is called "divergent thinking" which is a term coined along with "convergent thinking" by psychologist J.P. Guilford in 1956.[32] Divergent thinking involves the generation of many alternative responses to a problem or question, whereas convergent thinking involves selecting one correct response. To diverge means to develop in a different direction while to converge means to come together. While convergent thinking is the thought process rewarded in educational and vocational tests that have one correct answer, divergent thinking can be a key part of the creative process as it involves thinking of many possible answers and solutions.

There are a variety of problem-solving techniques that involve going through steps that begin with divergent thinking and finish with convergent thinking. The divergent thinking step is often called "brainstorming" or "design thinking," which is the generation of as many solutions as possible without any criticism or judgment. The reason that criticism and judgment are excluded from the brainstorming step is that the negative emotions that they foster may reduce creativity. After many answers or solutions to a question or problem have been generated, the next step is to use convergent thinking to choose the best one. This two-step process may be effective both for individuals and for groups or team settings.

Positive emotions may be another important part of the creative process. The broaden-and-build theory of positive emotions by Barbara Fredrickson predicts that positive emotions will build a variety resources including creativity.[33] Alice Isen did extensive studies on the effect of positive emotion (or positive affect as she called it) on cognition or thinking and found several ways that it may enhance the creative process.[34] First, positive emotion makes more thoughts available for processing which increases the number of ideas available for association. Second, positive emotion reduces the focus on any one solution and makes it possible for additional solutions to be brought to bear on a problem. Third, it increases the chance that the greater number of thoughts that arise may become associated making a novel solution more likely.

The other thing that may be an even more direct part of the creative process is the experience of flow. As I noted above when introducing the idea of flow, Mihaly Csikszentmihalyi discovered the experience when studying artists who seemed to get completely lost in their work.[35] The experience of flow may have been part of many of the greatest discoveries and advances in the arts and sciences. One reason why flow is often a part of the creative process is that it is usually necessary to continue to increase the challenge in order maintain a flow state. Another reason is that it involves very deep attention and concentration over long periods of time. The ability to push the limits of human time and energy while continuing to grow in skill and expertise may be a recipe for making new discoveries and putting things together in ways that have never been done before.

In addition to these processes that we can cultivate, there are several personal and social factors that have associated with creativity. Although some things have been related to creativity, it is important to keep in mind that they are not necessarily required for creativity. The personal characteristics that have been related to creativity include openness to experience, self-acceptance, self-efficacy, and cognitive flexibility. The environments that foster creativity are those that are more open, supportive, reinforcing, and informal. The environments and social factors that hinder creativity include stress, time pressure, micromanagement, constant evaluation, and constraints placed on the range of solutions.

There has also been a great deal of debate about the relationship of creativity with both intelligence and mental illness. To begin with, it is important to be clear that what is usually defined as intelligence is not the same thing as creativity. The relationship between creativity and intelligence probably depends on whether you are talking about one of the big C creativities that are rare and exceptional or the little c creativities that may be attainable for most everyone. There is some evidence suggesting that even the kind of Big-C creativity in famous artists and scientists may not require an IQ greater than 120. Overall, personal characteristics such as openness to experience and cognitive flexibility and exposure to diverse life experiences may often be more important than IQ.

The relationship between creativity and mental illness has been controversial and difficult to fully understand. First, there is no strong correlation between Big-C creativity and mental illness, although it may depend on the type of creativity. Creative artists may be more susceptible to depression than creative scientists who have generally been shown to be more stable. Most important, rather than having any inherent predisposition to mental illness, it may be that creative people sometimes experience more symptoms as a result of living in a culture that cannot fully accept their creative contributions. Second, it is also possible that some forms of creativity are higher in people with mental health problems because they are challenged to adapt and compensate due to the additional challenges that they face.

What Can We Do to Increase Creativity?

While I have already talked about some of the processes and factors that may feed into and be a part of creativity, what can we actually do to increase it in our lives? While we may have little hope in becoming the next Einstein or Picasso or even Steven Spielberg or J.K. Rowling, there is actually a great deal that we can do. While it may be useful to focus on increasing things that can foster creativity over the long run such as curiosity, intrinsic motivation, risk-taking, and self-management; there is also much we can do right now and we may have a lot of fun in the process. Because thinking outside the box has been a good metaphor for creativity, I would ask that you try to be open to thinking outside of the box in considering the ways that you may become more creative. Please feel free to be creative in doing and adapting the following exercises:

1. *Try new ways to experience flow.*

Make a list of things to do that enable you to experience flow. Remember that it is important to be clear about the goals of the activities, that they need to have clear and immediate feedback for you, and that there should be a good match between the difficulty of the task and your skills. Be sure to plan to do these things at a clearly defined time and place where you will not be interrupted. After you have finished, try to think of new ways to improve your performance of the task.

2. *Brainstorm with friends about a common problem.*

Contact friends who share a common problem that calls for a practical solution such as finding a good person to date, deciding on a career or major, teaching children to care for others, or managing your time better. You need at least one other person but the more you contact the better. Take at least

20-30 minutes to brainstorm and write down all the solutions that you can think of no matter how crazy they sound. Then take another 10-15 minutes to rank the different ideas. Finally, choose the top one and then see if the top choice works.

3. *Read an autobiography or biography of a famous creative person that you admire.*

Try to pick a person whose work you really love and appreciate and, if possible, someone who is doing something you would like to be more creative in doing. Find an autobiography or biography about the person that may help you understand how they got to be so creative. Read their story and take notes on what you think helped them to be creative while keeping a particular focus on what you could try. Try at least one of the ideas you came up to deal with a relevant task or problem.

4. *Write yourself into your favorite story as another hero.*

Think of a story that you love and that you would like to be a part of. Think about when and how you would most like to enter the story. Use your imagination by dialoguing with your favorite characters to determine how you could be a part of the story and how you could add something new. Then actually write the story as if you were adding another scene for a movie or chapter for a book. Finally, find at least one friend who is willing to act out the new scenes with you playing yourself.

5. *Pick one of the first small objects you see and think of as many new uses for it as you can.*

Open a drawer in an office, kitchen, or bathroom or go into your garage or closest. Pick one of the first objects you see that catches your eye or seems like it would be fun to think about. Then give yourself 10 minutes to write down as many new uses for the object as you can think of. See if you can think of at least three ways to use the object and try at least one of the new ways in the following week. Try to think of something that will be surprising to others but also makes sense as a way to use the object.

6. *Redecorate in a way that says something unique about you.*

Select a room or part of a room that you are free to decorate however you want. This should be any room where someone you know would be likely to notice a change. It could be at home, school, work, or anywhere else. First, try to decorate it in a way that someone else will be sure to notice and comment on. Second, try to decorate it in a way that says something unique and important about you.

7. *Find a new way to express your love to someone.*

Identify at least one of your friends or family members whom you love. Make of list of the ways you have expressed your love to them in the past. Now take at least 10-15 minutes to brainstorm about as many new ways you can express your love to them as possible. Rank them and try at least three of them in the next two weeks and see what happens. Afterwards, talk to the person about which one meant the most to them, and brainstorm together about the different ways you can express love to each other.

8. *Find positive meaning in a stressful event.*

Identify one of the most stressful events or times that you have had in the past 5-10 years. Pick one that definitely caused some negative feelings and had negative consequences. Then write about anything positive that you learned or can learn from the experience, any ways that you grew or could grow from it, and any benefits that you can see coming out of the experience. Then review what you have written and make a list of ideas for how you could learn, grow, and find benefits in similar stressful experiences that you may have in the future.

Using the Strengths of Wisdom for the Journey

This chapter has been about the strengths that can help us find our way to a life that brings lasting happiness, joy, meaning, and fulfillment. While there may be many times when things are going well and it seems easy to find our path, we will undoubtedly continue to face problems, challenges, stresses, losses, and crises that threaten us. As we noted at the beginning of the chapter, it was with the dementors looming in the background that Dumbledore offered the hope that happiness can be found in the darkest times if we remember to turn on the light.

At so many times in our lives, that light is that ordinary magic at the heart of what we talked about in this chapter. Wisdom is the ability to learn from our experience to choose the best path even when dealing with the most complicated and scary situations. This wisdom is fed by the curiosity that motivates us to learn all that we need to know, and love of learning is the systematic expression of our curiosity in the ways we continue to learn at school and in our daily lives.

Perhaps the greatest magic is in those two other strengths that may save us from war and help to heal our diseases. The open-mindedness that allows us to actively search for evidence that goes against our most cherished beliefs is at the heart of science and an approach to living that can help to free us from our blind spots. In addition, the boundless creativity that is possible for us all was the open door to J.K. Rowling, J.R.R Tolkien, George Lucas, Joseph Campbell, and others discovered in making their hero's journeys.

There are at least three ways that you can start to use the strengths of wisdom and knowledge to continue on your journey. The first is the very practical one of identifying a new activity that will enable you to better see and turn on the light. Review the activities under each of the strengths in this chapter and choose the one that you would most like to try and see what happens—and then try another.

The second way to use these strengths for your journey is to bring back to mind the picture of the kind of life that you would most like for yourself. Which of the elements of well-being have you most wanted to use in painting the picture of your best possible self and life? Put this at the forefront of your mind as you go back through the list of ways you can build each of the strengths in this chapter and choose the one that you think would most help you make the journey.

Finally, there is that simple notion of just reminding yourself that you may be on a long journey and that you have the capacity to continue to learn and grow in these strengths that bring light to your path. Although there are many short-term joys and rewards that you will experience, allow yourself that rare patience and confidence that trusts in your ability to eventually grow strong in those "better angels of your nature," and not only see the light, but bring it to others.

Chapter 9

The Courage to Overcome Obstacles

The only thing to fear is fear itself.
— *Franklin Delano Roosevelt*[1]

If wisdom is what enables us to turn on the light and find our way, then courage is what makes it possible for us to face and overcome our challenges and obstacles along the way. While wisdom may be a virtue that guides us in the choice of other strengths, courage may be what makes the use of all of our strengths possible. Winston Churchill helped give England the courage it needed to stand against Hitler during World War II and he said that, "Courage is rightly esteemed the first of human qualities, because, as has been said, "It is the quality which guarantees all others."[2] Similarly, the poet Maya Angelou said that, "Without courage we cannot practice any other virtue with consistency. We can't be kind, true, merciful, generous, or honest."[3] Wisdom may be the guiding light, but it is courage that enables us to move forward despite the dragons and dementors that we may face along the way.

The goal of this chapter is to give you a new opportunity to appreciate and grow in the essential courage that you may need to reach your goals. The Latin root of the word courage is "heart" and encouragement literally means to give heart or courage to someone. The *Character Strengths and Virtues* handbook includes courage as one of the six overarching virtues. The four strengths that underlie it are bravery, perseverance, honesty, and vitality which together "entail the exercise of will to accomplish goals in the face of opposition, either external or internal." (p. 199).[4] Bravery is what enables us to move forward in spite of fear, perseverance keeps us from giving up until we are successful, integrity makes it possible for us to move with honesty and authenticity, and zest is the energy and enthusiasm that we need to act with bravery, perseverance, and integrity.

9.1. Bravery

Bravery is a prominent theme in many of our greatest stories and movies. The movie *Saving Private Ryan* is about the courage of the soldiers who stormed the beaches of France to face death in taking Europe back from Hitler. The movie *Iron Jawed Angels* is about the women who experienced beating and imprisonment to confront the U.S. government and earn women the right to vote. The movie *The Insider* is about Jeffrey Wigand who risked his income, marriage, friends, and life to stand up to Big Tobacco. And of course there are the fictional stories of the cowardly lion in *The Wizard of Oz* who finally found courage within himself and Katniss Everdeen who volunteered to save her sister and battle the Capitol in *The Hunger Games*. But the same kind of bravery and courage may be just as important in our own lives.

What Are Bravery and Courage?

Although the VIA classification uses the word "bravery" for a strength underlying the virtue of courage, they are both generally defined as the same thing. *Dictionary.com* defines courage as "the quality of mind or spirit that enables a person to face difficulty, danger, pain, etc., without fear; bravery."[5] Similarly, the Human *Character Strengths and Virtues* handbook defines bravery as the "ability to do what needs to be done despite fear" (p. 199).[6] The *VIA Institute on Character* defines bravery as "not shrinking from threat, challenge, difficulty or pain; speaking up for what is right even if there is opposition; acting on convictions even if unpopular; includes physical bravery but is not limited to it."[7] While there are many similarities in the various definitions, the most common difference is whether fear must be present.

Earl Shelp presented three criteria for an action to be considered brave or courageous, that have been met with varying levels of acceptance and controversy.[8] First, there must be the presence of danger, loss, or potential injury. This criterion has been broadly accepted as part of nearly all definitions of courage. Second, the action must be voluntary. This has been debated in relation to some challenges where people may have little choice such as being drafted as a soldier or having a chronic illness. Third, the action must involve a judgment about the potential risks and benefits of it. While this is generally the case, there are certainly examples of people who have done things that have been considered to be courageous when they didn't fully consider the potential risks and costs.

Because of the differences and controversies in how to define courage and courageous actions, I want to offer a more specific and qualified definition. I will define courage as the willingness and ability to do what you think is best despite the presence of significant risk. While the presence of fear is not necessary in this definition, some fear and anxiety may almost always be present if there is a risk of negative consequences. What you think is best could be what you think is right in the moral sense or just what you think may lead to a better outcome for yourself and/or other people. The key parts of this definition of courage are that (1) there is a significant risk of harm or loss, (2) there is a judgment that the potential benefits may outweigh the risks, and (3) there is both the willingness and ability to carry out the action.

The other important issue is the relationship between wisdom and courage. Wisdom is what can enable us to make the best judgment about whether the potential benefits of an action are worth the risk of harm or loss. Courage is one of the possible responses to this judgment. When our best judgment tells us that the potential benefits are probably not worth the risk, then we could either (1) not act, which could be labeled appropriately "cautious," or (2) act, which could be labeled "rash." When our best judgment tells us that the benefits are probably worth the risk, then we could either (3) not act, which could be labeled "cowardly," or (4) act, which could be labeled "courageous." Thus, acting when the risks are worth it would be considered brave or courageous while acting when the risks are not would be considered rash.

What Are the Different Types of Courage?

Robert Biswas-Diener has written about what he calls "courage blindness."[9] He says that people tend to discount their own courageous acts with phrases like, "Oh I just did what anyone would have done," or "If I were really brave, I would have…" (p. 22). One of the reasons we may not recognize courage in ourselves or in others is that we define it narrowly in terms of physical risk or danger. However, courage has been defined in many ways including physical, moral, psychological, and personal courage. Physical courage involves the immediate risk of bodily injury, physical pain, or death, as we commonly think of with firefighters, police officers, and soldiers. Other examples are trying to prevent someone from being attacked, saving someone from drowning, or pulling someone from a car that might explode.

Moral courage involves trying to speak up and do the right thing in the face of negative consequences such as the loss of income, relationships, jobs, and social status. While trying to do the right thing can result in physical threats and danger, moral courage may more often lead to social consequences such as being embarrassed, criticized, rejected or ostracized. John F. Kennedy's wrote a book called *Profiles in Courage* that was about the moral courage needed in politics to stand up for what is right even if it may mean losing popularity or being voted out of office.[10] Other examples of moral courage are whistleblowers who speak out about unethical practices at work and people who stand up to those who bully and discriminate against other people based on their gender, ethnicity, sexual preference, or sexual identity.

Psychological courage was identified by Daniel Putman as the courage to face the painful and difficult parts of ourselves in dealing with mental health challenges and problems.[11] This has brought courage home to many people who deal with common problems such as anxiety, posttraumatic stress disorder (PTSD), depression, and substance abuse. The kind of exposure therapy that is effective for anxiety and PTSD can be very frightening and require tremendous courage to complete. For many dealing with depression, psychological courage may be required just to get out of bed, to go for treatment when feeling hopeless, or to resist suicidal thoughts and urges. Finally, the ability to deal with an alcohol and other substance abuse problem can require tremendous courage in facing the problem and in building a new life without the substance.

The additional kind of courage that I think is particularly important for positive psychology is what I would call "personal courage." I would define it as the courage to take the risks that are necessary in order to continue to grow as a person who can live a joyful and fulfilling life. These involve all of the kinds of risks that we have been talking about as part of a hero's journey to making the most of your life, becoming your best, and achieving the kind of well-being that is most important to you. This kind of courage may very well include aspects of the physical, moral, and psychological courage that we already discussed. It also includes the courage to take risks in being true to yourself, developing good relationships, finding satisfying and rewarding work, and finding ways to use your strengths to make the world a better place.

What Factors Are Related to Courage?

Before I focus on what we can do to increase courage, I want to say something about the personal characteristics that have been associated with acting courageously. These include self-confidence, an internal locus of control, valuing independence and freedom, low levels of arousal under stress, a sense of oneness with others, and a prosocial orientation. First, self-confidence is related to courage because the belief that you can do the task at hand makes it more likely that you will take the risk and perform the courageous act.

Second, an internal locus of control is the belief that the important things in your life are generally under your control. As with self-confidence, believing that you may have control over the outcome makes it more likely you will take a risk in acting courageously. Third, people who value independence and freedom are less likely to go along with social pressure and the status quo and more likely to speak out and take a stand when they or other people are being mistreated. Fourth, people with lower general levels of arousal under stress are more likely to act in a courageous way than those whose higher levels of arousal, anxiety, and fear may prevent them from acting.

The other two characteristics associated with courage have to do with social relationships. People who feel a sense of empathy, oneness, and solidarity with other people are more likely to be courageous. The power of a sense of community to foster courage can clearly be seen in team sports and probably even more with soldiers in battle. Many veterans grieve the loss of the sense of comradery that they have trouble finding again after they leave the military. Finally, a prosocial orientation is "psychology-speak" for the tendency to be positive, helpful, friendly, and constructive in relationships with others people. The desire to want to help and be good to others may be a strong motivation for courageous acts of self-sacrifice.

How Can Courage Be Fostered?

Although the study of courage has been neglected until recently, there are a wealth of promising new efforts to understand what increases our ability to act courageously. Robert-Biswas-Diener has written a book called *The Courage Quotient*.[12] He thinks that there are two major factors that determine whether we will act courageously when we have decided it is the best course of action. The first is how much we are willing to act, which is related to the brain's "behavioral activation system," and the second is how much fear we have, which is related to the brain's "behavioral inhibition system."

Biswas-Diener defines the "courage quotient" as the willingness to act divided by the fear we are experiencing. If the willingness to act is large enough in relation to the fear we are experiencing and the courage quotient is large enough, then we will perform the courageous act. Thus, there may be two primary ways to increase the courage for carrying out what we judge to be the correct course of action. The first is to increase our willingness to act by doing things like focusing on the benefits of acting and the second is to decrease the fear we are experiencing by doing things like practicing meditation and other relaxation techniques.

This two-factor theory of courage provides a very useful framework for understanding some of the interventions that may increase courage. First, there are several approaches for reducing anxiety and fear that are grounded in work done before the positive psychology movement. These include exposure therapy and a full range of relaxation techniques including meditation, guided imagery, progressive relaxation, biofeedback, and yoga. All of these techniques may be part of a general practice to reduce anxiety or could be used to specifically target fear or anxiety in the context of acting courageously.

Second, there are several approaches that have been emphasized more in the positive psychology movement that could be used to increase the willingness to act. These include cognitive reappraisal, behavioral activation, and boosting self-efficacy. Cognitive reappraisal could increase the willingness to act by increasing the focus on the benefits of a positive outcome. Behavioral activation could increase the willingness to act by connecting the outcome with things that are intrinsically reinforcing and rewarding. Boosting self-efficacy would mean increasing the confidence that the person can effectively perform the courageous act. This could be done by the ways to increase self-efficacy presented above including practicing the task, observing others do it, imagining yourself doing it, and receiving encouraging feedback from others.

What Are Practical Ways to Increase Courage?

1. *Focus on the possible benefits.*

If you have done a cost-benefit analysis and determined that the potential benefits are worth the risks of harm or loss, then focus on the benefits as a way to increase your willingness to act. Think about how what you do could be good both for you and for other people. Also, be sure to think about how what you will do could make you feel for having done it and how it fits with your values and the goals that you have for yourself.

2. *Practice relaxation to reduce your fear.*

Find a relaxation technique that you enjoy and that you can practice when you have decided to perform a courageous act. These could include practicing mindful breathing, using a relaxing guided imagery, or learning progressive muscle relaxation. First, master these techniques when you are not faced with a courageous act. Next, begin to use and practice them while thinking about and then actually carrying out the act.

3. *Learn about courageous people.*

Identify people who are similar to you and who are faced with similar acts of courage. These can be friends and family members, famous or historical figures, or fictional characters that you can relate to. Try to observe them or read about when they were acting courageously and try to learn and understand what may enable them to be courageous. When you are about to act with courage, remember and visualize them as a companion and role model that you want to imitate or honor.

4. *Get the support of others.*

Choose one or more of your most encouraging friends and ask if they would be willing to help you deal with a challenge that you are facing. Try to find people who have experience doing what you hope to be able to do. If possible, see if you can find someone who would be willing to act as either a formal or an informal mentor. Meet with them as regularly as you can to discuss your progress in becoming more courageous or in doing a specific kind of courageous act.

5. *Begin with a smaller task or risk.*

If the kind of courage that you want to display feels particularly large or overwhelming, break it down into smaller tasks that you can progress through in a step-by-step fashion. If the risks seems too great, see if you can first take smaller risks until you feel more comfortable and confident. This suggestion is built on the idea of increasing self-efficacy by practicing or doing something that is similar to the task that you want to perform.

6. *Get specific training.*

If the kind of courage you want to express is something you can receive specific practice or training for, then try to get the best class and teacher that you can. For example, for the fear of public speaking, there is an organization called *Toastmasters* where people who want to improve their speaking meet regularly to practice together. This kind of training is effective because it exposes you to the task with the support of others and allows you to learn new skills.

9.2. Perseverance

When I was 24 years old, I had to have major back surgery. Though the surgeon told me that I would be back to work in six months, after the surgery I could hardly walk and couldn't sit down without pain for months. I felt like I had been struck by lightning and had aged 50 years overnight. I had ran track in high school and to encourage me my brother gave me a poster of a long distance runner with a quote about the race not going to the swift but to those who persevere. Though I felt depressed and alone, I decided to take that to heart and learn to walk again by starting with walking to the house next door and adding a new house every day. After a year, I was walking more than five miles a day, was finally able to go back to work, and was a firm believer in the power of perseverance.

What Is Perseverance?

The artist and author Mary Anne Radmacher once wrote that, "Courage doesn't always roar, sometimes it's the quiet voice at the end of the day whispering I will try again tomorrow."[13] The *VIA Institute on Character* defines perseverance as "finishing what one starts; persisting in a course of action in spite of obstacles; getting it out the door; taking pleasure in completing tasks" and relates it to the synonyms persistence and industriousness.[14] The *Character Strengths and Virtues* handbook defines the word persistence as the "voluntary continuation of a goal-directed behavior in spite of obstacles, difficulties, or discouragement" (p. 229).[15] The way that I will define perseverance is that it is continuing to make the effort to reach a goal despite the obstacles along the way.

Perseverance not only makes it more likely that we will reach a goal, it also can build our self-efficacy, increase our sense of satisfaction in reaching the goal, and build the skills, talents, and strengths we can use for reaching other goals. When I was learning to walk again after my surgery, I was building my confidence that I could bounce back from a major stressor. I also gained a sense of satisfaction and gratitude for just being able to walk that I still have to this very day. Finally, learning to walk and sit down and drive again while I was in pain enabled me to build my strengths, such as the creativity that I needed to find new ways to function. In contrast, when a person reaches a goal quickly with little effort, there may be little benefit in terms of increased confidence and learning new skills or talents and also less satisfaction in reaching the goal.

What Else Can Help Us Understand Perseverance?

There are two other things that may help us better understand the value of perseverance and put it into perspective. First, there is the work of Angela Duckworth regarding what she calls "grit," which is defined as perseverance and passion for long-term goals.[16] The questionnaire that she created to assess grit includes items to assess both the perseverance of effort and the consistency of interests. The idea is that grit is the ability to both hold on to a long-term goal and continue to make the effort to pursue it. She completed a series of studies showing that grit was related to a range of better outcomes even when controlling for IQ and other personality factors. In fact, grit may be more important than basic intelligence in many occupations and educational settings.

Carol Dweck has also contributed to understanding the value of perseverance and sustaining our efforts in the face of adversity and set-backs.[17] She has identified two different mindsets that appear to have different effects on success. First, there is what she calls a "fixed mindset" where a person believes that their success is based on their innate ability, such as their IQ. Second, there is what she calls a "growth mindset" where a person believes that their success is based on their learning, hard work, and determination. Dweck has done research showing that children with a growth mindset had less stress and better academic performance than those with a fixed mindset. She argues that having a growth mindset may be beneficial for all aspects of living.

Together the work of Duckworth and Dweck suggest that perseverance may be valuable because it focuses on the effort needed to reach a goal rather than our innate ability. However, it is also important to know when to quit and "cut your losses." This is the wisdom to know the difference between what you can change and what you must learn to accept that is expressed in the *Serenity Prayer*. As the *Character Strength and Virtues* handbook says, "Persistence is only effective when used judiciously. The individual (or group) must make a correct appraisal of whether persistence in the face of failure will produce eventual success or simply more failure" (p. 240).[18] The strength of wisdom must be used to consider all of the factors involved and determine whether the potential benefits of persevering outweigh the costs.

The other ideas that may help us in fully understanding and appreciating perseverance are the ideas of the hero's journey, stages of change, and the PATH process presented in Chapters 5 and 6. Each of these help us understand how the journey towards a life of happiness and well-being can involve many steps requiring different kinds of effort, strengths, and skills. We may focus only on the perseverance needed for completing one step rather than following through with them all. Duckworth's idea of grit suggests that we need to keep in mind the long-term goal that may take years to accomplish and be sure to persevere to the end of the journey.

The author of the book *The Last Lecture* gives a wonderful example of the findings of both Duckworth and Dweck in his own life.[19] Randy Pausch was a college professor who knew he was going to soon die of cancer and wrote a book about the last lecture that he gave to his students. Not only was he a living example of how it is possible to persevere at being your best right up to the end of your life, he also left us with this quote about the obstacles that we face in life:

> The brick walls are there for a reason. The brick
> walls are not there to keep us out. The brick walls
> are there to give us a chance to show how badly
> we want something. Because the brick walls are
> there to stop the people who don't want it badly
> enough. They're there to stop the other people.[20]

The long-term goal that Duckworth shows us the value of is that thing that we want so badly and the mindset that Dweck emphasizes is how we can choose to see the brick wall as a challenge to growth rather than a dead end.

What Factors Are Related to Perseverance?

There is much that psychological research has learned about the factors that may increase perseverance. The first two may balance each other in supporting our continued efforts to reach a goal. The first is keeping the final goal clearly in mind and the second is taking small steps to reach it. Laura King's exercise of writing about your "best possible self" and the North Star step in the PATH process are ways of cultivating a real and sustaining vision of reaching a final goal.[21-22] At the same time, it is important to set small, clear, and specific goals that you can accomplish one at a time. Each time you make a small step you are rewarded and build self-efficacy for taking the next step. The challenge is not to err in either the direction of becoming so heavenly focused that you are no earthly good, or so earthly focused you lose sight of your vision.

The next two things that have been shown to foster perseverance can also be viewed together—they are optimism and hope. We will talk more about them in Chapter 13 about the virtue of Transcendence, but I will say now that both are essential for persevering to reach our goals. In the way I will be defining it, optimism is a positive expectation about the future and hope involves having both the will and the way to meet your goals. The more we expect good things in the future and are confident that we can reach our destination, the more effort we are likely to put in and the less likely we are to give up.

The third pair of things that can foster perseverance are creativity and flexibility in coping. There is a song from the 1970s by Kiki Dee called *I Got the Music in Me* with the simple line, "When something gets in my way, I go around it." Paul Baltes identified an effective way of maintaining well-being during old age despite the changes and losses of functioning. He called it "selective optimization with compensation" which involves selecting and optimizing what you can still do while also compensating for your declines and losses.[23] This is a very useful concept for the hero's journey in positive psychology because we have to be flexible in building and using our strengths and creative in finding new ways to use them to reach our goals.

The fourth pair of things that can foster perseverance have to do with our relationships—and are social support and positive reinforcement. Social support involves knowing there are people in our lives who support our goals and using their support when we need it. Robert Eisenberger has done work that dovetails with the importance of focusing on effort rather than ability, highlighted by Carol Dweck. Eisenberger found that what he called effort training, that involves receiving positive reinforcement, increases perseverance.[24] The kind of positive reinforcement that is most effective for increasing perseverance appears to be an intermediate or moderate amount which is given on a somewhat irregular basis.[25]

The fifth pair of things that can foster perseverance are cognitive reappraisal and a growth mindset. As we have seen from Dweck's work, when faced with a set-back, people are more likely to persevere if they have the mindset that they can improve with greater effort, than if they think that they failed because their ability is fixed and there is nothing they can do about it. Cognitive reappraisal is the process by which we can change our thinking or "mindset" to a healthier and more productive perspective. In other words, rather than seeing our "mindset" as fixed, we can reframe our thinking about our set-backs so that we can learn from our mistakes and improve in the future.

The final thing related to perseverance is "self-handicapping" which may reduce it. Self-handicapping is the name for what we do when we give up because we are afraid we will fail and we don't want to hurt our self-esteem. Essentially, we think it would be better not to even try, than to try and not only fail but feel like a failure as a person. This can be countered by several of the above ways to foster perseverance including imagining the positive outcome of reaching our goal, social support and positive reinforcement for our efforts, and reappraising the tasks with a growth mindset that sees failure as an opportunity to grow.

What Can We Do to Increase Perseverance?

1. *When you successfully persevered.*

Identify three times in your life when you persevered in striving for a goal and felt satisfied in reaching it. Make of list of the things that helped you persevere and plan to use one of them in reaching a current goal.

2. *When you should have given up sooner.*

Identify three times when you didn't know when to quit and you should have cut your losses sooner. Think about why you waited so long to give up. Try to identify the kinds of signs you had for quitting and think about the kind of signs you could look for in the future.

3. *Reappraising set-backs for a growth mindset.*

Identify three times in your life when one door closed and another door opened. Identify what at the time felt like it was a set-back or an end to something important to you, but where you later discovered it made a new opportunity possible.

4. *Simple positive self-feedback*

Think of a task that you want to persevere at in the next month. Break the tasks down into small and clear steps. Make a list of the small ways that you can reward yourself each time you take a step. Choose your favorite one and reward yourself for the task and see how it feels when you persevere.

5. *Positive support person.*

Identify a good friend or family member who can keep you accountable and reward you for persevering at a task. Identify a goal you can pursue in the next month and break it down into small manageable steps. Ask your friend to contact you regularly and see if you are continuing with the task and design a plan for them to reward you for each step you take.

9.3. Vitality

The movie *My Left Foot* is the true story of Christy Brown who lived in Dublin, Ireland during the 20th century and who was born with a severe form of cerebral palsy. Even though his condition was so bad that his only usable limb was his left foot, he became a painter and writer who wrote a popular and critically acclaimed autobiography. The scene that struck me the most from the movie was something that happened when Christy was a young boy and his family had no idea that he could communicate or understand what they were saying.

After seeing that his mother had survived a serious fall, Christy was so excited that he wrote his mother's name on the floor with a piece of chalk—with his left foot. His family was stunned when they realized that he could understand and communicate with them. This was the beginning of a whole new life where he was fully loved and appreciated by his family and where he even used his left foot to play soccer with his brothers. Christy Brown is a remarkable example of vitality in how it prevented his disabling condition from holding him back.

What Is Vitality?

Dictionary.com defines vitally in four different ways that reflect the life of Christy Brown and help us fully understand the meaning of this underappreciated human strength. It says that vitality is "(1) exuberant physical strength or mental vigor, (2) capacity for survival or for the continuation of a meaningful or purposeful existence, (3) power to live or grow, and (4) vital force or principle."[26] The *VIA Institute on Character* defines vitality as "approaching life with excitement and energy; not doing things halfway or halfheartedly; living life as an adventure; feeling alive and activated."[27] The *Character Strengths and Virtues* handbook also includes the synonyms zest, enthusiasm, vigor, and energy and says, "A vital person is someone whose aliveness and spirit are expressed not only in personal productivity and activity—such individuals often infectiously energize those with whom they come into contact" (p. 273).[28]

Although neglected in psychological research until recently, the idea of vitality has parallels in the Chinese concept of "chi," the Indian belief in "prana," and in the work of early psychologists. The word chi literally means "air" or "breath" in

Chinese but in Chinese medicine it refers to the flow of energy or the life force that runs through all things. In Hindu philosophy, Indian medicine, and yoga, the world prana refers to the life energy or life force that began in the sun and connects all of the Universe. For Sigmund Freud, there was an inherent instinct to live, which he called eros, and for Carl Jung there was the idea of psychic energy that was similar to physical energy and could be used wherever needed.

Vitality may be related to how much our basic needs are met. Self-determination theory developed by Richard Ryan and Edward Deci contends that autonomy, competence, and relatedness are three basic psychological needs.[29] Autonomy is the need to be a causal agent and act in harmony with who we are, competence is the desire to control and master our environment, and relatedness is the desire to interact and connect with other people. Ryan and Christina Frederick defined vitality as a positive feeling of aliveness and as having energy available.[30] They predicted and found that the fulfillment of the need for autonomy, competence, and relatedness were related to greater vitality.

Vitality may also involve a particular combination of mood states. Robert Thayer developed a theory relevant for understanding how mood may be involved in vitality.[31] He thinks that there are two dimensions to how we experience mood. The first is a continuum from energy to tiredness and the second is a continuum from tension to calmness. This is important for understanding vitality because it may not just involve high levels of energy but also low levels of tension. When we have a lot of caffeine or sugar we may increase our energy level but may also feel tense, and when we sit down to listen to relaxing music we may not feel tense but also may not have a lot of energy. But doing an activity such as yoga or tai chi may involve both high energy and low tension which would be a good example of an expression of vitality.

What Increases or Decreases Vitality?

There are a variety of things that have been identified which may influence vitality. First, there are social and environmental factors that promote the fulfillment of basic psychological needs such as autonomy, competence, and relatedness. This might mean having a school or work setting where you can use your gifts and strengths, continue to grow and learn, and develop positive relations with others. This might also mean being in an environment where there are rewards that boost your energy and also times and places where it is possible to relax and reduce your tension.

Second, there are personal factors that decrease vitality such as illness, pain, and smoking and those that increase it such as a healthy diet, good sleep habits, and regular exercise. Robert Thayer did research comparing the effects of eating a candy bar to walking fast for 10 minutes in relation to the dimensions of energy and tension.[32] He found that walking was associated with higher energy and lower tension after one hour and also two hours later. In contrast, eating a candy bar was associated with higher energy and higher tension after one hour and lower energy and higher tension after two hours. Exercise may be a good way to both increase energy and reduce tension.

Third, the combination of practicing mindfulness and behavioral activation may be a good way to foster vitality by addressing both of Thayer's dimensions. Practicing mindfulness may reduce the tension you experience in your daily life as you learn to calmly focus on the present moment. If you remember from Chapter 6, behavioral activation involves finding the kinds of activities that you find most intrinsically rewarding and reinforcing and then incorporating them into your life. Doing what you enjoy can bring you more energy and the feeling of being alive.

What Can We Do to Increase Vitality?

These suggestions flow directly from the ideas about what we discussed about personal factors, mindfulness, and behavioral activation:

1. *Exercise regularly.*

It sounds so simple but can be so hard to do for many of us. The keys are to find something you enjoy that increases your heart rate and that you can fit in your schedule. Do it at least 30 minutes three times a week. Find a good friend to either do it with you or hold you accountable for doing it. After one month, see if you are feeling more energy and less tension.

2. *Practice mindfulness.*

Practice mindfulness regularly using the kind of progression of mindfulness exercises presented in Chapter 7. Begin by practicing alone in a quiet place and then find ways to practice during your daily activities. Whenever you notice yourself becoming tense during the day, practice mindful breathing until you begin to feel calm.

3. *Pleasant events scheduling.*

Make a list of all the things that you enjoy doing. They should be a variety of activities that reliably make you feel good. Pretend you are a doctor and prescribe yourself one activity a day for the next two weeks. Try each activity to see how it affects your energy level and your excitement and enthusiasm for life.

4. *Develop a passion.*

This is related to Mihaly Csikszentmihalyi's idea of flow and Joseph Campbell's idea of following your bliss. Find something that you love to do that you can do on a regular basis. Try to make it something that reliably puts you in the flow state described in Chapter 5 and that involves a long-term goal you can continue to pursue.

9.4. Integrity

In June of 2003, the American Film Institute reviewed the past 100 years of movies made in the United States and created a top 100 list of the greatest heroes in American film. Although Indiana Jones, James Bond, Clarice Starling from *Silence of the Lambs,* and Ellen Ripley from *Aliens* were all in the top 10, the top choice was a much more down to earth character from an old black and white film. That hero was Atticus Finch from the movie *To Kill a Mockingbird*—a prime example of the honesty, authenticity, and integrity that is so lacking in flashy Hollywood action heroes and the glitzy culture that creates them.

Atticus Finch lived in a small southern town when the United States had not begun to really face the racism we still struggle with today. Atticus was a lawyer who was a widower with two small children. He lived a quiet life until the mayor asked him to defend a black man who was falsely accused of raping a white woman. Even though he knew it was a lost cause, Atticus took the job because he wanted to be true to himself and his values in doing the right thing. Even though he lost the case, the black people in town and his children gained great respect for him, as have so many who have come to love the story.

What Are Integrity, Honesty, and Authenticity?

While courage, perseverance, and vitality are more directly about overcoming obstacles; integrity, honesty, and authenticity involve bringing the truth of who we are to our path. As the *Character Strengths and Virtues* handbook says, "Honesty refers to factual truthfulness and interpersonal sincerity, authenticity refers to emotional genuineness and psychological depth, and integrity refers to moral probity and self-unity" (p. 250).[33] The *VIA Institute on Character* defines them together as "speaking the truth but more broadly presenting oneself in a genuine way and acting in a sincere way; being without pretense; taking responsibility for one's feelings and actions."[34]

As I will define them, honesty is about speaking or telling the truth as we know or see it versus simply lying or distorting the truth to suit our purposes. Integrity includes honesty but is broader and also about whether the different things we do are consistent, whether they fit with our values, and whether they match what we say. The opposite of someone with integrity might be a hypocrite who professes strong moral values but actually behaves in a very different or immoral way. Authenticity is communicating and being what we know ourselves to be with other people as opposed to presenting a false front.

What Good Are Integrity and Honesty?

I will consider honesty and integrity together because honesty is an inherent part of integrity. Both involve challenges to doing the right thing and come with risks and benefits. There may be times when it is justifiable to tell a lie or act in an inconsistent way. The classic example is when German citizens were lying to the Nazi's about hiding the Jews that would die if they were caught. A common example is what you might say to a sensitive friend who asks you whether they look old or overweight. But while there may be times and places when not telling the truth may be justified, it is all too easy to fall into self-serving biases and rationalize that it is all for the best when it may really just be the easy way out.

There is a long debate on the cost-benefit ratio and evolutionary significance of being honest and living with integrity. On the cost side, we may get into trouble presenting ourselves honestly but in a less favorable light. It may be harder to "win friends and influence people" as the title of the popular old Dale Carnegie book suggests if we tell them what we really think. Living your values and speaking truth to power are not always good for your health as many martyrs have discovered.

On the benefit side, being honest may make us more trustworthy to others, more likely to be a good mate, and more likely as parents to survive the B.S. detectors of adolescents. In addition, we may be more likely to want to be friends with and lend our help and support to someone we can believe and trust.

But there is another way to look at honesty and integrity in relation to happiness and well-being. If we define well-being as the hedonic pursuit of pleasure and avoidance of pain, then being honest with our date about their breath may not always serve our immediate purpose. But if we define well-being as the eudaimonic pursuit of joy, meaning, and fulfillment, then it may be a completely different story. The short term losses in immediate pleasure may be outweighed by the longer term gains that come in being honest and living with integrity. Despite the small risk of becoming a martyr, life may be more meaningful when doing something that supports our highest values and we may end up with much more supportive and giving friends.

The other thing is that it may be more important to feel good about yourself and be like Atticus Finch than to feel like that person who hurt you or your best friend. One of the lasting contributions of the positive psychology movement is giving us a new lens through which to see the best in us. As we have begun to see in many studies, not only does identifying and using our strengths improve our well-being, it can also be a valuable and rewarding end goal in and of itself. As the Buddha discovered, many of the external things that we trust in for happiness will pass away. In contrast, no one can take away the satisfaction of having been true to our values and done the right thing.

What Good Is Authenticity?

I am dealing with authenticity separately from honesty and integrity because it has been treated separately in psychology and self-help and may represent a unique application of the virtue of courage to our personal lives. Authenticity has often been defined by the words in Shakespeare's *Hamlet* "to thine own self be true" and the words of Soren Kierkegaard "be that self which one truly is."[35-36] While there is much popular appreciation of the value of "being yourself" and "being true to yourself," there is less of an understanding of what that may actually mean.

There are scientific theories and traditions suggesting that we may not actually have much of a self to be true to. Behaviorists have argued that the self is only a product of conditioning and that there is no self that underlies our behavior. Some sociologists have contended that the self is only part of a group of empty masks, roles, and performances determined by social norms. Some neuroscientists have argued that because there is no central control center in the brain there is little to support the idea of an integrated sense of who we are.

There are also theories and traditions in psychology supporting the idea of a unique self that is relatively consistent in many attitudes and behaviors. Humanistic theories have often provided support for the idea of a unique person who has the potential to grow and become self-actualized. Personality theories have focused on personal characteristics and stories that make us unique. Some neuroscientists have suggested that the unique ways our brains are structured and function probably correspond with unique attitudes, behaviors, and personalities.

While it may be easy to take sides on this debate, I think these sides represent important poles and that the truth is somewhere in the middle. The critics of the idea of a stable self help us see how we are influenced by our environments, how we are changing and evolving, and how difficult it is to fully know and understand who we are. The advocates of the idea of a relatively stable self help us to see the ways that we are unique and consistent in our thoughts and behaviors across different times and situations.

Thus, the question about authenticity may not be about being true to a completely stable self that is set in stone. The real question may be about living in a way that makes the best use of the relatively consistent but also changing person that we are. The truth is that people who are as tall, fast, and can jump as high as Michael Jordan are better suited to basketball than those of a lesser height, speed, and vertical leap. There are also differences in intelligence, personality, personal history, values, interests, and strengths that can greatly influence our path in life.

Because all of these differences can affect how we experience happiness and well-being, it is important to be true to ourselves in doing what fits the best for us. While it is difficult to do research on this kind of matching because it requires such large samples, the success of intelligence and ability testing in organizational psychology has depended on it. The strength of authenticity is what enables us to discover what is unique about ourselves and what fits the best in enabling us to experience happiness and well-being.

How Can We Be More Authentic?

There are few people in the history of psychology who have had a greater understanding and appreciation of authenticity than Carl Rogers.[37] He was a humanistic psychologist whose primary goals were much aligned with positive psychology. He wanted to enable people to become what he called a "fully-functioning person," which is very much akin to the positive psychology goal of making the most of our lives and living them to the fullest. A central process in enabling people to do this was to help them learn to be more authentic or "congruent" as he defined it.

In understanding what Rogers meant by congruence, it is important to understand how it relates to three aspects of our lives.[38] The first is what we actually say or communicate to another person. The second is what we are aware of about our own inner experience including our sensations, feelings, and thoughts. The third is our actual experience which includes both what we are aware of and what we may not yet be fully aware of.

Rogers chose the word congruence because it means "coming together" and identified two kinds of congruence. The first is "intrapsychic congruence" which involves the coming together of our awareness and our experience. The more we are aware of everything that is going on within ourselves, the more intrapsychic congruence we have and the more aware we are of that inner self that we can be true to. Intrapsychic congruence between our awareness and experience can be fostered in a variety of ways including practicing mindfulness, journaling, having honest friends, mentoring, coaching, and psychotherapy.

The second kind is "interpersonal congruence" which involves the coming together of our awareness and our communication. Interpersonal congruence is when our communication about our self with others matches what we are aware of about our self. The more we communicate the true aspects of our experience that we are aware of, the more we are being authentic in our relationship with another person. Interpersonal congruence can be fostered by practicing it in close relationships with people we trust by being vulnerable in sharing our inner experience with them. Social work researcher Brené Brown has written about the value of this kind of vulnerability in her popular book *Daring Greatly: How the courage to be vulnerable transforms the way we live, love, parent, and lead.*[39]

For Rogers, it was important to work on both kinds of congruence in order to be an authentic and fully-functioning person. First, it was important to become as aware as possible of the full breadth and depth of your inner experience—your true feelings, thoughts, preferences, interests, and desires. Second, it was important to communicate as much of it as you can with people who are important to you. The more you are congruent in these ways, the more you will come to fully know and understand yourself, the more energy you will have in not having to hide, and the more you will be able to discover and achieve what really makes you happy.

Finally, the ideas of Carl Rogers about authenticity and the importance of a good match between values, goals, and behavior has found support in recent theory and research.[40] Self-determination theory supports the idea of authenticity where an autonomous self is more satisfied if there is freedom to do what is personally interesting and meaningful. Ken Sheldon and his colleagues have found that pursuing authentic goals leads to greater effort and goal attainment.[41] Finally, Brené Brown has shown that the willingness to take risks in being authentic and vulnerable is related to a greater sense of love and belonging.[42]

How Can We Practice and Build These Strengths?

There are some general principles about ways to practice and increase each of these three things. Practicing honesty can be a kind of exposure therapy where you do what may at first feel uncomfortable and later may feel just right. Practicing integrity can involve clarifying your most important values and determining whether what you do and say is consistent with them. Authenticity involves increasing your awareness of your thoughts and feelings as well as being vulnerable in sharing them with others. Here are a few more specific ways to practice each:

1. *Refrain from telling small lies.*

Try to go through a day without telling small white lies—as long as it won't obviously be harmful to someone. See how other people respond and how it makes you feel. Think about how, where, and when these small lies may be justified and when they may not be.

2. *Say what you think to someone who you think will disagree.*

Think of people and situations in your life where you may not feel free to honestly give your perspective. Think about whether there are any truly dangerous risks involved. If not, then experiment with sharing your perspective and see what happens.

3. *Identify principles you want to live by and see if your behavior matches.*

Write down three to five principles that you would most like to live by. Review what you said and did over the previous week and rate how well your behavior matched your principles. Continue to review your principles and try to raise your rating.

4. *Learn about an example of integrity you admire.*

Identify a person of integrity you admire and who can be a model for you. Learn as much as you can about them. Think about the situations where it may be hardest for you to be true to your values and imagine what they would say or do.

5. *Build intrapsychic congruence by practicing mindfulness.*

Practice mindful breathing and then pay attention to and note whatever thoughts cross your mind. Continue to practice on a regular basis and begin keeping a journal of what surprised you as well as the things you were not aware of.

6. *Build interpersonal congruence by practicing vulnerability.*

Watch Brené Brown's TED Talk about *The Power of Vulnerability*[43] and identify three ways that you can be vulnerable with another person in the next week. Identify situations where there is some risk but where you also feel safe with the person. Try it and see what happens.

Using the Strengths of Courage for the Journey

Whereas the last chapter was about how the strengths of wisdom can enable us to turn on the light and see our path, this chapter has been about the primary "force" that can sustain us on our journey. There are four strengths that compose the virtue that has enabled us to survive, thrive, and grow through even the greatest challenges and obstacles that we have faced.

Courage is what makes it possible for us to boldly move ahead despite our greatest and most fearsome dragons. Perseverance is what enables us to continue to try no matter how many set-backs we experience and stay with our goals until we achieve them. Vitality is the excitement and enthusiasm that makes us feel good to be alive and provides the motivation and muscle that fuels our courage and perseverance. Integrity is the ability to bring all of who we are to the task at hand and experience the satisfaction of being true to ourselves and our values and beliefs.

At so many times and in so many ways in our lives we may feel like we have come to that brick wall that Randy Pausch describes or come face-to-face with that most fearsome dragon or dementor. It is at those times when we can remember that we are not alone, that our brothers and sisters on the journey have been there before. We can trust that so many of our fellow travelers have taken heart and found the courage to go on. Harry faced Voldemort, Luke faced Darth Vader, Wonder Woman faced Ares, and Frodo felt the full power of the ring and prevailed. Mother Teresa faced the poverty of Calcutta, Nelson Mandela faced that small cell in prison, and Gandhi faced one of the most powerful nations in the world with only a small white robe and the discipline of non-violence.

The strengths that we talked about in this chapter are not lofty academic words or abstract concepts that are destined to be removed from our daily experience. They are things that we can actually learn, practice, and turn into the habits and strengths that can make a critical difference. They can make all the difference between a life of quiet desperation or comfortable numbness, and a life of joy and fulfillment that the darkness cannot touch and that makes our lives worth living. They are the ways that we can say yes to our most frightening and challenging tasks and prevail in knowing that we have brought the best of who we are to our most sacred journey.

Chapter 10

The Humanity to Connect with Others

Be kind, for everyone you meet is fighting a hard battle.

—Unknown[1]

There are many heroes in *The Lord of the Rings* trilogy. There is the wizard Gandalf who beat the Balrog, there is the mysterious Strider who became the king who returned, and there is Frodo who carried that dangerous ring to cast it into the fire to destroy it. But there is one more than all of the others who shows what this chapter is all about. Samwise Gamgee is a shining example of what is truly a best friend for life. He was that friend who made the journey that made saving Middle Earth possible. He was the one who carried Frodo when he was exhausted and overwhelmed by the enormity of the challenge.

But can also find friends that may be just as important in our other favorite hero's journey stories. For Harry Potter, it was Ron and Hermione. For Dorothy in *The Wizard of Oz*, it was the cowardly lion, that awkward scarecrow, that man made of metal, and that feisty and furry little version of "man's best friend." For Luke Skywalker, it was Princess Leia, Han Solo, a couple of robots made of metal, and that feisty and furry big thing that few could understand. These characters are in these archetypal stories because they reflect something that is essential for our journey and play such a vital role in our overall happiness and well-being.

We have talked about the wisdom that can show us the way and the courage that gives us the strength to go forward, but in this chapter we will talk about what enables us to find and cultivate the people who walk with us and help make the journey worth it. When I worked in a psychiatric unit before going to graduate school, there was one thing that seemed to keep deeply depressed and suicidal people alive more than anything else—they had someone to live for. The beginning of the 13th chapter of the first book of Corinthians in the Bible gives a list of the many great things that a person could do and ends with the simple words—"but without love I gain nothing."

In the VIA classification, the virtue of Humanity was included as a testament to the universal value of human relationships across all times and cultures. The three strengths associated with Humanity make it possible to have the kind of friendship and love that may more than anything else make our lives worth living. We will begin with social intelligence as how we can best relate to other human beings. We will continue with love as how we can cultivate the relationships with those who mean the most to us. We will end with kindness as the strength that enables us to be a positive and friendly presence in the world.

10.1. Social Intelligence

The great actor, entertainer, and writer Will Rogers is famous for saying, "I never met a man I didn't like."[2] My father said the same thing—which I thought was technically true but for some reason didn't apply to his relationship with our little Yorkshire terrier. I would sometimes find my father angrily shouting at the little beast when it had him backed into a corner in our house. Whether or not you believe there are actually people who like everyone, there are people who seem to like and get along with almost everyone. Are they just born that way? If not, what is their secret?

Then there are also people who have a much harder time getting along with others. They just rub others the wrong way or have a habit of saying the wrong thing at the wrong time. While there are some people you are always glad to see, there are others who you may actively screen on your phone or go out of your way to avoid running into. While most of us probably fall somewhere in between these two extremes, the study of social intelligence has tried to help us understand these differences and whether we can be a little more like Will Rogers.

What Is Social Intelligence?

Dictionary.com defines social intelligence as "the ability to form rewarding relationships with other people."[3] The *Character Strengths and Virtues* handbook says that "social intelligence concerns one's relationships with people, including the social relationships involved in intimacy and trust, persuasion, group membership, and political power" (p. 339).[4] The *VIA Institute on Character* says that people who are socially intelligent are aware of the motives and feelings of other people, know what to do to fit into different social situations, and know what to do to put others at ease."[5] They further say that social intelligence involves social awareness or being aware of others and social facility or knowing how to use this awareness.

The *Character Strengths and Virtues* handbook also associates social intelligence with personal intelligence and emotional intelligence and all three together can be referred to as hot intelligences. The term hot intelligence is used to describe the forms of intelligence that involve emotion and motivation in relation to personal and social issues directly relevant for survival. In contrast, cold intelligence is that which is normally assessed in IQ tests. Personal intelligence has to do with the ability to accurately know and understand yourself and emotional intelligence is the ability to effectively understand and use emotional information as it applies to yourself as well as to your relationships with others.

There are at least two kinds of problems in using the word "intelligence" in relation to our social lives and relationships with others. First, although Howard Gardner developed a theory of multiple intelligences, there is still debate about whether intelligence is basically one thing or consists of separate kinds of intelligences that aren't always strongly related.[6] There is some evidence that differences in what some think of as social intelligence may really be explained by differences in general intelligence, personality, and experience in social relationships. Second, using the word "intelligence" often carries with it the idea that it is an innate ability that cannot be changed or modified.

In contrast, I will define and use the term social intelligence as an ability that can be modified. I will slightly extend the *Dictionary.com* definition to say that social intelligence is the ability to form and maintain beneficial and rewarding relationships with other people. This actual ability as it is expressed in our relationships is a combination of inherent biological factors that are more difficult to change with a broad array of knowledge and skills that are more subject to change. This ability includes both the awareness and understanding of social relationships and the more practical knowledge of how to use them in creating and maintaining the kind of positive relationships that are an important part of well-being and can foster other kinds of happiness and well-being.

What Are the Foundations of Social Intelligence?

Our ability to establish and maintain good relations with other people may first and foremost be rooted in the evolution of our brains. Many scientists think that the main reason the human brain evolved to be so large was to negotiate the social world. The archeologist Steve Mithen thinks that the first big jump in brain size from 450cc to 1000cc occurred about 1.8 million years ago when we started living together in larger and more complex communities.[7] He thinks the second big jump from 1000cc to 1200cc happened more recently from 200,000 to 600,000 years ago when the use of language really took off. It is ironic that there have been arguments about whether there is such a thing as social intelligence that is different from the "general intelligence" that we use for doing things like math and science. More likely, the ability to get along with others was the original intelligence that later also came to be used for math and science.

There are parts of our brains that may have evolved specifically to enable us to get along with others. Anyone who has raised a large family, led solders in combat, or been a resident advisor in a freshman dorm knows how much these challenges push us to develop more brain power. There is strong evidence that at least parts of the fusiform gyrus in our brains may have evolved primarily to recognize the faces of other people. Moreover, along with some of our more social skilled primates, we may also have "mirror neurons" that fire both when we act and when we see the same action performed by another person. In essence, part of our brain is doing the same thing that our friend's brain is doing when we are watching them doing jumping jacks and possibly even when we see that they are happy or sad.

The evolution of our brains as complex social creatures living in large communities with other complex creatures has resulted in two phenomena that may be foundational for social intelligence. The first is what enables us "to walk a mile in another person's shoes" and may more than anything else be at the heart of our ability to relate to other people: empathy. Whereas sympathy has been defined as feeling sorry for the suffering or distress of another, empathy may involve much more. While sympathy may rely on the fusiform gyrus to help us know when another person is sad or upset, empathy probably also involves the mirror neurons that enable us to begin to actually feel their pain. Empathy is the ability to project ourselves so much into the experience of another person that we can begin to really experience what they are experiencing.

Tania Singer and her colleagues did a study demonstrating how the brain may be involved in empathy.[8] Using functional magnetic resonance imaging (fMRI), they compared brain activity in women when they received a painful stimulus with when they saw their male partner receiving the same painful stimulus. When the women were experiencing pain, both the parts of the brain that give us sensory information about where the pain is and the parts of the brain involved in emotional unpleasantness of pain were active. Not surprising, when the woman saw that their partners were in pain, their sensory areas were not active. However, their emotional areas were active, suggesting that they experienced the same unpleasantness when watching their partners receive the painful stimulus as when they received it themselves.

The second phenomenon that may be foundational for relating to other people has been called "theory of mind." This somewhat strange and awkward term does not mean a theory of how the mind works thought up by psychologists. It refers to the predictions that each of us make in real-time about what another person is thinking and feeling and what they are going to say and do next. While empathy enables us to walk a mile in another person's shoes, our theory of mind aims to predict where they are going to walk next. It can be a tremendously complex and demanding task that relies on a good part of our large brains. Making good predictions about what someone is going to do next can be a life or death skill when we are in battle or even when deciding whether to approach a man on the street or how to drive through an intersection.

How Are Personal and Social Intelligence Related?

Personal intelligence and emotional intelligence include a variety of things that may enable us to get along well with others. While the term "personal intelligence" has been used little in the history of psychology, the accurate self-knowledge and understanding that it refers to has been a primary focus in psychotherapy and is informed by many subareas of psychology. The goal of many theories and psychotherapeutic techniques has been to facilitate a better understanding of our emotions, motivations, needs, and desires and to use this in better relating to other people. Subareas like developmental, personality, social, and abnormal psychology are certainly also useful in increasing our self-understanding.

So what are the ways that knowing and understanding ourselves may help us get along better with others? First, the capacity to understand and appreciate the depth and breadth of our own experience gives us a window into the lives and experiences of other people. Second, being aware of our own preferences, needs, values, and goals can enable us to choose those who are the best match for us on our journey. Third, learning how to love and care for our self may go a long way in teaching us how to better love others. There is a reason why every world religion has a version of the golden rule: knowing what we want done unto ourselves helps us know better how to treat others.

How Are Emotional and Social Intelligence Related?

What about emotional intelligence? How can it help us get along better with others? The use of the term "emotional intelligence" has been much more common in psychology than "personal intelligence," especially since the publication of Daniel Goleman's book *Emotional Intelligence* in 1995.[9] This book popularized the term and defined it as including the different domains of knowing your emotions, managing your own emotions, motivating yourself, recognizing and understanding other people's emotions, and managing relationships.

Later, Peter Salovey and John Mayer began a program of research focusing on emotional intelligence and developed a more concise and better integrated definition.[10] They defined it as the following four abilities:

1. *Perceiving emotions*—the ability to perceive and understand emotions in ourselves and other people.

2. *Using emotions*—the ability to use emotions to improve our thinking and solve problems.

3. *Understanding emotions*—the ability to understand emotional concepts, languages, and meanings.

4. *Managing emotions*—the ability to regulate emotions both in ourselves and other people.

Mayer and Salovey also developed a test called the Mayer-Salovey/Caruso Emotional Intelligence Test (MSCEIT) which assessed each of these four abilities.[11]

Although the definitions and measures of emotional intelligence have varied, the studies that have used them have generally found positive relationships with a range of beneficial outcomes. A review by Mayer found that emotional intelligence was generally related to better social relationships in both children and adults, being better liked by others, better academic achievement, better social dynamics at work, and better overall psychological well-being.[12] Another review by Nicole Schutte of the use of several measures of emotional intelligence found that, on average, it was positively related to mental health with a correlation of $r = .29$ and physical health with a correlation of $r = .22$.[13]

What are the reasons that emotional intelligence may help us in our relationships? Let's take Salovey and Mayer's four types of emotional intelligence. First, the ability to perceive our emotions in ourselves and others can provide important clues about what we need from another person and what they may need from us. Second, the ability to use our emotions in making decisions can provide us with added perspective in deciding how to relate to another person. Third, understanding a broader range of emotions and ways of expressing them may help us more fully and accurately understand and communicate what we need from another person. Fourth, being able to manage emotions such as strong feelings of anger or fear may help us better deal with the conflicts and problems that may arise in relationships.

What Can Enable Us to Relate Better to Others?

Although there has been some promising recent work to better define and measure aspects of emotional intelligence, much of the basic research and theory relevant for social intelligence has not been directly connected with specific ways to help people learn to relate better. However, there have been several separate interventions and programs that have helped people improve their relationships. Some of the most important include active constructive responding, anger management, assertiveness training, reflective listening, and a range of other useful social skills.

Active constructive responding was developed by Shelley Gable and has often been a part of interventions developed by those in the positive psychology movement.[14] Active constructive responding involves learning to better respond to another person who has good news to share and has been linked to improved relationships. Active constructive responding involves both being active in verbally and non-verbally affirming the good news and constructively giving positive feedback that enables the person to elaborate and more fully share and celebrate the good news with you.

Anger management has been a part of many cognitive behavioral therapies and directly addresses the emotion management part of emotional intelligence in the Salovey and Mayer framework. It may be particularly useful in preventing road rage and in relationships and professions where interactions can escalate into violence. It generally involves a three step process of identifying the triggers for becoming angry, learning relaxation techniques for when the triggers occur, and role-playing the situations when future triggers may occur.

Assertiveness training has also been a part of many cognitive behavioral therapies and is used to help people communicate more clearly and directly. The goal is to help people find a good balance between being aggressive and demanding and being passive and not standing up for themselves. Assertiveness training is thought to be an effective intervention especially for people who have trouble expressing anger. But it may also be generally helpful for most people in enabling them to communicate more directly in both their interpersonal and work relationships.

Reflective listening was originally part of the client-centered therapy developed by Carl Rogers, which increases empathy and the ability to understand the emotions of others. It involves first trying to understand what the speaker is saying and then offering it back in the listener's own words to see if their understanding is correct. It is different from active listening which involves trying to understand, respond, and remember what the speaker says but not actually checking with them to see if the understanding is accurate.

The term "social skill" has been used to refer to any skill that facilitates interaction and communication with others. These skills can include all of the above as well as leadership and mentorship training, conflict management and resolution, public speaking and writing, and the interpersonal skills needed for dating and maintaining a healthy couple's relationship. These skills are often targeted at people in various professions or with various mental health problems but may be more generally useful for most people in a variety of situations.

What Can We Do to Improve Social Intelligence?

These interventions provide a good foundation for what we can do to improve our ability to find and maintain good relationships. Here are some practical things that may be easy to try:

1. *Just listen mindfully.*

When you are alone with a good friend or family member, pay full attention to what they are saying and observe their facial expression, tone of voice, and body posture. When they pause, check with them to see how well you are listening and understanding them.

2. *Active constructively respond to good news.*

Read more about active constructive responding or google "active constructive responding" to find the instructional video. Practice active constructive responding in the next two weeks whenever someone tells you good news and notice how they respond.

3. *Catch them being good.*

Whenever one of your friends or family members does something that you like, admire, or appreciate; tell them just what you like and why you like it. Be specific about what you like and why, and see how it affects how you both feel.

4. *Practice pausing when angry.*

Think about what triggers your anger and imagine yourself pausing and either taking three deep breaths or thinking about something really funny. Then, when you notice yourself becoming angry, try each a few times and see what works the best for you.

5. *Increase your emotional vocabulary.*

Google a list of emotion words with many options for common emotions such as happiness, anger, fear, and sadness. Carry the list in your wallet. Set your phone to randomly go off three times a day for a week and when it goes off find the word that best matches your current emotion.

6. *Watch TV without sound.*

Watch a dramatic television show or movie with the sound turned off. Pay attention to the facial expressions, postures, and movements of the characters and try to figure out what they are feeling and thinking. Finally, try to predict what they will do next.

10.2. Love

On the one hand, love is probably the most common and popular theme in books, movies, and music, the thing that brings us more happiness and pain than anything else, and the one thing that many of us would be willing to give our lives for. On the other hand, love remains a mystery to us, psychology and science have long stayed away from it, and many have thought we would be much better off focusing on other things.

When the psychologist Ellen Berscheid got one of the first government grants to study love in 1975, Senator William Proxmire gave her a *Golden Fleece* award for wasteful government spending. Berscheid wanted to understand why people fall in love and Proxmire responded: "I believe that 200 million other Americans want to leave some things in life a mystery, and right on top of the things we don't want to know is why a man falls in love with a woman and vice versa" (p. 306).[16] Berscheid was not phased and along with other psychologists began to study love and learn about what for many of us may be the most important thing in our lives.

So it is with a bit of fear and trembling that I begin to talk about something that can be as powerful, painful, hard to define, hard to understand, and hard to find as love. But it is also with a great sense of anticipation and hope that I address something that may play such a central role in our journey. There are few things that have been both more a source of a mystery and pain and also of joy, fulfillment, and a life worth living.

What Is Love?

It sounds strange even to ask the question. What is love? That has been the subject of endless philosophical debate—and probably also marital arguments and counseling sessions. In trying to start with the usual suspects in defining it, I found that *Dictionary.com* has no less than seven different definitions, including (1) "a profoundly tender, passionate affection for another person," (2) "a feeling of warm personal attachment or deep affection, as for a parent, child, or friend," (3) "sexual passion or desire," and (4) "sexual intercourse or copulation."[16] Part of the problem in understanding and studying love is that we define it in so many different ways.

Ellen Berscheid, who received that early government grant, went on to focus on two primary types of love that we can see reflected in the above definitions.[17] She defined passionate love as a state of intense emotional attachment to another person that is highly pleasurable but can also be obsessive and difficult to maintain and sustain. In contrast, she defined companionate love as the affection and friendship experienced between two people when their lives are deeply intertwined. While the metaphor for passionate love may be fire, the metaphor for companionate love is vines gradually growing together and forming an ever stronger bond.

Cindy Hazan says that "love represents a cognitive, behavioral, and emotional stance toward others that takes three prototypical forms. One is love for the individuals who are our primary sources of affection, protection, and care... Another form is love for the individuals who depend on us to make them feel safe and cared for... The third form is love that involves passionate desire for sexual, physical, and emotional closeness with an individual whom we consider special and who makes us feel special" (p. 304).[18] These are analogous to the love of a child for a parent, the love of a parent for a child, and the love shared by an adult couple.

John Lee took it even further in reviewing references to love throughout history and across cultures.[19] He used Greek words to distinguish the six different types of love that he identified. Eros is the passionate love where the lover idealizes the partner. Ludus is love played as a game for mutual enjoyment but without the intensity of eros and with little commitment. Storge is the emotionally intimate kind of love and affection that is shared between friends. Pragma is practical or convenient love often based on rational and realistic choices about sharing similar interests and goals. Mania is the possessive and obsessive kind of love often felt as an intense need for the other. Agape is the purest form of love based on a strong and unconditional commitment to give oneself for the well-being of someone else.

In summary, while there are many types of love, they all involve a mutually beneficial close relationship. In addition, there are two dimensions that stand out among the various classifications of love. The first is the common distinction made between friendship or companionate love and passionate or sexual love. The second is whether the love is between two people who are relatively equal in maturity and experience or whether it is between a parent and child or a teacher and student, for example.

How Is Attachment Theory Related to Love?

The theory that has probably done the most to unify and integrate the thinking about these different kinds of love is attachment theory. Attachment theory was developed by John Bowlby who discovered that orphans who had their basic needs met did poorly if they didn't also develop enduring emotional bonds with parental figures.[20] Attachment theory is the idea that the early attachment of a child with at least one parent is critically important for their development and may have strong implications for the quality of their relationships for the rest of their lives.

Mary Ainsworth developed a creative way to study the relationship between children and their mothers to identify whether they had a healthy attachment relationship.[21] Ainsworth used what she called the "Strange Situation" which was a research protocol where a child is separated from their mother, a stranger enters the room, and the parent returns. Ainsworth saw that children tended to react three different ways to the parent when they returned. Secure attachment was how she described the children who, although they were upset when the parent left, were happy to see her when she returned. Avoidant attachment was how she described those who avoided or ignored their mother and showed little emotion when she left or returned. Anxious-ambivalent attachment was term for the children who showed distress even before separation and were clingy and difficult to comfort when their mother returned.

Ainsworth also used the Strange Situation to understand what a parent does that causes their children to be insecurely attached. She saw that securely attached children not only trust their parents to return but also trust that they would respond to them in a sensitive and consistent way. The insecurely attached children had parents who were not very good at reading the signals of distress in their children and were not consistent in how they responded to their distress. Years later, in 1995, Dymphna van den Boom did a study where she trained parents to respond more sensitively to infants who were irritable.[22] Months later she tested them using the Strange Situation and found that the ones with parents who had the sensitivity training were three times more likely to be securely attached compared with infants whose parents did not have the training.

Ainsworth thus provided a way to study and classify attachment styles in infants. Before long, social psychologists studying adult romantic relationships began to wonder if these patterns of attachment were similar in adults. During the mid-1980s, Cindy Hazan and Phil Shaver ran a newspaper ad asking how many could identify with statements expressing the three attachment styles that Ainsworth had identified with infants using the Strange Situation.[23] They found that out of 579 responses, 59% could be classified as securely attached, 25% avoidant attached, and 19% anxious/ambivalent attached. In addition, they found that the securely attached reported higher levels of friendship, trust, and happiness and lower levels of jealousy, emotional extremes, and fear of closeness than the avoidant and anxious-ambivalent groups that represented insecure attachment.

Later, Kim Bartholomew took it a step farther in developing a four category model of adult attachment that is related to whether a person generally has positive or negative thoughts of themselves and their partner.[24] The four categories are the same as those of Ainsworth and of Hazan and Shaver except that avoidant attachment is split into two categories:

1. *Secure attachment* involves being comfortable with intimacy and autonomy, with positive thoughts of the self and positive thoughts of the partner.

2. *Preoccupied attachment* is similar to anxious-ambivalent attachment which involves a preoccupation with relationships, with negative thoughts of the self and positive thoughts of the partner.

3. *Dismissive attachment* is an avoidant attachment style that involves dismissing intimacy and strong independence, with positive thoughts of the self and negative thoughts of the partner.

4. *Fearful attachment* is an avoidant attachment style that involves fear of intimacy and social avoidance, with negative thoughts of the self and negative thoughts of the partner.

Overall, there are several aspects of attachment theory that may help us understand the nature of love relationships. First, we may have evolved a biological urge for attachment that continues to affect us across our lives and influence all of our love relationships. Second, the same urge for attachment that causes an intense and emotional connection between children and parents may also explain some of the passion and obsessiveness of adult romantic relationships. Third, a major cause of poor relationships and the unhappiness they often cause may be the expectation that others will be as insensitive and inconsistent as early caregivers. Research suggests that people develop working models of attachment that can become a "self-fulfilling prophecy" for continuing the same insecure patterns of relationships in adulthood. Fortunately, there is much we can do to alter these patterns in adulthood.

What Is Most Important for Love Relationships?

Before we begin to talk more about how we may be able to improve our love relationships, I want to present what is one of the best developed theories about what is important for a healthy and rewarding adult love relationship. Ellen Berscheid has already given us a clue in focusing on both passionate love as the erotic sexual love that is like a fire, and companionate love that is characterized by friendship and affection and is like two vines growing together.[25] Robert Sternberg has developed what he calls the "Triangular Theory of Love," which adds one other component that is often neglected in Western culture but which may be a critical ingredient for building a relationship that can stand the test of time.[26]

The three primary components of love for Sternberg are passion, intimacy, and commitment. Passion is equivalent to Berscheid's passionate love and John Lee's eros love style. Intimacy is similar to Berscheid's companionate love and Lee's storge love style. Commitment is the additional component and bears some resemblance to Lee's pragma and agape. Sternberg's name for relationships with both passion and intimacy is romantic love and his name for the kind of love that involves passion, intimacy, and commitment is consummate or complete love. While consummate love may be hard to create and maintain, he thinks a key to doing it is to continually translate it into behavior and action. We will examine some things that we may be able to do to intentionally translate commitment into action that may help sustain all three components.

How Can We Improve Our Love Relationships?

In the first section of this chapter, regarding social intelligence, I told you about several things that may be beneficial in all relationships—including adult couples. Active constructive responding can be a great way to use good news to bring a couple closer together. Assertiveness training helps to keep two people on a level playing field by finding the right balance between communicating in a passive and an aggressive way. Anger management can be critical in slowing our reactions enough to avoid saying those things that we can't take back.

Reflective listening may actually be hardest to do but also most rewarding with those we are closest to.

We have also learned something about what we can do to foster a more secure attachment. We may come to feel more secure in a relationship where distress is responded to in a sensitive and consistent manner. Kirsten Cronlund has written about how to use mindfulness in loving another person which may foster this sensitivity and consistency.[27] She suggests that attending mindfully to everything that happens with the other person may be the best path to a satisfying relationship. We will naturally find some things that a partner does annoying and irritating. The key in using mindfulness is to simply observe what is happening without judging it and buying the precious time that may allow us to better accept them for who they are.

Some of the most rigorous and fruitful research with couples has been done by John Gottman. He has identified many things that couples can do to increase the likelihood that they will be satisfied in their relationship and stay together. He developed an intervention where these things are taught to couples and found that it greatly reduces the chances of getting divorced. The following are the principles presented in his book *The Seven Principles for Making Marriage Work*.[28] Most are relevant for any love relationship.

1. *Enhance your love maps*—by becoming intimately familiar with your partner's world including their worries, hopes, and goals in life.

2. *Nurture fondness and admiration*—by meditating on what you love, appreciate, and cherish in your partner.

3. *Turn toward each other*—be there for them through big and small events and respond well when they ask for attention, affection, and support.

216

4. *Accept influence*—share power with them by deciding things together and taking their feelings into account.

5. *Solve solvable problems*—learn to resolve problems and conflicts in ways involving tolerance and compromise and prevent the escalation of negative feelings.

6. *Overcome gridlock*—when you are stuck in solving a conflict, be patient in finding and exploring the issues that may be causing the gridlock.

7. *Create shared meaning*—create a shared inner life that involves rituals and symbols about what it means to be a part of the relationship.

The final point I want to make is about using wisdom and commitment to find a balance between passionate and companionate love in the course of adult romantic relationships. Jonathan Haidt writes about how passionate love typically reaches the maximal intensity in the first few months of a romantic relationship and may be destined to fall back down nearly as fast but not quite as much as it rose after six months or so of a new relationship.[29] In contrast, he argues that companionate love has the potential to continue to grow steadily for as long as two people remain together.

Haidt thinks that there are two danger points in the course of most adult romantic relationships. The first is when passionate love is at its peak before it has had the chance to drop back down to where we have enough time to pay our bills and reestablish our relationships with our friends. The danger here is to think that the intensity of the passion you are experiencing must mean that you are meant to be together forever and then to quickly do things like getting pregnant, engaged, or married. The most important thing to do here may simply be to expect and wait for a natural drop in passion and then pay attention to what you have in common and focus on the development of companionate love.

The second danger point occurs right after the passionate intensity comes down to a level where you may still have time to keep your job and your friends. The danger here is to assume that the reason the raging fire has been reduced to a gentle flame is that this person cannot be "the one" and that you may as well just break up now and try to light a match with someone else. The most important thing here is to realize that this may just be the naturally waning of a raging fire that just couldn't last at the initial intensity. The best goal here may be to pay attention to what you have in common, focus on developing companionate love, and find creative ways to rekindle the passion in the light of a budding friendship that may continue to grow.

What Can We Do to Practice Love?

While the seven principles by John Gottman may provide a place to start for many, here are a few simple things to try.

1. *Share your top strengths.*

Have each person take the *VIA Survey* and get together to talk about the results. When you get together, share your top five strengths and talk about how you have seen them in each other. Talk about how you can support each other in spotting the other's strengths and using them to build your relationship.

2. *Share a rose and a thorn every day.*

Set aside a time at the end of every day or every time you get together. During this time talk about one bad thing that happened and one good thing that happened for each of you since you last talked. Repeat this at the end of every day or every time you get together for two weeks and talk about how it has affected your relationship.

3. *Give them the gift of time.*

Give the gift of time to a person that you love. Tell them that you just want to be with them and ask them what they would like to do. When you get together, do your best to make them happy and savor the things that you like about them.

4. *Find new ways to express love without words.*

Find new ways to express your love through non-verbal expressions, physical gestures, or affectionate touch. First brainstorm a list of at least 10 things that you could try. Then try at least five of them in the next two weeks and see what happens.

5. *Practice mindful acceptance when you are annoyed.*

When you begin to feel annoyed or irritated with something about them, practice mindful breathing and try to pay attention to them without judgment. Observe your irritation as it comes and goes without acting or saying anything. See if you can notice anything new about them or about your own feelings as they come and go.

6. *Directly express your unconditional love.*

Make a list of all of the things that you appreciate about them and how you would miss them if they were no longer here. Then think about the best way that you can clearly and directly tell them that you will continue to love them no matter what happens. Be sure to look into their eyes and observe their response when you tell them.

10.3. Kindness

Before the *Hunger Games* books and movies became a popular example of a world gone wrong, Aldous Huxley wrote the classic dystopian novel *Brave New World* which came to serve as a symbol of superficial happiness. He also wrote a book called *The Perennial Philosophy* where he identified the greatest common teachings of the world's spiritual and wisdom traditions. So

Huxley seemed to know a lot about the things that can enable human beings to be both at their worst and at their best. So much so that others couldn't avoid asking him one particular question: "People often ask me what is the most effective technique for transforming their life. It is a little embarrassing that after years and years of research and experimentation, I have to say that the best answer is—just be a little kinder."[30]

What Are Kindness, Compassion, and Altruism?

The *Character Strengths and Virtues* handbook says, "Kindness, generosity, nurturance, care, compassion, and altruistic love are a network of closely related terms indicating a common orientation of the self toward the other… Kindness and altruistic love require the assertion of a common humanity in which others are worthy of attention and affirmation for no utilitarian reasons but for their own sake" (p. 326).[31] I will use the words kindness, compassion, and altruism because they have been the main focuses for research and theory in psychology. Altruism is an unselfish concern for or devotion to the well-being of other people, compassion is having empathy or feeling for the suffering of others, and kindness is being friendly, generous, and considerate.

Together they encompass a self-giving willingness and ability to behave in ways that benefit other people. The affirmation of this willingness and ability can be seen in world religious traditions in the use of the word "agape" in Christianity which means divine self-giving love, "hesed" in Judaism which means steadfast love, and the word "karuna" in Buddhism which means compassionate action. The value of kindness and compassion has even been affirmed in modern psychotherapy. Carl Rogers thought that effective psychotherapy may depend on whether the therapist has "unconditional positive regard" for the client.[32] William Miller is the founder of motivational interviewing, which is an empathetic way of talking with another person that has been shown to help them reduce alcohol and substance abuse. He has written about how "agape love" may be a critical element in human change and transformation.[33]

What Does the Research Say About Kindness?

If all you did was watch the news, you might wonder whether human beings are capable of much kindness. The way that we have evolved to watch out for threats may make it difficult for us to recognize some of the kindness around us. Dacher Keltner is the founder and faculty director of the *Greater Good Science Center* in Berkeley, California that focuses on altruism, compassion, kindness, forgiveness, and gratitude. He has written about research suggesting that we may have evolved with an instinct for kindness and compassion that we can do much to cultivate.[34] He highlights research showing how the reward centers of our brains react the same way to helping others as when we experience pleasure and that we have a signature physiological response in our bodies when we feel or express compassion.

There have been many interesting studies that have tried to examine the human capacity for giving and what may affect it. There was the classic study that John Darley and Bibb Latané did to try to understand why bystanders didn't help a woman who was being murdered.[35] They found that having more bystanders made it less likely for anyone to respond, illustrating what they called the "diffusion of responsibility." Then there was the clever study where students training to be ministers were asked to give a talk about the Biblical story of the Good Samaritan.[36] This is a story about religious leaders who pass by a man in distress without helping. However, the students didn't realize that on the way to giving the talk, they would encounter a man slumped in an alley in distress. Overall, only 53% stopped to help the man and whether they helped was highly dependent on how much of a hurry they were in.

Other research has examined the question of what motivates people to help others. The empathy-altruism hypothesis states that if someone else is feeling empathy towards another person they will be more likely to help them regardless of what they may gain from them. Daniel Batson and his colleagues did an experiment where they had undergraduate students watch another student receiving a shock and then gave them the chance to help by taking the shock themselves.[37] Batson found that the students were more motivated to help out of unselfish reasons if they were experiencing more empathy. Netta Weinstein and Richard Ryan did several studies to compare the effects of giving motivated by the free desire to give versus being forced to give. They found that both the giver and their recipients were better off when the giver was free to give.[38]

Why Do People Do Kind Things?

There are at least four personal characteristics that make it more likely that a person will be more altruistic, compassionate, and kind. First, they tend to be higher on the Big Five personality characteristic of agreeableness. Agreeableness is itself defined as being kind, sympathetic, cooperative, warm, and considerate. Second, they have higher than average levels of empathy and sympathy for the suffering of other people. Third, they use higher level moral reasoning that involves focusing on the needs of other people rather than only thinking about the consequences of helping for themselves. Fourth, they are more likely to have a sense of social responsibility that involves caring for all kinds of people whether they know them or have things in common with them or not.

There are also several different possible motivations people have for helping others. These include being aware of direct tangible benefits to ourselves, such as impressing other people, making friends who will give back to us, or getting a tax deduction for a charitable contribution. These may also include things that may be less tangible and more internal such as being true to our values, feeling like we can make a difference in the world, or just wanting to feel like a good person. The motivations for helping others may also be less about what we can get out of it and more about the needs of other people. These include being motivated to do something by seeing the distress or suffering of another person, or just wanting to do something for someone even if you don't see their distress or know them, such as sponsoring a poor child in another country.

Finally, in addition to how much empathy we may be feeling, there are several other things that may make it more likely for us to help another person. There is strong and consistent evidence that people who are in a positive mood are more likely to help other people. This may be because they are not focused on a negative problem that they have to solve or that they have more energy and time to spare in doing something for someone else. One specific emotion that may be particularly conducive to helping others is elevation. If you remember, Jonathan Haidt gave the name elevation to the emotion we experience when we see or learn about a beautiful act of kindness or giving. The combination of elevation and empathy may make it particularly likely that a person will act in a kind or compassionate way.

What Are the Benefits of Kindness and Compassion?

Stephen Post has written a book called *Why Good Things Happen to Good People* where he talks about all the ways that kindness and helping behavior may be beneficial for our health.[39] He discusses the growing body of research showing that helping others is related to better mental and physical health as well as living a longer life. For example, Doug Oman found that elderly people who volunteered for two or more organizations were 44% less likely to die within five years even when controlling for age and health behaviors such as exercise and smoking.[40] Rachel Piferi and Kathleen Lawler found that people who gave support to others had lower blood pressure than those who did not give support to other people.[41] Maria Pagano and her colleagues found that alcoholics who helped others during their treatment were more likely to remain sober.[42]

There are many reasons why altruistic behavior may improve our health and longevity. First, it may expand our social network and increase the social support available when we need it. Second, it may distract us from our own problems and help reduce the self-focused attention that may be a risk factor for anxiety and depression. Third, it may increase our sense of meaning in life which may give us more of an incentive to take care of ourselves and live longer. Fourth, it may increase our sense of self-efficacy and confidence that we can make a difference in the world. Fifth, it may increase positive emotions which may reduce our stress response and increase our resilience. Finally, it may lead to a more active lifestyle if we are doing something that requires more physical activity.

Researchers in the positive psychology movement have identified several interventions that may increase thoughts and feelings of kindness and compassion and also have an effect on our happiness and well-being. Barbara Fredrickson found that using meditation to increase feelings of lovingkindness increased positive emotions, social support, and reduced illness symptoms.[43] Kathryn Buchanan and Anat Bardi found that increasing acts of kindness over a 10-day period increased life satisfaction and Keiko Otake and colleagues found that just counting acts of kindness for a week increased happiness.[44-45] Sonja Lyubomirsky thinks that doing more acts of kindness may be one of the simplest and most effective ways to beat the hedonic treadmill and raising our happiness to a new level.[46]

What Are the Dangers of Kindness and Compassion?

There are at least two primary dangers in misdirected kindness or helping behavior. The first is that it may not be what the other person needs. The idea of "tough love" is that sometimes love may involve doing something that the other person may not like but may ultimately be the best for them. In deciding when and how to express compassion and kindness, it is important to use wisdom in determining whether you are doing something that will ultimately result in more happiness and well-being for the other person. At the time, it may not feel kind to tell someone that you think they have a problem with alcohol or that you do not think they should stay with the person who is abusing them, but it may ultimately be the kindest, most courageous, and best thing you can do for them.

The second danger is that trying to help others may, in some cases, be harmful to yourself. While self-giving and sacrifice may be necessary in some situations, taken to an extreme they can result in a level of burnout and compassion-fatigue that may make it very difficult to continue to give. Kristin Neff has developed the idea of self-compassion which can be a great antidote to compassion fatigue and a way to balance giving to others with taking care of ourselves.[47] Neff has developed a website where you can assess your own level of self-compassion and she also provides practical ways to learn self-compassion in taking care of yourself. Other ways to combat compassion fatigue include practicing mindfulness, being aware of your limits, learning when to say no, getting the support you need from others, and being sure to take time to rest and rejuvenate.

How Can Kindness and Compassion Be Fostered?

There are at least six different kinds of things that may be helpful. The first is finding ways to increase empathy. Generally, the way to begin is with having empathy and compassion for your own pain and suffering and then extending it to a larger and larger circle of people. Rather than focus on the ways that people are different, focus on the common human experiences of wanting to be happy and well and what it feels like to suffer the pain and loss that makes this difficult.

Second, focus on the potential positive effects of helping other people. In an interview that the Dalai Lama had with the emotion researcher Paul Ekman, he spoke of a way to do this when he said, "First you deeply reflect upon the downside of narrow-minded self-centeredness. Then you reflect upon the positive consequences and the potential of more other-centered perspectives. On the basis of these reflections, you cultivate compassion" (p. 278).[48]

Third, find good models and mentors. As we have learned, seeing someone else do what we want to be able to do is a great way to build self-efficacy and find new ways to help and give to other people. Also, finding and reading about others who can show you good examples of kindness and compassion may give you the feeling of elevation which you can draw on for inspiration and motivation in helping others.

Fourth, "Just do it," as the *Nike* commercial used to say. As several studies have shown, just performing more kind acts for other people is self-reinforcing and rewarding because it increases your happiness and well-being and your motivation for continuing to be kind. Doing acts of kindness can be a powerful catalyst for beginning an upward spiral to a higher level of well-being and to more satisfying and rewarding relationships.

Fifth, practicing lovingkindness meditation may foster both kind intentions and behavior and also be one of the best ways to increase positive emotions. Usually lovingkindness meditation involves a progression of trying to increase feelings of lovingkindness with different kinds of people. It may start with you or someone easier to feel love for and progress to more neutral people and eventually to those you find hardest to love.

Sixth, write about and meditate on the best acts of lovingkindness that you have experienced with other people. These can help you learn to be more loving and compassionate with yourself, produce feelings of elevation that can motivate you to be kind to others, and serve as examples for how you can practice love and kindness with others. It may help to think of being kind to others as a way of honoring the kindness you have received from them and "paying it forward."

These six methods lend themselves to an integrated and logical progression of ways to become a kinder and more compassionate person. You could think about this progression as moving from thoughts to feelings to behaviors. The initial step is to think of ways that people have been kind to you along with moving examples that you can remember and use to reflect on and guide you. The next step is to reflect and meditate on these examples to increase your feelings of empathy, elevation, and motivation to perform acts of kindness and compassion. The final step is to perform new acts of kindness and focus on how it makes both the other person and you feel during and after each act. The positive feelings and relationships that this builds can start a feedback loop providing more motivation to begin the cycle again.

How Can We Practice Kindness and Compassion?

The 2001 movie *Amelie* shows what can happen when you undertake the seemingly simple experiment of doing something kind for another person. Try to watch it if you haven't already. Or, better yet, try these exercises for yourself:

1. *Keep a kindness journal.*

For the next two weeks, write down the kind things that you do for other people. Review the list at the end of each week and reflect on how it affected you and the other person.

2. *Do your favorite kind acts.*

Google one of the many lists of kind things on the Internet and choose your ten most favorite. Try to do at least two a week for the next two weeks.

3. *Kindness for friends and strangers.*

For one week, alternate days of doing something kind for someone you know and for someone you don't know. See how they both affect you and how they feel similar or different.

4. *Kindness and candy.*

For one week, on alternate days treat yourself to your favorite candy or do something kind for someone else. Think about how you felt at the time and at the end of the week.

5. *Kindness for yourself.*

Write down at least 10 kind things you can do for yourself and choose three to do over the next week. Think about how each felt and what you enjoyed the most.

6. *Write about loving and kind acts.*

Write down three to five of the most loving and kind acts you remember someone doing for you. Choose your favorite and give yourself at least 20 minutes to write freely about it.

7. *Be a compassionate warrior.*

Wonder Woman is great example of a heroic character who combines courage and compassion. Do something for someone else that is compassionate and also involves courage.

Using the Strengths of Humanity for the Journey

If wisdom shows us the way and courage enables us to sustain our journey, the strengths of humanity help us to build the relationships that can be the source of our wisdom and courage. It is our parents, teachers, mentors, and friends who often show us the way and teach us wisdom in the first place. It is that one person who believes in us and loves us no matter what who gives us the encouragement we need and makes it all worthwhile.

In this chapter, we began by learning about social intelligence as the ability to form and maintain beneficial and rewarding relationships, we proceeded by covering that mysterious, powerful, and multi-faceted thing we call love, and we ended with kindness—which may have so much power to transform ourselves and our world. All three enable us to form the human connections that may be essential for our happiness.

Social intelligence will help us recognize and develop a relationship with the Rons and Hermiones we may meet and also recognize and deal with the Malfoys. It can help us to find and cultivate our friendships, to be wise and strong in dealing with our enemies, and perhaps even as Lincoln suggested, to "destroy our enemies by turning them into friends."[49]

The kind of love we talked about can enable us to sustain, deepen, and enrich the relationships that are most important to us. These are the people we most want to give ourselves for and who may bring some of the greatest joy and meaning that we will know in our lives. They are our fellow travelers but also, in some ways, may be a destination itself.

And kindness, as Aldous Huxley said when asked, "What is the most effective way to change the world?... I have to say that the best answer is—just be a little kinder."[50] As has been attributed to Mother Teresa, "If you are kind, people may accuse you of selfish ulterior motives, be kind anyway."[51] As the Dalai Lama said, "My religion is very simple. My religion is kindness."[52] And who could forget the quote at the beginning of the chapter, "Be kind, for everyone you meet is fighting a hard battle."[53]

We may all be fighting a hard battle, but we are also all on the same great journey—and it may be one of the greatest gifts in life to know that we are not alone.

Chapter 11

The Justice to Do the Right Thing

We must be the change we wish to see in the world.

—Mahatma Gandhi[1]

Martin was born in Germany in 1892. He became a Lutheran minister and supported Hitler's rise to power—at least at first. But he changed his mind as he saw what Hitler wanted to do to the church. He joined a group of ministers who opposed Hitler and in 1937 was arrested and confined to the Sachsenhausen and Dachau concentration camps until he was released in 1945 when the war was over. During the 1950s, he wrote the following poem:

> First they came for the Socialists,
> and I did not speak out—
> because I was not a Socialist.
>
> Then they came for the Trade Unionists
> and I did not speak out—
> because I was not a Trade Unionist.
>
> Then they came for the Jews,
> and I did not speak out—
> because I was not a Jew.
>
> Then they came for me—
> and there was no one left to speak for me.[2]

His full name was Martin Niemöller and he wrote several versions of this text during his life. But each of them started with the smallest or most distant group and moved to the largest group and then finally to himself.

The virtue of Justice and the three strengths associated with it are what enable us to move beyond ourselves to that most distant group and see that our happiness might intimately be tied to theirs. In the last chapter, we learned about the mirror neurons that support empathy and the innate human capacity for compassion. The neuroscientist Vilayanur Ramachandran has studied mirror neurons and called them "Gandhi neurons" because they enable us to actually experience what other people are experiencing.[3]

With the extreme emphasis on the individual in Western culture, it is easy to forget our common humanity and think that all we need to be happy is to look out for ourselves. Psychology has often fallen into that trap as it focuses on individual behavior but the worst offenders may be self-help books that only focus on pleasing yourself. Because we can feel for others and know that we could feel the same way and experience the same thing, our happiness is tied to theirs. As we have seen, the things that may ultimately bring us the greatest satisfaction, gratification, and reward may be living a life of meaning that involves doing something to make the world a better place for us all.

Fortunately, the creators of the VIA classification helped broaden the focus of psychology to include what may truly be some of what is noblest and best about us. The strengths of fairness, citizenship, and leadership may be easily neglected in psychology but have been vital for creating a civilization where we can enjoy as much happiness and well-being as many of us have. Fairness is what guides us in making our most difficult moral choices, citizenship is what makes it possible for us to work together in building a better society, and leadership is necessary to organize and guide us and make it happen.

11.1. Fairness

If you haven't already seen it, you may want to view the TED Talk video of an experiment done by Sarah Brosnan and Frans de Waal with capuchin monkeys.[4] There are two monkeys in cages side-by-side and the monkeys can see each other. The experimenter trained the two monkeys to do a simple task that involved giving them a rock to get a reward. The first time the monkeys do the task they both get a piece of cucumber for their reward. First one does the task and gets the cucumber and then the second one does the task and gets the cucumber.

For the next round, the experimenter is going to reward the first monkey with a grape and the second monkey with a piece of cucumber. Monkeys like grapes a lot more than cucumbers. The first monkey does the task and then the second monkey sees the first monkey get the grape. Next, the second monkey does the task and is once again handed a piece of cucumber. As soon the second monkey gets the cucumber this time, it immediately throws it back at the experimenter and violently shakes the cage.

In the TED video, the experimenter makes a joke about how this looks like a recent human protest about economic inequity.[5] He also pointed out that the same experiment has also been done with dogs, birds, and chimpanzees. But the point is clear, capuchin monkeys—like human beings—have evolved with a sense of fairness and react very strongly when it is violated. In this section, I will talk about how we determine what is fair and right and what we can do to get better at it so we will have a more just and ultimately happy world.

What Is Fairness?

The Oxford online dictionary says that fairness is "impartial and just treatment without favoritism or discrimination" and that justice is "just behavior or treatment" or "the quality of being fair and reasonable."[6-7] The *Character Strengths and Virtues* handbook defined fairness as "treating all people the same according to the notions of fairness and justice; not letting personal feelings bias decisions about others; giving everyone a fair chance" (p. 30).[8] It also says that fairness is "the product of moral judgment—the process by which people determine what is morally right, what is morally wrong, and what is morally proscribed" (p. 392).[9]

Just as with the monkeys in the experiment, it may not be hard to think of times when we felt like other people were not being fair to us. We were unfairly graded on a paper or test or pulled over for forgetting to use our turn signal. We don't get the same opportunity or pay as someone else. We were discriminated against because of our gender, race, religion, or sexual orientation. We were diagnosed with a terminal illness at a young age or hit by a drunk driver or blindsided by a breakup or the betrayal of a friend. If we had a cage to shake or a cucumber to throw at whoever was responsible—we probably would.

But while we are often faced with how to respond to an injustice done to us, we are also sometimes faced with difficult choices that may result in someone else feeling just as unfairly treated. The process of determining what is right and wrong was fairly easy in the experiment with the monkeys, but, of course, can be much harder in real life situations. Psychologists and neuroscientists have tried to study this by examining how we respond to the common and challenging moral dilemmas that we may face. This is similar to the way that Paul Baltes used challenging questions to ask research participants to come up with a wise response.

Here are some questions that may be challenging and begin to shed light on how we may make decisions about what is fair and right:

1. Is it okay to go through a red light in the middle of the night?

2. Is it right to cheat on your taxes if your rate is too high?

3. Is it okay to buy from a company that breaks child labor laws?

4. Is it right to lie if it will enable you to help people?

5. Is it okay to keep money you find in a billionaire's wallet?

It turns out that there are at least two primary processes involved in making these kinds of decisions that have been represented in what have been called the Justice and the Care traditions of moral reasoning. The Justice tradition focuses on the use of logic and moral principles to make these decisions and was founded by Lawrence Kohlberg.[10] The Care tradition focuses on the use of emotion and human relationships to make these decisions and was founded by Carol Gilligan,[11] who was a graduate student of Kohlberg's.

What Is the Justice Tradition of Moral Reasoning?

The foundation of the Justice tradition is Kohlberg's six stages of moral development. Kohlberg's theory gave a primary place to human reasoning and was built on Jean Piaget's theory of cognitive development. Piaget thought that people must pass through a series of stages including moving from simple concrete ways of thinking to more complex abstract thought.[12] Kohlberg assumed that the way people make moral and ethical decisions is based on their stage of cognitive development.

In addition, Kohlberg's idea of justice was based on the philosophy of Immanuel Kant and his idea that there may be universal ethical principles that apply across all situations. His theory of stages is well suited for positive psychology in that the highest stages have been embodied by moral exemplars such as Gandhi, Martin Luther King, Jr., and the Dalai Lama. Thus, his stages run the range between the most self-centered and self-serving ways of making decisions on the left side of the proverbial "bell curve," through the middle stages where more of us operate most of the time, to the right side of the curve representing the best of what is possible and what may be most beneficial for society and humanity as a whole.

I will go through each of the six of Kohlberg's stages of moral development and relate them to probably the most famous example of a moral dilemma that he used. It has been called the Heinz dilemma and is as follows:

> A woman was near death. There was one drug that the doctors thought might save her. It was a form of radium that a druggist in the same town had recently discovered. The drug was expensive to make, but the druggist was charging ten times what the drug cost him to produce. He paid $200 for the radium and charged $2,000 for a small dose of the drug.

> The sick woman's husband, Heinz, went to everyone he knew to borrow the money, but he could only get together about $1,000 which is half of what it cost. He told the druggist that his wife was dying and asked him to sell it cheaper or let him pay later. But the druggist said: "No, I discovered the drug and I'm going to make money from it." So Heinz got desperate and broke into the man's laboratory to steal the drug for his wife.[13]

> Should Heinz have broken into the laboratory to steal the drug for his wife? Why or why not?

Kohlberg asked people to respond to these kinds of dilemmas and had a well-developed system for classifying their responses into one of the six stages.[14] The important thing was not the final decision, in this case whether or not Heinz should have stolen the medicine, but what reasons the people gave for their final decision. In addition to having six stages, Kohlberg also divided moral development into three levels which each consisted of two of the stages.

1. *The Preconventional Level*

The first level was called the pre-conventional level which is most common in children but can also occur in adolescents and adults. This is where a person judges whether something is right or wrong by the direct consequences of the action or by what may be of greatest benefit to the individual.

Stage 1: *Obedience and punishment driven*—this is where you think something is wrong because you *will* get punished. The assumption is that if someone is punished, then they must be bad. An example is that Heinz should not steal the medicine because he *will* get punished and that would mean he is a bad person.

Stage 2: *Self-interest driven*—this is where something is wrong because someone *might* get punished or because you *might* get punished. This is a "what's in it for me" approach to making a moral decision. An example might be that Heinz should steal the medicine because he will be happier if he saves his wife even if he has to go to prison.

2. *The Conventional Level*

The second level is called the conventional level and is common for both adolescents and adults. This is where what is right and wrong is judged by comparing it to the expectations of other people and the norms of society. Whereas the pre-conventional level and stages one and two primarily involve considering what is best for the individual, the conventional level involves obeying rules and principles even when there are no direct benefits or consequences for doing so.

Stage 3: *Good intentions as determined by social consensus*—this is where what is right and wrong is determined by whether it will help or harm an important relationship. It involves trying to conform to what other people expect and want. Heinz might decide to steal the medicine because that is what his wife wants and he wants to do right by her.

Stage 4: *Authority and social order obedience driven*—this is where what is right serves the larger social system and the rules and laws that society is based on. The individual no longer needs the approval of others but obeys the laws because they are necessary to maintain a civil and functioning society. Heinz might decide not to steal the medicine because it is against the law or if he does he might be sure to take the punishment given by law.

3. *The Postconventional Level*

The third level is called the post-conventional level, also called the "principled level" and involves the idea that the perspective of the individual can take precedence over the views of others and society. The driving forces of this level are having internal principles of justice that one uses to determine what to do and questioning the norms, rules, and laws of society. Although they may be seen as valuable for maintaining order and civility, rules and laws are not seen as absolute but are designed by imperfect people and subject to modification and improvement.

Stage 5: *Social contract driven*—this is where what is right is determined by fulfilling the obligations and commitments that we have agreed to as members of our society. There is an appreciation that while people may have different perspectives on what is right and wrong, it is also necessary to have laws that promote the greatest good for the greatest number of people. Heinz might decide to steal the medicine because everyone has the right to choose life even if it means breaking a law. Or he might decide not to steal it because he thinks the druggist has a right to get paid fairly.

Stage 6: *Universal ethical principles driven*—this involves the adherence to universal ethical principles above all else. While laws and social contracts are necessary and important, they should be subject to the highest principles held by the individual. Thus, there may be unjust laws that need to be challenged and even disobeyed. Examples might be when Gandhi and King challenged the existing laws and social order in the treatment of native Indians and African Americans. In the case of Heinz, he could have placed ultimate value on the principle of preserving human life. In one case, he might reason that he should steal the medicine because his wife's life is worth more than the property rights of another. Or, he could decide not to steal the medicine because stealing it could deprive others whose lives are just as worthy of the drug.

What Is the Care Tradition of Moral Reasoning?

Carol Gilligan thought that Kohlberg's approach placed too much emphasis on logic and reason and did not fully take into account the role of emotions and relationships in making moral decisions.[15] Thus, she developed a theory of moral development that gave greater importance to the role of empathy and compassion and to having a personal relationship with the people involved. She offered a three-stage theory that began with (1) the orientation to individual survival where the self is the sole object of concern, then moved to a stage where (2) goodness is conceived as self-sacrifice and taking responsibility for others, and finally to a stage of (3) nonviolence where the rule against doing harm or hurting people was the highest guiding principle.

She thought that these three stages may better reflect how women progress in their moral development than Kohlberg's stages. As with Kohlberg, the individual begins by focusing on what is best for the self but then for Gilligan there is a stage where the person focuses so much on taking care of the other that it involves too much self-sacrifice. This may represent what women experience more often than men when they focus too much on others at the expense of themselves. The third stage is where a person achieves a better balance between taking care of oneself and others and not seeing good as only sacrificing for others but as seeking truth for the self and refraining from both harming others and oneself.

What Do the Justice and Care Traditions Offer?

Although they have different emphases, the Justice and Care tradition generally complement each other and have much to offer. The Justice tradition focuses on how we may use reason and logic, which may better represent the way that men have been socialized than women. It can enable us to understand how our thinking may evolve from only focusing on ourselves, to considering others in our social group, and then encompass all of humanity, which may represent a worthy goal for many people. There is also a great deal of research that has validated the progression through Kohlberg's stages, showing that children and adults can be taught to improve their moral reasoning, and that this kind of training can have beneficial effects on well-being and functioning.

The Care tradition can help us better understanding the ways that our emotions and social relationships can influence our decisions about what is right and wrong. The work of Antonio Damasio demonstrating the influence of "gut feelings" on decision-making suggests that our emotions may play a strong role even when we are not aware of them.[16] The work of Jonathan Haidt in identifying what determines our political perspective suggests our social connections may often play a greater role than logic or reason.[17] The powerful influence of social and emotional factors may help explain whether or not a person follows through in actually doing what they think is right.

The best approach based on both the Justice and Care traditions may be to become more aware of how emotions and social relationships may influence our decisions and to use the stages of moral development as a guide for thinking through them. Using the stages as a guide could involve learning how people in the more advanced stages have thought about dilemmas similar to the ones we are facing. This could lead to the integration of both our awareness of our emotions and relationships and the kind of thinking that may involve a higher level of moral decision-making.

A common example is trying to mediate a dispute between two children to determine who is telling the truth. Let's say you have a five-year-old son and he and a neighbor boy of the same age were playing and just broke your favorite vase. They both blame the other and it is up to you to decide who was responsible and what the consequences will be. You not only have to fully listen to both sides of the story but also be aware of any strong feelings that may bias you for or against your own child—or the neighbor child if you also know him well. The more aware you are of your strong emotions and biases, the more you will be able to fairly consider and weigh everything they tell you. This may help you do the best job of determining how much each is responsible and decide on the consequences that might be best for each.

What Fosters Fairness and Doing the Right Thing?

There are several things that may generally help us become better in deciding what is fair and doing the right thing. First, it may help if we come to see ourselves as a moral or ethical person who values doing the right thing. This can occur when our parents and peers recognize us for doing the right thing, when we decide to imitate or follow a strong moral example, or when we learn more about our strengths and capacity for goodness. The more you see yourself as a person who does the right thing, the more likely you will be to try to do what is fair.

Second, we can find ways not only to increase our empathy but also to really understand what other people are going through. While empathy often focuses more on knowing what another person is feeling, perspective-taking is the name given to trying to actually see things from their point of view. This extra step may reveal more of the specifics and details of their situation and enable us to see just how and why something may or may not be fair. Perspective-taking can be an effective way to challenge the myside bias where we only see things from our point of view.

Third, the strength of open-mindedness can both facilitate perspective-taking and directly impact our ability to make a judgment about fairness. You may remember that selective exposure is our natural tendency to only expose ourselves to the people and perspectives we are comfortable with. The way we defined open-mindedness was to actively search for evidence that contradicts our most cherished values and beliefs. Trying to play devil's advocate and examining both sides of an issue can help us do this.

Fourth, the strength of integrity may be the perfect complement to strength of fairness. When faced with a morally challenging situation, our initial goal may be to use the best of what we have learned about how to be fair in determining what is right and the best course of action. But the next step may be to actually take action. An important part of integrity is that our values and beliefs are well-integrated with our behavior. Having the motivation and courage to be true to our values enables us to follow through in our behavior in the world.

What Can We Do to Increase Fairness?

1. *Write down the important rules or principles that you live by.*

List at least three rules or principles, but no more than 10. Think about how much they were determined by emotions and relationships versus logic and reason. Think about how they have been involved in determining what is fair or right in your past and how you can better use them in the future.

2. *Read a biography or watch a movie about a moral leader.*

Watch a movie or read a book about someone like Gandhi, Martin Luther King, Jr., Mother Teresa, Eleanor Roosevelt, or Abraham Lincoln. Try to identify both what they think is right and how they determined the right thing to do.

3. *Write about a time when you were treated unfairly.*

Identify a time you felt like you were treated unfairly by another person. Write down your reasons for why you think you were treated unfairly. Go back over Kohlberg's stages and see if you can identify what stages your reasons fall under.

4. *Write down times when you treated someone else unfairly.*

Identify a time you think you treated someone else unfairly. Write down your reasons for why you think you treated them unfairly. Write down what you could do to prevent treating someone unfairly this way again in the future.

5. *Do something kind for someone who is an underdog.*

Identify someone you think that life has in some way been unfair to. This can be something large such as having a major illness or disability or something small or even a one-time thing. Do something kind for them that doesn't call attention to itself and see how it feels to you to do it.

6. *Ask an honest friend when they thought you were acting unfairly.*

This is for those who are feeling particularly bold and courageous. Ask them first when they thought you were unfair in some way with them. If they can't think of anything, ask them if they can think of other ways that they thought you were being unfair with anyone else.

11.2. Citizenship

One of the most thrilling moments in the original *Star Wars* movie occurred when Luke Skywalker was honing in on the target to destroy the Death Star. At the same time, Darth Vader was honing in on him and almost had him in his sights to destroy him. Then out of nowhere the Millennium Falcon appears with Han Solo who fires a shot at Darth Vader's ship that causes it to go spinning out into space.

At the beginning of the movie, Han Solo lives up to his name in only looking out for himself. He was the quintessential rugged individualist, mercenary, cowboy that is so idealized in Western culture. But during his new adventure something happens, like Martin Niemöller he changes his mind and is now willing to risk himself against the dark forces to help those other than himself. How did this happen and what can we do to make this happen?

What Is Citizenship?

The word citizenship is one of the most easily misunderstood of the VIA strengths with one of the most boring and uninspiring dictionary definitions. *Dictionary.com* defines it as "the character of an individual viewed as a member of society; behavior in terms of the duties, obligation, and functions of a citizen."[18] It doesn't bring near the sense of excitement of Han Solo bursting in out of nowhere to blast the evil one out into space.

The *Character Strengths and Virtues* handbook definition is almost equally dry but brings out the transformation that Han Solo underwent: "Citizenship, social responsibility, loyalty, and teamwork represent a feeling of identification with and sense of obligation to a common good that includes the self but that stretches beyond one's own self-interest" (p. 370).[19] The *VIA Institute on Character* avoids some of the problems with the word citizenship by naming this strength "teamwork." It defines this in terms of "citizenship or responsibility toward one's community, loyalty as unwavering trust for a group, and patriotism as unwavering loyalty toward one's homeland/nation without hostility toward other nations."[20]

As I have taught positive psychology during the past 12 years, I have seen many students who have had a problem with this strength because of the word citizenship and other words like patriotism and loyalty that have been associated with it. The problems have been around the way that it can foster an "in-group" vs. "out-group" mentality that may have caused many wars and conflicts in the world. One particularly bright and engaged graduate student told me about a YouTube video called the *Empathic Civilization* by the economist and social theorist Jeremy Rifkin. In the video and in his book of the same name, Rifkin talks about how humans may have gradually evolved to see people outside of their group as part of their group and argues that embracing this tendency may be the key to the future health of humanity and the planet.[21]

Thus, in using the word citizenship and in defining this strength, I think it is important to make a distinction between two kinds of citizenship. As I did with creativity, I will distinguish between Big-C citizenship meaning working for the greatest good of everyone and little-c citizenship meaning focusing only on one's country, state, city, country club, church, or sports team.

The historical movement from only working for oneself or one's family to the larger community probably brought greater happiness and well-being for all involved. Now, with how interconnected and interdependent we have become with everyone else around the world, Big-C citizenship may be useful for avoiding the negative connotations of little-C citizenship and will be the best focus of this section.

What Is Big-C Citizenship?

Even with this initial distinction in mind, there are three other points that may help to illustrate what Big-C citizenship means. First, there is that very useful phrase in the speech of John F. Kennedy to "ask not what your country can do for you—ask what you can do for your country."[22] When people talk about being a citizen, they often differentiate between the rights of being a citizen and the duties or responsibilities of being a citizen. Big-C citizenship is not about making sure you get all that is coming to you as much as making sure that you do your part in contributing to the overall human community. In risking his life, Han Solo was less concerned about getting and spending a paycheck for helping to destroy the Death Star than he was about doing something to help his friend and beating the dark side of the Force.

Second, Big-C citizenship is not about win-lose or winning at all cost as much as it is about using the maximum creativity in working towards solutions that are win-win for everyone. I remember how strong the rivalry was when I was growing up between the Washington Redskins and the Dallas Cowboys football teams. It was wonderful to win a great victory over the other team but that also meant that millions of people in the other city would be depressed the next day. Overcoming win-lose thinking can be a great challenge when we grow up separating people into us and them, winners and losers, and friends and enemies. But at the heart of Big-C citizenship is the motivation to create a community where all can benefit and where the common enemies might be things like the war, poverty, disease, hatred, and violence we can all suffer from.

Third, Big-C citizenship goes beyond the attitude embodied in the saying "my country, right or wrong." This represents a kind of unthinking patriotism that never allows us to question the powers that be or the established order. During the 19th century in the United States, this would mean thinking that questioning the institution of slavery would be unpatriotic or not being a good citizen. Even if we are trying to find win-win solutions and considering the well-being of everyone, we can fall into the danger of thinking that the established ways of doing them are set in stone or sacrosanct. Big-C citizenship assumes that the best way "to love our country" or the whole family of humanity is not to unthinkingly obey our leaders and institutions but to hold us all accountable to a higher standard that will make our country and our world better.

What Are Ways to Cultivate Big-C Citizenship?

If we define citizenship as doing those things that foster the well-being of humanity as a whole, then what can we do to increase these behaviors in ourselves and in others? First, the most simple and straightforward way for many to increase Big-C citizenship is to volunteer to do something that may help the larger community. This might be different from some of the things people do to boost kindness or compassion that focus on just one or two people. It may be optimal if it is something that impacts a larger number of people or even affects the larger social or political system. The goal is to choose something that fits with our strengths, interests, and values so that it will be self-rewarding and reinforcing.

Second, as often happens with volunteer work, we can look to do something that involves working together towards a common goal or task. The idea of the hero's journey carries with it the notion that we are all on a most sacred and profound journey to live life to the fullest, to fully realize who we are, and to use it for all we are worth in making the world a better place for others. The movie *Places in the Heart* won the Academy Award for the best screenplay with Sally Field winning the best actress in 1985. It is the story of how common challenges brought a struggling widow, her children, a blind man, and a black man together to raise the cotton that would save the family farm and create a new family.

Third, we can raise the awareness of the suffering of others who are very different from us and far out on the circle of our common humanity. The movie *Paper Clips* is the true story of a school principal in a small Tennessee town where there was almost no awareness of those who lost their lives under Hitler during World War II. The principal was struggling to find a way to help the students comprehend the number of people who lost their lives in concentration camps and came up with the idea of collecting paper clips to represent each life lost. They began with what they thought was the impossible goal of collecting 6,000,000—one for every Jewish person who lost their life. After the media heard about it and publicized it, they ended up with 11,000,000 to represent all who lost their lives and created a beautiful museum to store them in.

Fourth, we can boost our empathy and compassion for people who are different from us. A young high school teacher in California did just this by teaching her students of different ethnicities how to understand each other better. In the movie *Freedom Writers*, based on a true story, Erin Gruwell uses a game to help her students see how much they had in common. The game involved having them step forwarding onto a line on the floor whenever they had a common experience. In the process of doing this, they realized that they were suffering from many of the same traumatic experiences and losses. As a result, instead of fighting each other as they had been, they started to become more like a family and began to support each other.

Fifth, we can help people understand just what it feels like to be a part of a less powerful out-group. One of the most famous examples of this is what the third grade teacher Jane Elliott did with her students the day after Martin Luther King, Jr. was killed.[23] She divided the class up into blue- and brown-eyed students and gave special treatment to the blue-eyed students before reversing the process and giving special treatment to the brown-eyed students. What the students wrote about their experiences was published in the local newspaper and Elliot received lots of positive media attention as well as some criticism in the town where she taught. The blue- and brown-eyes exercise was modified and repeated in many settings and Elliott became a pioneer of diversity training and devoted the rest of her career to it.

Sixth, we can increase our motivation to give ourselves to others when we remember what others have sacrificed to give us the things that we value and cherish. These are part of what national holidays and memorial days are for but can be extended to all of humankind. One day a couple years ago I was sitting in a church next to a 91-year-old man when someone said it was the anniversary of D-Day in World War II. The man next to me started to cry and I asked him why. He said that he still remembered the day when he was almost drafted to go on the D-Day mission where the largest percentage of people died. When the men were gathered together to announce who would be drafted, the person sitting right next to him was called to go and he wasn't. He said that in the 70 years since that day he has tried to live his life as a gift to honor the sacrifice of those sitting around him that day who died so that others could be free.

Finally, Phil Zimbardo recently started what he has called the Heroic Imagination Project (HIP) that combines many of these methods.[24] Zimbardo is famous for the Stanford prison

248

experiment that showed how social pressure can influence people to behave badly and he designed HIP to teach children how to become "ordinary heroes." The program has a four week curriculum where students learn about both what can increase and what can decrease being a good citizen. They learn about the power of prejudice and negative social influence as well as how to increase empathy and reduce the tendency to blame the victim. Finally, they use real and fictional heroes such as Martin Luther King, Jr., and Harry Potter as models for their behavior and are encouraged to put what they learn into practice.

What Can We Do to Become a Better Citizen?

1. *Volunteer for a community project that fits with your values, interests, and strengths.*

Think about this as an experiment. Make a list of the kinds of things you could volunteer for. Identify the one that fits best with your values, interests, and strengths. Then try it for a few hours and reflect on how it makes you feel.

2. *Pick up litter where you live, work, or go to school.*

There are rewards in doing this in secret and other rewards in doing in a way that is more obvious to others. Doing it in secret helps you know what it feels like to do something without the recognition of others. Doing it in an obvious way with a litter bag may inspire others to do the same.

3. *Become a blood or an organ donor.*

This can be a wonderful way to think about how we are all connected. Think about how there are people out there who may really be able to use your blood or organs in the future. Try donating blood once and see if you want to make it a regular thing.

4. *Write your congressperson about what you think your community needs.*

Identify the senator or congressman for your state or local government and get their email address. Write about a specific issue you are aware of or just tell them you are glad for their service. Share any ideas you have for improving the community.

5. *Read about someone who made a sacrifice to give you the freedom and rights that you enjoy.*

Think about those who either gave their lives, or sacrificed in some other way, so that you could live in a better society or world. Make a list of what they did that made your life better. Think about what you can to do honor them and "pay it forward."

11.3. Leadership

Many people don't know that Martin Luther King, Jr. went off script near the end of his famous *I Have a Dream* speech. It was a hot August day during the summer of 1963 and 250,000 people were gathered around the foot of the Lincoln memorial to hear him. He was nearing the end of his prepared speech and the gospel singer Mahalia Jackson shouted, "Tell them about the dream, Martin!" It was then that he went off script in finishing the speech with the poetic vision and words that were so memorable.[25]

This speech is not only often cited as one of the greatest speeches of all time but also one of the greatest examples of transformational leadership. What was it about these words and who King was and how he gave this speech that made it such a powerful and transformative moment in American history? What is it that makes a great leader and how can we all be better leaders?

What Is Leadership?

The strength of leadership is one of the simplest to define but may be one of the hardest to do. *Dictionary.com* defines a leader as "a person or thing that leads."[26] The *Character Strengths and Virtues* handbook gets a little more specific in saying that leadership involves, "encouraging a group which one is a member to get things done and at the same time maintain good relations within the group; organizing group activities and seeing that they happen" (p. 30).[27] It further defines it later in more precise academic language as "an integrated constellation of cognitive and temperament attributes that foster an orientation toward influencing and helping others, directing and motivating their actions toward collective success" (p. 414).[28]

I will take the broader approach in defining leadership here as enabling others to move towards their goals and would add a distinction between two kinds of leadership. As with creativity and citizenship, I would distinguish between Big-L leadership as the formal leadership of a relatively large number of people in larger groups and little-l leadership as the everyday leadership we all exercise in facilitating group activities and even in leading and influencing other individuals.

What Are the Different Types of Leadership?

There are many kinds of leadership and researchers and theorists have identified a full range of leadership types and styles. They most often involve dichotomies that represent two different approaches or contrasting styles of leadership.

1. *Task-Oriented vs. Relationship-Oriented Leadership*

Task-oriented leaders focus on the specific job that needs to be done to reach a goal or meet performance standards while relationship-oriented leaders focus on the satisfaction, motivation, and well-being of members of the team. The task-oriented leader places more emphasis on planning and monitoring the steps it takes to meet specific goals and may be more useful when team members are not as good at managing themselves or their time. The person-oriented leader places more emphasis on supporting and motivating team members and enabling them to work well together. The effectiveness of either style may depend on the work setting and it may often be optimal to find a good balance between focusing on completing tasks and supporting workers.

2. *Autocratic vs. Democratic Leadership*

This dichotomy depends on how much decisions are made by the leader alone or jointly with members of a team or work group. The extreme example of an autocratic leader is a dictator who makes decisions completely alone. A less extreme example is a military leader where it may be necessary to retain a large degree of authority and control.

In contrast, a democratic leader places the highest priority on collective opinions and the will of the people they are designated to lead. In the *I Have a Dream* speech, King was acting as a democratic leader in expressing the deepest hopes, wishes, and desires of others. There is a place for both autocratic and democratic styles depending on the need for quick action and the maturity of the followers.

3. *Transactional vs. Transformational Leadership*

Transactional leadership is also known as management leadership and it involves using rewards and punishments to motivate team members to meet the current goals of an organization. Transformational leadership involves working with the team to identify the needs for change, creating an inspiring vision for change, and following through in working with the team to bring the joint vision of change about.

The goal of transactional leaders is to get the current job done whereas the goal of transformational leadership is to achieve a mutually beneficial better future. The metaphor of a dream in King's speech is a prime example of a vision of a better future and how a leader can cultivate, articulate, and use that in transformative leadership.

4. *Destructive vs. Constructive Charismatic Leadership*

Charismatic leadership involves the ability to inspire and motivate through the leader's personality in speaking to the emotional experience of others. Because charismatic leadership can be so powerful, there has been a distinction made between constructive and destructive charismatic leaders. Constructive charismatic leaders such as King and Franklin Delano Roosevelt are oriented towards serving, empowering, and transforming others. Destructive charismatic leaders such as Adolph Hitler, who was responsible for the genocide of millions of Jews, and Jim Jones, who led his followers to kill themselves in the 1978 Jonestown Massacre, use their charisma and ability to persuade people to submit to them so they can increase their own power and status in serving their own ends.

5. *Servant vs. Self-Serving Leadership*

Robert Greenleaf identified a servant leader as an ideal type of leader that puts the needs of others first and helps them develop and perform as optimally as possible.[29] The contrast between such a leader and a self-serving leader may help us put the other styles in perspective. The servant leader balances getting the job done with nurturing the development of the team and also is democratic in that the will of the people is their highest concern.

While transactions may need to be made, the servant leader is ultimately transformative in moving everyone toward a shared vision of a better tomorrow. Any charisma they possess is used constructively in serving the greater good of everyone. King, Gandhi, and Mandela are examples of servant leaders in how they balanced caring for the people with their long-term vision of a better world.

What Characteristics May Be Useful for Leadership?

There have been many efforts to identify the personal characteristics that may be involved in leadership. While their relative importance may vary across leadership style and situation, there are several characteristics that may consistently be useful for leaders.

First, there is a moderate positive correlation between IQ and becoming a leader. However, becoming a leader in many domains may not require a high IQ. There are many who think that having greater social or emotional intelligence may compensate for a low IQ or even be more important. There are others who think that having too high of an IQ may make it more difficult for a leader to relate with a broad segment of workers or team members.

Of all of the Big Five personality characteristics, extraversion generally appears to have the strongest relationship with leadership followed by conscientiousness, emotional stability (being low in neuroticism), and openness-to-experience while agreeableness is not correlated with leadership. Other personal characteristics that have been related to leadership include autonomy, assertiveness, dominance, and risk-taking. Autonomous leaders are more common and valued in Western cultures. Having an assertive and dominant personality may be useful in developing more forceful leadership but could also be used in the abuse of power.

Finally, there have been several studies that have tried to determine which of the other VIA strengths may be more common in leaders. As we have mentioned, these strengths can become more stable personal characteristics but also involve specific attitudes and behaviors that can be cultivated. The ones that have emerged as being most common and potentially important for leadership are social intelligence, creativity, prudence, honesty, bravery, hope, humility, and teamwork.

Social intelligence, honesty, humility, and teamwork may make it possible for leaders to understand and work well with other people. Balancing prudence and hope may enable them to both develop an inspiring vision and a thoughtful plan for how to accomplish it. Creativity and bravery may enable them to discover new paths and take the necessary risks to follow them.

How Can Good Leadership Be Fostered?

There have been many successful interventions and programs designed to foster leadership in a variety of settings. These have included formal leadership training programs in businesses and other organizations, programs that focus on using ongoing experiences in the process of learning to become a leader, and self-help programs consisting of books, seminars, and workshops. I will highlight some of the approaches that have been taken by these programs.

1. *What are your interests, values, and goals?*

The first step for many people is to be clear about what they are most interested in and what they want to accomplish. If you want to become a good leader, it may be critical to either try to lead in an area that you care about or find some way to connect what you are doing with what you care about. Many of the greatest leaders were not born with an extroverted or assertive personality, but came to behave in a much more extraverted and assertive way when they were trying to get other people involved in something they cared about. This draws on Csikszentmihalyi's idea of flow and Joseph Campbell's idea of following your bliss.[30-31] If you find something that you love to do, then you will be intrinsically motivated to learn more about it and other people who share your interest may be more likely to want to listen to you to learn more about it.

2. What is your natural leadership style and personality?

There are two main reasons for determining this. First, knowing your natural leadership style and where you stand in relationship to personal characteristics related to leadership may help you identify the areas where you are strong and what you may need to work on. Second, knowing these things may make it a lot easier to find the setting that may best match your personality and where your natural style can grow and flourish.

If you are more naturally focused on getting the job done rather than spending a lot of time getting to know people, then you may work better in a setting that requires task-oriented leadership. If you are a more agreeable person who likes to please other people, then you may be happier in a setting that requires a more democratic leader who takes a relationship-oriented approach.

3. What are your strengths and how can you use them to lead?

It may be particularly useful to identify your top strengths in relation to the VIA classification or the *Strength Finder 2.0* set of strengths that are specifically geared to business and organizational settings.[32-33] First, you can determine how well your top strengths match up with the strengths presented above that have been most associated with leadership. Second, knowing your top strengths can be the beginning of finding new ways to use them.

As we discussed above, the sailboat metaphor has been used to describe the difference between focusing on weaknesses, which is like trying to fix all of the holes in your boat; and focusing one strengths, which is like simply lifting the sails. Once you identify your strengths, then you can look for new ways to use them in becoming the kind of leader that fits best for you and what you have to offer.

4. *How can you build your strengths and learn new skills?*

Once you have a good idea of who you are and what you have to work with, then you can make the best judgment about how to increase your strengths and what new skills you need to learn. If you are more task-oriented and focused on getting the job done but need to work in a more relationship-focused environment, then it may be important to focus on increasing your social intelligence, for example, through assertiveness training or active constructive responding.

While something like being very introverted may be more difficult to change, there are wonderful resources such as Susan Cain's book *Quiet* which has much to say about how you may be able to use being introverted to your advantage.[34] This is where it is also important to remember the idea of the Gandhi ladder that by continuing to practice you can develop almost any new habit or strength.

5. *Is your motivation to be a Big-L leader or to make a difference?*

This is not only a critical question for anyone who will become a leader but also for anyone who is already a leader. It also gets at the difference between a destructive and constructive leader and at the heart of the idea of a servant leader. The history books are filled with narcissistic people whose main goal in becoming a leader was to exercise power and control and gain wealth and recognition. Someone like Rosa Parks is a good example of a different kind of leader. She was a shy person who was no longer willing to sit in the back of bus and who exercised little-l leadership which made a big-D difference. Jane Elliot took the same path in doing what she believed was right by teaching third graders in a way that led to diversity training that has helped broaden the circle of understanding for millions.[35] The best way to become a good leader may be to do what you think is right and trust that others will follow.

What Can We Do to Become a Better Leader?

1. *Use your top strengths for leadership.*

Take the *VIA Survey* to identify your top strengths and google Tayyab Rashid's *340 Ways to Use VIA Character Strengths.*[36] Go through the lists under your top five strengths and brainstorm about which of them you could use to help you become a better leader. Then try it and see what happens.

2. *Organize an activity with friends with a common interest.*

Try to identify a few of your friends who are interested in the same things that you are. Make a list of activities related to your interests that you would all enjoy. Then decide which you want to do and find a time when you can all do it together.

3. *Identify the strengths of the people you already lead.*

If you are in a leadership role, ask your team to take the *VIA Survey* and organize a time when you can meet to talk about the results. When you meet, ask them to share their top strengths and brainstorm together on how each person can better use their strengths to achieve your common goals.

4. *Invite your friends to join you in volunteering.*

Try to identify something you can do to serve your community that some of your friends may be interested in doing with you. Keep inviting people until you have at least a few people to join you and invite them to volunteer again if you enjoy doing it together the first time.

5. *Learn about a leader who is like you.*

Try to identify either a fictional or a real character in a book, play, or movie who was a leader and who has a similar personality or similar strengths as you. Identify and write down the things that they said and did to lead other people. Use them as a guide for yourself.

Using the Strengths of Justice for the Journey

While the strengths of Humanity enable us to connect with and care about individual people, the strengths of Justice enable us to do what may have an impact on the larger human community. The strengths of fairness, citizenship, and leadership help us to expand our circle of empathy and compassion to all people and make the difficult choices that face us in serving the greater good. Like Han Solo before he met Luke and Leia, many of us find ourselves lost and alone in the old Western myth of the rugged individualist who never looks beyond themselves.

In this chapter, we saw how Han Solo and many others may have developed the strengths that helped them bring new hope to others. Robert Niemöller was a supporter of Hitler until he risked his own life and challenged us to act. Erin Gruwell was a naïve and idealistic young high school teacher until she found a way to build a bridge where there had been so much hatred. Jane Elliott was trying to help her white third graders understand why King was killed and ended up on a new adventure. Finally, that very same man—King—lives on in holidays, the names of streets, and most of all in the dream that would not die.

But the call to adventure in the hero's journey is not just about Luke and Han or Robert, Erin, Jane, and Martin. It is about me as I write this sentence and you as you read it. This call is not just for isolated individual cowboys and cowgirls and the individual pleasures that we seek. The call to Luke, Harry, Frodo, and Diana in *Wonder Woman* was to something larger. The call to expand the circle of citizenship in finding ways to work for the well-being and justice of all is just as real for us as it was for King the day he gave his most famous speech.

The virtue of Justice and the strengths in this chapter are about so much more than the "don't worry, be happy" philosophy that came with the "me-generation" of the 1980s. These strengths are for those of us who choose to expand our circle of empathy and compassion as a part of our vision of the best life we can seek for ourselves. While there is no denying that choosing such a path can bring great risks and sacrifices, there is also no denying that such a meaningful path can bring great rewards.

Chapter 12

The Temperance to Find the Balance

Between stimulus and response there is a space.
In that space is our power to choose our response.
In our response lies our growth and our freedom.

—*Viktor Frankl*[1]

In many great stories, there is a young hero who seems to possess all of the right stuff for meeting the challenge and completing the journey. But as with Luke Skywalker in his training with Yoda, they are impatient and tempted to rush off before they are ready. In *The Lord of the Rings*, Boromir overestimates his ability to deal with the temptation of the power and greed that the ring represents. In contrast, the elf princess Galadriel shows us a very different response. She had great respect for the power of the ring and had long thought about how she might respond to it. When she finally faced its temptation and prevailed, she grew taller and more beautiful and now could fully bestow her gifts on those working to destroy the ring.

In the stories of Jesus and Buddha, there are similar great temptations that must be faced and are necessary in preparing them for their great missions. After he was baptized, Jesus went to the desert in order to fast for 40 days and 40 nights. Satan tried to tempt him by offering him food, power, and wealth; but each time Jesus resisted by pointing to the God who was calling him to a higher purpose. In the story of Buddha, the demon Mara assaults him as he sits seeking enlightenment under the

Bodhi tree. Mara tries to tempt Buddha with promises of glory and pleasure and beautiful women but the Buddha prevails and touches the earth as his witness that he has defied Mara and achieved enlightenment.

The strengths under the virtue of Temperance in the VIA classification are easily underestimated and all too often neglected and forgotten in our culture of immediate gratification. They are also the least popular but ironically for many contain the missing key for a better life. They are also consistently among the lowest ranked of all the VIA strengths with self-control being the least endorsed strength by both children and adults around the world. While it is important to raise the sails in using our top strengths, it may also be necessary to fix a few holes in the boat by working on our weaknesses. For some of us, these strengths may be at the top of our list. For many more, they represent some of our greatest weaknesses that threaten to sink our ships and keep us from sailing at all.

The four strengths that we will focus on in this chapter may help all of us find and maintain the necessary balance we may need to successfully make our journeys. We will begin with self-control, which is the internal discipline that we need to reach any goal. Second, we will focus on prudence, which means learning to make the best judgments about when to delay our gratification and when to "party hardy." Third, we will focus on humility, not as a weakness but as the ability to accurately view all of our strengths and weaknesses. Finally, we will focus on forgiveness, which for many may be one of the most challenging strengths of all, but also one that can free us to fully experience the happiness we seek.

12.1. Self-Control

As I sit here writing, I think about whether to go downstairs and get the last piece of that German chocolate that my sister-in-law brought us. There is something about it that makes my mouth water and my stomach growl even more than the familiar *Snickers*, *Reese's Peanut Butter Cup*, and *Butter Finger* that call out to me when I wait in line at the grocery store. The consequences are clear, if I indulge now I may feel good for a few minutes, but will certainly want to take a nap before dinner. I decide to wait, but the more I try not to think of it, the more it pops back into my awareness until I start writing about it for this chapter.

What Is Self-Control?

Dictionary.com defines self-control as "control or restraint of oneself or one's actions, feelings, etc." That can be a big "etc." that includes so many things. The *Character Strengths and Virtues* handbook defines self-control or self-regulation as "regulating what one feels and does; being disciplined; controlling one's appetites and emotions" (p. 30).[2] Something about that word "appetite" struck a nerve. I'll think I'll go have a piece of that German chocolate…

Okay, back after the nap and now I need to work extra hard to catch up! The *VIA Institute on Character* defines self-regulation as "the practiced ability to monitor and manage one's emotions, motivation, and behavior in the absence of outside help."[3] I guess I was lacking the help I needed for the chocolate. While I think this is the most complete definition, I think it is better to use the term "self-control" rather than "self-regulation" because self-regulation often refers to body processes we are not aware of, whereas self-control is the conscious and deliberate effort not to eat any more chocolate.

Whether or not a person is able to exercise self-control may actually be determined by two different systems in our bodies. Janet Metcalfe and Walter Mischel have proposed hot and cool systems that may be involved in the delay of gratification.[4] The hot system includes the impulses, emotions, and reflexes that urge us to go ahead and do something quickly.

The cool system includes our ability to think things through in a slower and more deliberate fashion. In this framework, whether someone exercises self-control may depend on whether the cold system is strong or developed enough to override the hot system. There may be large individual differences in the strengths of both systems but the cool system may be much more subject to shaping and strengthening during our lives.

Why Is Self-Control Important?

The behaviors we need self-control for can range from the more obvious health behaviors such as diet, exercise, smoking, alcohol, and drugs to the others things that are equally important such as finishing our work and refraining from saying those angry words on the tip of our tongue. There can be tremendous individual differences in what we have a difficult time controlling. Research has shown that women generally have a harder time refraining from eating too much and men find it harder to control their sexual impulses. I once worked with a student who wanted to do research about why some people are so unmotivated to exercise while others find it so easy.

Roy Baumeister thinks that we can divide self-control into the four broad categories of thoughts, emotions, impulse control, and performance.[5] Controlling thoughts includes getting certain thoughts out of our minds, such as those of German chocolate or that annoying song, and getting ourselves to pay more attention to other thoughts, such as focusing on our work. Controlling emotions may involve trying to reduce our feelings of fear or sadness, or trying to refrain from an angry gesture at the person who just cut us off in traffic. Impulse control is what I didn't have enough of in eating that chocolate, or many don't have when gossiping about other people. Finally, we also use self-control to improve our performance on a full range of tasks from hitting a golf ball to playing a video game or singing and playing a musical instrument.

Regardless of what kind of temptations are most difficult for us to resist, it is clear that self-control can be a challenge for all of us and that self-control may have sweeping implications for our happiness and well-being. There are countless studies that have shown that self-control can both help us avoid bad things happening and also enable us to make progress in obtaining the good things that can make us happy. A lack of self-control has been linked to all kinds of problems such as alcohol and substance abuse, obesity, and a whole host of related chronic illnesses, and problems with money and interpersonal relationships. Conversely, those with high levels of self-control have often been shown to be more successful at school, work, and athletics.

What Does the Research Say About Self-Control?

The classic psychological study demonstrating the potential long-term positive effects of self-control is what has come to be known as the "marshmallow experiment" conducted with four-year-old children in the 1960s by Walter Mischel at Stanford University.[6] The experiment involved giving the children a choice between eating a large marshmallow now or waiting until the experimenter came back 15-20 minutes later and receiving a second large marshmallow if they hadn't eaten the first one.

In this case, self-control was the ability of the children to delay their gratification. The remarkable thing about this experiment is that they were able to follow up 14 years later with many of the children in the original experiment. They compared those who waited for the second marshmallow with those who grabbed the first marshmallow and ate it before they could get another one. They found that the "waiters" were doing better than the "grabbers" on a full range of variables including better coping with stress, better relationships with their peers, and even higher college entrance examination scores. Thus, this kind of self-control was begun to be seen as very important.

There is also an important paradox in the exercise of self-control. Daniel Wegner did a fascinating study where he asked people to try not to think of a white bear while they were verbalizing their thoughts.[7] Wegner found that not only were people not able to *not* think about the white bear, but that there was a rebound effect where they thought about it more later. This is similar to what people experience when they are trying not to think of German chocolate or not to think about drinking if they are trying to abstain from alcohol. There may be times and ways that our efforts at controlling our thoughts, emotions, or impulses might backfire and have the paradoxical effect of increasing rather than decreasing them over the long run.

Roy Baumeister has used the metaphor that self-control is like a muscle to explain two of the most common findings by people who have studied it.[8] First, the amount of self-control that a person has at one time may be like a muscle in that it can be depleted with overuse. Second, the general capacity for self-control can be increased just as muscle strength can be increased through exercise.

Baumeister and others have done studies suggesting that self-control may be a limited resource that can be depleted over time with too much effort. In a typical study, Baumeister had people watch a film that brought out strong emotions and asked them to either try to increase or decrease their emotional response. Then the researchers had them use a hand grip to test their stamina and found that those who tried to control their emotions performed worse than another group who watched the film without trying to control their emotions. However, a large scale replication by Martin Hagger and colleagues using a similar experiment only found a small but non-significant reduction in self-control after it had been used in another task.[9] Researchers are trying to understand the conflicting results and have suggested that depletion of self-control may only be likely after the most demanding tasks.

While it is uncertain when and how much self-control may be depleted, there is little doubt that there is much we can do to improve it. Not only is there evidence that practicing self-control in one area of our lives may improve our self-control in that area. It is also possible that increases in self-control in one area may generalize to other areas of our lives. Mark Muraven and his colleagues had people increase self-control in relation to their postures, their emotions, or their diets and found that improvements in one area was related to improvements in the other two areas.[10] Similarly, researchers studying meditation have argued that increases in self-control fostered by regularly practicing meditation may generalize to other areas of our lives. In addition, the improvements in self-control and discipline that many athletes report often appears to generalize to other areas of their lives.

How Can Self-Control Be Fostered?

For those of us who may be struggling with controlling our thoughts, feelings, impulses, and behaviors, this may be one of our most important questions. Fortunately, there has been a great deal of attention focused on it and there seem to be many good ways to strengthen our self-control.

1. *Self-Monitoring*

While this may not work as well with thoughts of white bears and reducing some other thoughts and feelings, it is one of the best supported ways for changing behaviors such as eating and drinking. Many studies have found that monitoring our behavior may be all that is needed for an important change or that it may be the key factor in a program with many components. Self-monitoring will get that cool system in the habit of waking up before that candy wrapper is off and half the bar has disappeared. The key with self-monitoring is to have a convenient real-time system where you can write down or enter into a smart phone reports about what you want to monitor.

2. *Implementation Intention*

Peter Gollwitzer introduced the idea of an "implementation intention" as a way to make it more likely that you will reach a goal.[11] Research has supported the hypothesis that implementation intentions increase the likelihood of reaching a variety of goals including exercising more and better emotion regulation. The idea here is that you try to set a goal for yourself that involves increasing or improving your self-control. Then you think about the steps you may have to take to reach that goal and what obstacles you may face. Next, you develop a plan for just what you intend to do when faced with each step and potential obstacle. If you want to stop eating dessert, for example, then you develop a plan that includes the intention of not driving by *Baskin-Robbins* and thinking about what you will say to that "friend" who offers you a piece of your favorite pie.

3. *Mental Contrasting*

Gabriele Oettingen introduced this technique of improving self-control that involves visualizing a positive outcome.[12] Research has shown that it improved academic performance, diet, and exercise, and increased help-seeking and help-giving behavior. There are three steps. The first is to identify an important change that you want to make; the second is to identify and imagine the most positive and successful outcome that may result from the change; and the third is to imagine the greatest obstacles that may stand in the way of you reaching your goal. If your goal is to exercise three times a week, you could imagine how much it might improve how you look and feel and then imagine all of the barriers that make it harder to exercise.

4. *Stimulus Control*

This means that you reduce the likelihood of indulging a thought, feeling, or impulse by making it less likely you will be tempted. This could include obscuring the stimulus by not having the German chocolate in your house, distracting yourself externally by watching your favorite television show, distracting yourself internally by dreaming about your vacation, or replacing the stimulus with something that is even more sensually enticing such as taking a long hot bath or getting a massage. For many people trying to refrain from alcohol, for example, an effective approach might involve avoiding people and places where there may be any alcohol.

5. *Urge Surfing*

Urge surfing is a way of trying to deal with recurrent thoughts that may tempt us to do something that we don't want to do. Alan Marlatt used it to treat people with alcohol problems when the craving for alcohol began to rise like a mighty wave.[13] Urge surfing is a type of mindfulness technique that involves (1) focusing on where in your body you are experiencing the craving or urge, (2) acknowledging where and how you are experiencing it, (3) continuing to focus on the areas where you experience it, and (4) releasing tension as you breathe each breath. This may also be one of the best defenses against the rebound effect of trying not to think about the "white bear." Rather than fighting thoughts of the bear you simply allow them to come and go until they pass.

6. *Reducing Conflicting Goals*

One of the most unrecognized causes of poor self-control may be trying to do too many things at once or not being able to decide what to do. Research has found that being ambivalent or conflicted about what goals to strive for may make it harder to attain any goals and lead to poorer psychological and physical well-being. People may set themselves up for failures of self-control when they have so many goals that they do not have enough attention or energy to be successful in all of them. A good first step for many of us may be to prioritize our goals and manage our time so we can fully focus on one thing at a time.

What Are Ways We Can Practice Self-Control?

There are many ways to use and combine the techniques that I have talked about. Here are a few simple things that you may want to start with:

1. *Exercising more.*

Identify a specific and realistic goal for exercising at least three times in the next three weeks. Develop a plan for what to do and use both implementation intentions and mental contrasting in thinking about it. Tell a friend about what you plan to do and ask them to check with you to make sure you do it. Finally, write down when and how long you exercise and note how you feel before and after exercising.

2. *Not having a specific food or drink.*

Think about a kind of food or drink that you would like to avoid for the next three weeks. Don't keep them around where you live and develop a plan for what you will do or say when you are near them away from home. Think of how you can distract yourself externally and internally whenever you think of the food or drink. When distraction doesn't work try urge surfing.

3. *Reaching a specific goal.*

Use the SMART acronym to identify a goal that is (1) Specific, (2) Measurable, (3) Achievable, (4) Relevant, and (5) Time-bound. Use mental contrasting to imagine the best outcome and the most likely obstacles. Verbalize your implementation intentions to reach your goal, take each step, and deal with obstacles. Monitor and reward your progress at each step.

4. *Not gossiping about other people.*

State your commitment to yourself not to gossip for the next three weeks. Identify the situations where you are most likely to gossip. Use mental contrasting by thinking about how you will feel if you are successful and what obstacles might arise. Make a plan for both reducing the likelihood that you will be tempted and for how to handle the temptations when they arise.

5. *Exercising self-compassion.*

Whenever you notice that you make a mistake or fail in exercising self-control, simply note it and use it as an opportunity to practice self-compassion. Be aware of any self-defeating thoughts such as "I just don't have enough self-control" and replace them with thoughts of self-compassion and the idea that you will improve with time.

12.2. Prudence

First, let's just get this out of the way. The word prudence is a problem. People associate it with being a prude, which is not accurate. I had a student once go into a long rant about how he hated prudence when he was really angry about people who were shocked and offended by the free expression of sexuality. Others think of the old *Saturday Night Live* skit where one of Dana Carvey's signature lines in doing an impression of the first President Bush was "wouldn't be prudent." Then there is the *Beatle's* song called *Dear Prudence*, which was written about Mia Farrow's sister "Prudence," who became so serious about meditation that John Lennon wrote the song to get her to come out and play. So there is all kinds of confusion about the word prudence.

What Is Prudence?

Dictionary.com defines prudence as "the quality or fact of being wise in practical affairs, as by providing for the future."[14]

Similarly, the *VIA Institute on Character* says that prudence involves "far-sighted planning as well as short-term, goal-directed planning. It is often referred to as cautious wisdom, practical wisdom, and practical reason. Early in the *Character Strengths and Virtues* handbook, prudence is defined as "being careful about one's choices; not taking undue risks; not saying or doing things that might later be regretted" (p. 30).[15] So you see that these are not exactly the same thing as being that person who was teased for being a prude in school.

But the best definition and understanding of prudence I have come across is the one by Nick Haslam who wrote the chapter about prudence in the *Character Strengths and Virtues* handbook. He defined it as "a cognitive orientation to the personal future, a form of practical reasoning and self-management that helps to achieve the individual's long-term goals effectively."[16] But the most important point he made for me was how the idea of prudence is rooted in the concepts of balance and harmony that are expressed in the Greek idea of the golden mean and the Buddhist idea of the middle way. Haslam talks about how this meaning is derived from Aristotle's use of the Greek word "phronesis" which means practical wisdom and Thomas Aquinas' use of the Latin word "provideo" which means foresight. One English scholar even thought that the best translation of the Latin word prudential is the word mindfulness.

My goal is not to argue over the definition of the word prudence, but to try to discover the meaning that people thought was so important that they made it a virtue or strength across time and culture. It seems that the original meaning has become lost in a culture that is out of balance and has morphed into the word prude to describe those who are excessively concerned about sex or trivial moral questions. But the heart of prudence in the original and best sense of the word may not be something trivial at all, but something that may be a missing piece in today's culture of extremes and immediate gratification. So I will focus on the following sense of the word prudence, that it is our ability to prioritize and balance our desires and goals so that we will be able to achieve the maximum happiness and well-being in the long-run.

This balance does not mean only focusing on planning for a tomorrow that may never come. It means weighing the very good chance that a lot of tomorrows will come with the ever present danger of never learning to enjoy ourselves now. Prudence, in this sense, does not mean *always* delaying gratification and *never* "partying hardy" now, it simply means using our brains to decide what may be the best balance between the two. Some might say "eat, drink, and be merry, for tomorrow we die" but if we spend all of our money doing that now, we may not be able to afford the eating and drinking part for the many tomorrows that we are likely to have. But others may live so much in the thoughts and dreams of possible tomorrows that they miss some pretty good parties and the chance to really be present to their lives in the here and now.

Prudence in this sense is also very different from self-control. While self-control is the ability to manage our emotions, motivation, and behavior in the present; prudence is the ability to decide when and where to try to do that. While self-control includes being able to delay gratification, prudence includes being able to decide when it is best to delay. We might use our prudence to decide that we have worked enough today and that now is *not* the time to use our self-control in trying to avoid that chocolate bar. We might decide we haven't been enjoying ourselves and living in the present moment as much as we would like and that we need to spend *less* time working three jobs and saving for the future. Prudence is the foresight to take the broader and long-term perspective that enables us to decide when to hold back and when to indulge.

The other thing that is sorely needed that prudence may provide is the ability to find the best balance in prioritizing our desires and goal. There are psychologists such as Robert Emmons who have found this to be important as they have studied goals.[17] As we discussed above, reducing conflicting goals can be a way to increase self-control while prudence is the strength that is used in balancing and reconciling our conflicting goals. It is hard to imagine a strength that might be more important in enabling us to negotiate a modern world where we are constantly presented with choices and demands on our time and attention. In this world, prudence is that forgotten unsung hero of a strength that may come to our rescue.

How Can Prudence Be Fostered?

So if prudence involves prioritizing and balancing our desires and goals so we can be happy both now and in the future, what can we do to improve it? While the word prudence has rarely been used in psychology circles, there are a variety of interventions and approaches that may be a good place to start. Since prudence involves both prioritizing our current desires and demands and balancing our present and future, the most useful interventions may enable us to do this in a more thoughtful and systematic way.

1. *Values Clarification*

This first intervention has been called values clarification and it can be useful in building many strengths and in fostering many different kinds of happiness and well-being. But it may also be an important foundation for prudence in enabling us to determine our priorities. Once we know what is most important, it may be much easier to balance our efforts in achieving it. Values clarification usually involves going through a list of values and rating or ranking them in terms of their importance. Milton Rokeach, for example, has developed a list of more than 20 common values that include things like love, wealth, family, success, friends, power, and fun.[18] The goal is to enable us to become clearer about what is most important to us so that we can better prioritize our time and energy.

2. *Goal Clarification and Conflict Resolution*

The second intervention could be used as a next step after values clarification and involves the more specific process of clarifying and deciding among conflicting goals. For example, Robert Emmons developed a technique that involves creating a matrix where you list your most important goals along the left side of the page to form separate rows and you list the same most important goals along the top to form separate columns.[19] Then you fill in a number indicating how much each goal has a harmful or helpful effect on reaching each of the other goals. Averaging the rows or columns can provide an indication of which goals are causing the most harm in reaching other goals. It can be a good place to start in deciding how to change your life so that you will have a better chance to reach your most important goals.

3. *Setting Long- and Short-Range Goals*

The third intervention is an elaboration of short-term techniques for accomplishing goals such as those recommended in the SMART acronym. As I already noted, the SMART approach involves identifying goals that are Specific, Measurable, Achievable, Relevant, and Time-bound.[20] The PATH process presented in Chapter 6 is a good example of how SMART goals can be extended to include longer periods of time.[21] After identifying a vision of what you want most in life and identifying where you are now, you can identify longer-term goals, shorter-term goals, and the first steps to take. In order to increase prudence, you could begin with the perspective gained by clarifying values and goals and then developing lists of long-term, intermediate, and short-term goals while keeping in mind the value that you place on enjoying yourself in the present.

4. *Goal Directed Time Management*

The fourth intervention is time management, which involves prioritizing your time and energy over the short run in order to best accomplish your overall plan. The danger in trying to manage your time is to begin without a good sense of your goals and priorities. Once you are clear about what is most important to you through values clarification, what goals you want to accomplish, and what you need to change to avoid goal conflicts, then you are ready to get more organized in structuring your daily and weekly schedule to make it happen. Books such as David Allen's *Getting Things Done* are resources that can help you do this once you have identified your most important goals and how much time you want to devote to them.[22]

What Are Ways We Can Practice Prudence?

1. *Stop and breathe before you say it.*

If you feel like expressing anger at someone, stop and breathe and give yourself the chance to notice the thoughts and feelings that pass by. Give yourself more time to reflect before you say it. If you feel like sending an angry email, sleep on it first.

2. *Do a risk-benefit analysis.*

If you are trying to make an important decision, make a list of the pros and the cons and rate each one on a scale of one to ten from least to most important. Then come back to it at another time and read each item while mindfully paying attention to how you feel. Be open to what the combination of your ratings and your feelings about them lead you to decide.

3. *Hold off on a big decision if you are tired or stressed.*

If you are having trouble making a big decision, give yourself the time and space you need to feel as rested and relaxed as you can. If you are exhausted, take a nap or wait until after you've had a good night's sleep. If you are depressed, do something that makes you feel better before trying to make a final decision.

4. *Consult a trusted friend.*

Get into the practice of identifying a good friend or two you can rely on to listen and help you think through important decisions. Try to find people who don't necessarily tell you what to do but are willing to hear you express your thoughts out loud and help you clarify them.

12.3. Humility

Of course no powerful leader will ever be liked by everyone. Often people will point to the many mistakes and failures of those in public life. However, there is no doubt that there are a lot of people who really admire Pope Francis and probably at least some of this admiration has to do with his humility.

He is the first pope to take the name Francis after St. Francis of Assisi because of his devotion to humility and the poor. He lives in a regular apartment when he could live in luxury and has traveled in a 1984 Renault rather than a fortified Mercedes; and he has openly called himself a sinner. He has washed the feet of the elderly, the disabled, refugees, and criminal offenders. He let a small boy interrupt his sermon because he wanted to see him, declined eating with leaders in Congress to have lunch with the homeless, and invited 200 homeless people he met in the violent slums of Rio de Janeiro to visit him at the Vatican.[23]

Like prudence, humility is neither a popular nor a common strength and not one that is very often talked about or rewarded in our Facebook and reality TV culture. But, as with prudence, we have lost the original meaning of the word and what was at the heart of this strength that has been appreciated through thousands of years and across many cultures. Pope Francis may be that rare reminder of what we may be missing.

What Is Humility?

The problem is that now there are both positive and negative meanings associated with the word humility. On the one hand, humility has come to sometimes mean being weak and passive and lacking in self-respect and self-confidence. On the other hand, it is used to refer to people like Pope Francis who are strong and active and live in a way that brings the greatest confidence and respect of other people.

Not surprisingly, the *Character Strengths and Virtues* handbook defines humility along more positive lines as "letting one's accomplishments speak for themselves; not seeking the spotlight; not regarding oneself as more special than one is" (p. 30).[24] The *VIA Institute on Character* says that if humility is a top strength then, "you do not seek the spotlight, preferring to let your accomplishments speak for themselves. You do not regard yourself as special, and others recognize and value your modesty."[25]

However, the definition that may best capture what has been most important about humility is the one by Lauren Kachorek and her colleagues. They defined it as "a non-defensive willingness to see the self accurately, including both strengths and weaknesses" (p. 463).[26] The willingness to accurately see and appreciate your strengths and positive qualities is the necessary safeguard against the common tendency to associate humility with weakness and inferiority. The willingness to see your weaknesses addresses the need to recognize our limitations rather than artificially trying to inflate our self-importance. Kachorek and her colleagues use the word "non-defensive" to mean that you are open to accurately seeing all of yourself even if it is uncomfortable and the word "willingness" means that you are willing to at least try even if you will never know yourself fully or perfectly.

Why Might Humility Be Valuable?

There are many benefits to humility in this sense of the word. First, the willingness and ability to see and acknowledge your strengths and weaknesses may be good for your mental and physical health. People who cannot see anything good about themselves may be vulnerable to a low sense of self-worth and depression, while those who cannot see anything bad may have an inflated sense of self-esteem and the grandiosity that can fuel manic states. In addition, the energy that it takes to be defensive in hiding your strengths or your weaknesses can be exhausting and may eventually lead to chronic health problems.

Second, people who are non-defensive about who they are with other people are more likely to be loved and appreciated by others. People who are only aware of their weaknesses may come across as not having much to offer and may feel undervalued and underappreciated. People who present a false positive front and deny their weaknesses may cause others to feel inferior or second best. Narcissism involves having an inflated sense of self-importance and of what you can do. Research has shown that while narcissistic people may get more attention, their desire to be the center of attention and sense of entitlement is often a big turn off that pushes other people away.

Third, people who are able to see and acknowledge their strengths and weaknesses may be better able to reach their goals. The Greek aphorism "know thyself" may be particularly applicable to understanding the value of humility. Knowing about our weaknesses may help us be more realistic about what tasks to undertake and what to do in order to compensate when our limitations may be a problem. Similarly, knowing our strengths may help us determine when a particular goal is achievable and just what to do in order to achieve it.

What Is the Role of Self-Acceptance in Humility?

There is also a curious paradox about the kind of humility we are talking about and the kind of pride that is sometimes used to compensate for feeling inferior with other people. The term Napoleon complex refers to the idea that some short people may compensate by being domineering and aggressive. The same may be true of someone who is worried they are not good enough and think they have to compensate by showing off or bragging that they are better than others. In contrast, humility as the non-defensive willingness to see all of who you are is rooted in the assumption that you are acceptable and worthy just the way you are. You can be open about your strengths and weaknesses because there is nothing you need to do to earn, show, or prove your value or worth as a person.

The underlying sense of self-acceptance at the heart of humility means that we do not ultimately have anything to hide. This self-acceptance is reflected in some ancient traditions and may be the driving force of some of the most transformative interventions in psychology. The theologian Paul Tillich has suggested that the idea of grace in Christianity may be understood simply as the experience of "accepting your acceptance."[27] The Buddhist idea of "metta" or lovingkindness, as expressed in a mindful approach to living, takes for granted that it is good and right to fully accept ourselves.

The value of self-acceptance at the heart of true humility can also be seen in modern psychology. Albert Ellis developed a form of cognitive therapy based on the idea that people are worthwhile just for being and that making your self-worth depend on anything you do is a recipe for feeling anxious and depressed.[28] Carl Rogers believed that "unconditional positive regard" helps free us from external conditions of worth so we can accept ourselves and begin to change and grow.[29] Group psychotherapy and support groups work by enabling us to be more honest and self-accepting in our relationships with others.

How Can Humility Be Fostered?

If we define humility as the non-defensive willingness to see ourselves in all of our strengths and weaknesses, then it may not be hard to find things that will increase it. First, having a history of warm and satisfying relationships associated with a secure attachment style may be vital for the development of humility. As Mary Ainsworth discovered, children who trust that their parent can be sensitive and consistent in their caring are more likely to develop a secure attachment style. Knowing that you can trust others to be there for you when you succeed or fail may make it possible to accept your strengths and weaknesses.

Second, humility may be modeled by having parents and peers who openly acknowledge both their successes and failures and their positive and negative qualities. It will probably be much easier for the next pope to admit he is a sinner and drive a 25-year-old car after seeing Pope Francis do it. History and literature are full of stories of men who felt like failures because they felt they could never live up to the image of their fathers who themselves were often very flawed. There may be equally as many stories of women who never fulfilled their potential because the stereotypical female did not provide a good model for their strengths.

Third, there are intentional efforts that can be made to gain a more realistic view of your whole self. You may be able to turn to psychology for help in identifying some of the self-enhancement biases by which you may try to maintain a fragile sense of self-esteem and which prevent you from seeing some of your weaknesses. Conversely, you can use some of the tools introduced by the positive psychology movement to begin to identify your strengths and see what is best about you. In addition, you can use the practices of mindfulness and journaling to see yourself more clearly and you can use psychotherapy to help you see your blind spots.

Fourth, there is simply cultivating an openness to your everyday experience and all the ups and downs you are bound to face along your life's journey. There are few things that would teach you more about your weaknesses, and maybe even strengths you didn't know you had, than being a parent. Many of us could probably say the same thing about so much else we go through that confronts us with who we are rather than what we thought we were. Just like the friend who will always tell you if you have a piece of lettuce in your teeth, or that you are just full of it; it is hard not to come to a more realistic appreciation of who you are if you are just open and show up to your life.

What Are Ways We Can Practice Humility?

1. *Compliment someone who does something better than you.*

When someone does something better than you or something you are not good at, tell them how well you thought they did it and that it was better than you had done it or could do it. Ask them if they can give you any pointers about how you might be able to do it better.

2. *Tell someone about a time you were genuinely proud of what you did.*

This is to emphasize the part of humility that involves the ability to see and acknowledge your strengths as well as your weaknesses. It is also to acknowledge a kind of pride that can be a healthy and good thing. The key is to only do it when you are genuinely proud of something you did rather than doing it because you need to show you are better than someone else.

3. *Admit to someone you were wrong and say you are sorry.*

You can either wait until the next time you make a mistake or do something wrong, or you can think of something that you did in the past. Get together with the other person involved and tell them you want to take responsibility for your actions and that you appreciate their willingness to listen to you.

4. *Reward others when they are honest about who they are.*

Try to do this both when someone talks about a strength that may be hard to admit and also when someone talks about a weakness. It can be a different person each time but use this as a way to get in the habit of reinforcing people for being honest and authentic about themselves.

12.4. Forgiveness

In the year 2000, Everett Worthington's 76-year-old mother was sexually violated and violently murdered in Knoxville, Tennessee.[30] His brother Mike got so depressed that he killed himself five years later. Everett was a licensed psychologist and not only struggled to forgive his mother's killer but to forgive himself for not being able to save his brother. He was so angry that he wanted to beat the killer's brains out with a baseball bat.

But over time, Everett learned to forgive his mother's killer and forgive himself and began to study forgiveness at Virginia Commonwealth University. He said that, "Chains fell off, a weight was lifted off my shoulders. I felt free. From research, I can tell you that it helps with physical health, mental health, relationships, and spiritual life." While he wanted justice for the killer, he had already found a way to free himself from his own personal prison through forgiveness.

There can be many different kinds of hero's journeys. There is the lifelong journey we have talked about to make the most of our lives and live them to the fullest. There are the many smaller journeys that many of us embark on such as going to school, getting married, having children, growing old, and facing death. There are few hero's journeys that are as challenging as finding the freedom from hatred and sense of peace that can come with forgiveness.

The sacred Hindu scripture called the *Bhagavad Gita* says, "If you want to see the heroic, look at those who can love in return for hatred. If you want to see the brave, look for those who can forgive." There are few instances where the great ordeal of the classic hero's journey is more challenging and more real —but also potentially more surprising and transforming.

What Is Forgiveness?

The great danger in thinking about forgiveness is that it is so often mistaken with what it is not. It is easy to see how we can get confused and turned off by the idea of forgiveness by reading definitions such as those in *Dictionary.com* that define the verb forgive as "to grant pardon or remission of (an offense, debt, etc.); absolve" and "to cancel an indebtedness or liability to."[31] The *Character Strengths and Virtues* handbook takes a somewhat broader view in defining forgiveness as "forgiving others who have done wrong; accepting the shortcomings of others; giving people a second chance; not being vengeful."[32]

As with prudence and humility, it is important to understand what is at the heart of this strength as distinct from what may be an unhealthy distortion. In the best and most constructive sense of the word, forgiveness is the process by which we replace anger and resentment for someone who hurt us with the kindness and compassion that enable us to move on with our lives. It involves an inner change and transformation by which we are no longer obsessed with what someone did but experience a new sense of freedom and peace. The kindness and compassion are for both the offender and for ourselves but does not mean that we have to have a relationship with the offender or that we have to excuse, justify, deny, or forget what they did.

Let me try to expand on the things that are easily confused with forgiveness. First, forgiveness is not excusing or pardoning what another person has done or keeping them from facing the consequences of their actions. There is a story of a mother who forgave the killer of her son and ended up living next door to him but that was only after the killer had been in prison for many years and the mother worked through her anger. That the killer was remorseful and paid a price for what he did made it easier for the mother to forgive him.

Second, forgiveness is not justifying what someone has done or rationalizing that it was okay for them to do it. Although having empathy and understanding why someone hurt you can make it easier to forgive them, forgiveness is not the same thing as understanding what someone did or coming to believe that it was justified. In the movie *Dead Man Walking*, Susan Sarandon plays a Catholic nun who came to forgive a murderer played by Sean Penn. But she forgive him not because she understood why he did what he did but in spite of the fact that she couldn't understand.

Third, forgiveness does not mean denying the harm of what someone has done to you, trying to ignore that it was done, or trying to deny that it had negative consequences. If your best friend is killed by a drunk driver or you become paralyzed in the accident, it would not be fair to yourself to pretend that it wasn't a tragedy with lasting consequences. Kim Phuc is a Vietnamese woman who still suffers the consequences of being burned over 66% of her body by a Napalm attack during the Vietnam war.[33] She will never be able to deny the permanent effects on her skin but she has found a way to forgive the pilots who dropped the bombs.

Fourth, while forgiveness can mean no longer being overwhelmed with anger and resentment and obsessing about revenge, it does not mean having to forget what another person did to hurt you. In many cases, such as being in an abusive marriage or relationship, it is critically important to be able to remember what someone did to avoid going back to them and to notice the warning signs in someone else who may be abusive in the future. The philosopher, poet, and novelist George

Santayana said that "those who cannot remember the past are condemned to repeat it."[34] Remembering what caused you harm without being obsessed by it can keep you safer in the future.

Fifth, forgiveness does not necessarily mean reconciling, getting back together, continuing to relate to someone, or even ever seeing the person who hurt you again. Many people have confused forgiveness with being a doormat and allowing someone to continue to hurt them when it would be obvious to other people that they should stay away. At the same time, we can all make mistakes in hurting others and there are many times when it may be worth the risk to try to reconcile and continue to relate to someone we really care about. This is where great wisdom may be needed but it is important to remember that forgiveness is possible without reconciling with another person.

Sixth, the kindness and compassion cultivated in the process of forgiveness does not mean that you have to like or feel affection for the person who hurt you. It just means that you are free from your own anger and ill will towards them. The idea of tough may be useful in relation to someone you want to forgive. That is, the kindness and compassion you cultivate is not a superficial "niceness" that lets them off the hook. It can include the tough love that allows them to make amends and face the consequences of what they have done. The main thing is that what the person did to you can no longer keep you from being happy and feeling good about yourself and your own life.

What Factors Are Related to Forgiveness?

There are a variety of personal and situational factors that can make it more or less likely that a person will be able to forgive someone who hurt them. The personal factors include being higher on agreeableness and lower on neuroticism in the Big Five personality characteristics. People high on agreeableness tend to be more kind, sympathetic, cooperate, warm, and considerate and may try harder to understand why the other person did what they did and be more willing to try to reduce their feelings of anger and resentment. People who are low on neuroticism may experience less anger and hostility and see the transgression in a less negative light. However, the strongest personal predictors of forgiveness are empathy and perspective-taking because they make it possible to put yourself in the offender's place and understand their need for forgiveness.

The situational factors related to the ability to forgive include the severity of what was done to you, the intention of the offender in doing it, whether they apologize to you or not, and whether they are willing to make amends. Research has shown that the stronger the intention to do you harm and the worse you are hurt, the harder it is to eventually forgive another person. For this reason, it could be so difficult to forgive the intentional killing of your own child or someone else you love very much. There is also evidence suggesting that getting an apology or having the other person at least try to make amends for what they did can make forgiveness easier. The mother of the boy whose son was killed talked about how much it helped that her son's killer apologized and tried to make amends.

How Can Forgiveness Be Fostered?

The process of forgiveness and the things that might facilitate it have been the focus of several prominent forgiveness researchers including Everett Worthington, Michael McCullough, and Robert Enright.[35-37] They have all written books about it and I refer you to them to fully do justice to the process and guide you through it. You may be thinking about forgiving someone for doing something that is relatively minor or it may be something that was much more painful and traumatic. If at any point you think you are in danger of harming yourself or another person, please reach out to a counselor or therapist who can provide you with the professional help you may need to go through the whole process safely.

Here are some of the most important tools that have been suggested for the process of forgiveness:

1. *Social Support*—While it is best to have several support people, be sure that you have a least one person whom you can trust to understand and talk with you as needed when going through this process. Ask them if they are willing to support and talk with you during the process of trying to forgive another person.

2. *Journaling*—Doing focused writing exercises such as those developed by James Pennebaker can be very useful at several points in the process of forgiveness.[38] This writing can involve keeping a daily journal, specifically writing about the experience of being hurt by another person, expressing your thoughts and feelings about them, and eventually writing about what you may have learned or gained from the whole experience.

3. *Meditation*—Mindfulness meditation can be a way of dealing with the intensity of thoughts and feelings that you may experience as well as helping you relax and calm down when you are feeling distressed. Lovingkindness meditation may be even better as it involves cultivating feelings of kindness and compassion that you could direct initially towards yourself and eventually towards the offender.

Here are some of the common elements that are often mentioned as being most important in the process of forgiveness:

1. *Building Self-Compassion*—Going through the whole process of forgiveness can be very demanding and difficult and may require great patience and compassion for yourself. You may need to be patient and kind to yourself if your feelings are stronger than you expect, if you become discouraged and decide to quit, or if it takes you several tries before you feel like you are making any real progress. One way to work on self-compassion is to go to

Kristin Neff's website and take the self-compassion assessment and do the exercises that she recommends.

2. *Acknowledging Your Anger*—Anger and resentment are natural consequences of being hurt by another person. For many, this element may be the most important part of the process of forgiveness, the one that is most painful and difficult, and the one we are most likely to avoid or deny. It involves being willing to fully experience the anger, resentment, and pain as a result of being hurt. Because this can be a long and unpredictable process, it is especially important to be patient and compassionate with yourself and make use of a good friend or counselor when necessary.

3. *Developing Empathy*—While it is not always possible to feel empathy for and take the perspective of the offender, it can make it easier when it is possible. The important thing is not to feel like you have to justify or fully understand what they did. If it is someone who you know and want to continue to have a relationship with, it could be beneficial to hear their perspective if they are capable of talking with you about it in a non-defensive way. In addition, sometimes it may help for you to imagine when you may have done something similar.

4. *Finding Benefits*—This is under the category of stress-related growth that we talked about in Chapter 7 where you learn, grow, finds benefits, or experience some kind of a positive change as a result of stressful events. It is important not to feel like you have to find any benefits unless you are ready and they are genuine. There may be a danger of using this as a way of denying your hurt or anger. It may be difficult to do this if you haven't fully or acknowledged your anger or how much you were hurt.

5. *Demonstrating Forgiveness*—This involves actually doing something to demonstrate your willingness and commitment to forgiving another person or to confirm or express that you have

actually forgiven them. Behavioral psychology emphasizes the value of taking action as a way of changing our thoughts and feelings. This may involve telling the other person that you forgive them when you think you are ready, writing a letter that you don't send if the person has died or if don't think it would be a good idea to talk to them, or just doing something to show your commitment to beginning the process of forgiveness.

What Are Ways We Can Practice Forgiveness?

1. *Forgive yourself for a mistake you made.*

Begin by practicing forgiveness in a small way with yourself. Acknowledge your feelings of anger and frustration with yourself. Practice self-compassion by accepting what you did and give yourself another chance as you would a good friend who you love.

2. *Remember a time you hurt another person and forgive someone who did something similar to you.*

Identify something you did that clearly hurt another person and try to think of another person who hurt you in a similar way. If you can't think of anyone, then imagine how you could respond in a forgiving way if someone does to you in the future something similar to what you did to someone in the past.

3. *Ask someone for forgiveness for something that you did.*

Think of someone to whom you have done something that was hurtful or harmful. Try to think of someone who you like and trust and can talk with about it. Then get together with them and tell them what you thought you did, ask for their forgiveness, and be open to however they respond.

4. *Write about any benefits that came out of being hurt by another person.*

Try to identify a time when you were hurt by another person where you learned something, grew in some way, or noticed some kind of benefit or positive change. Allow yourself to write freely for at least 15 minutes about the benefits, how they make you feel, and how you can use them to make your life better in the future.

5. *Forgive someone you are holding a grudge against.*

Try to identify one thing that someone did to you that you have been holding on to for a long time. See if you can find something with someone who you still see on a regular basis. Whether or not you talk to them, do something to show that you intend to forgive them and let it go.

Using the Strengths of Temperance for the Journey

The strengths of Wisdom help us turn on the light to see the path and those of Courage enable us to face and overcome the obstacles we face. The strengths of Humanity enable us to connect and care for those who are close to us and those of Justice help us make a difference in the larger world. It is easy to underestimate and undervalue the strengths of Temperance that are in such short supply in today's instant gratification culture where there can be so much pressure to show off.

Yet what a tragedy if we were to overlook these often misunderstood, forgotten, and distorted strengths. They offer us so much in restoring balance to our lives. As Luke did when he first held a light saber, we can get so excited by what is flashy and enticing that we rush off before we are ready. We can't even get our boats out of the harbor because we are held back by our lack of self-control, our poor planning, our refusal to honestly face who we are, and our inability to let go of our grudges.

There may be few better examples of the power of Temperance than in the slow but intensely focused process of becoming a martial artist. The original *Karate Kid* movie provides a wonderful example of this when the wise old Kensuke Miyagi teaches a young boy how to learn karate by doing his chores. "Wax on, wax off," he taught the boy to do as he waxed his car.

But it wasn't until Mr. Miyagi went to strike him that the boy realized that he now had the skill needed to deflect the punch and that all along Miyagi had been teaching him to become a master by the simplest everyday task.

The strengths of Temperance are like that. Wax on, wax off. "What the hell am I doing this for?" we might ask. And then it all makes sense. Hone that self-control muscle just by meditating. Prepare to amass a lifetime fortune of happiness by practicing prudence and foresight. Become a great leader by being humble and realistic about who you are. Set yourself free by forgiving. Lift your sails and allow your strengths to carry you forward in the flow and bliss of the wind. But don't forget to take the time to "wax on, wax off"—and realize that this is where you may win some of your greatest battles.

Chapter 13

The Transcendence to Go Above and Beyond

I am the master of my fate, I am the captain of my soul.
—William Ernest Henley[1]

"Keep your feet on the ground and keep reaching for the stars," as we remember the *American Top 40* radio announcer Casey Kasem saying back in Chapter 7. Just as we learned that mindfulness can keep us grounded and self-efficacy is the confidence to reach our goals, so the strengths of Temperance allows us to hone our skills and those of Transcendence enable us to fly. "Wax on, wax off," Mr. Miyagi said to his young protégé.

There are few people whose practice of simple daily disciplines paid off more in reaching for the stars than the man who lived in a seven by eight foot room, slept on a straw mat, and whose job was breaking rocks into gravel. He was first known by the guards as prisoner 46664 and was in prison for 9958 days or 27 years, 10 months, and four days. The prison on the isolated Robben Island where he spent most of his time in prison later came to be known as Mandela University.

Rather than becoming bitter and depressed about his situation, Nelson Mandela "waxed on" and "waxed off" as he became a Big-C citizen and graduated with honors with a triple major in kindness, humility, and forgiveness. His kindness won the respect and admiration of the prison guards, his humility enabled him to become the epitome of a servant leader, and his forgiveness made it possible to avoid great violence and build bridges of compassion where there had only been walls of hatred.

Nelson Mandela went from experiencing the guards urinating around him as he broke rocks into gravel to being elected the president of South Africa. He is a prime example of how it is possible for a person to transcend their humble circumstances and reach for the stars. We may never be the president of a country, just as we may never go to *Hogwarts* or train to be a Jedi knight. But we can learn to fly in the same way that Mandela did as we stay true to our own hero's journey.

This final chapter is about the VIA strengths that, more than anything else, can enable us to reach beyond what we may have ever thought possible. Optimism and hope give us the vision, humor is the ordinary magic that brings laughter and joy to every moment, appreciation and gratitude enable us to see the goodness and beauty all around us, and meaning, purpose, and spirituality make it all worthwhile and enable us to reach for the stars.

13.1. Optimism and Hope

The most unforgettable phrase from the movie *Field of Dreams* is undoubtedly "If you build it, he will come." At first glance, the movie appears to be about baseball, but it is really about something much more universal—the power of hope. From building the Egyptian Pyramids to the Great Wall of China to the Panama Canal to going to the moon, the human ability to envision a better tomorrow and work to make it happen has consistently brought about things that previously would have been considered miracles. There may not be a better explanation for how we can do these kinds of things than the twin strengths of optimism and hope.

What Are Optimism and Hope?

Dictionary.com defines optimism as "a disposition or tendency to look on the more favorable side of events or conditions and to expect the most favorable outcome" and hope as "the feeling that what is wanted can be had or that events will turn out for the best."[2-3] The *Character Strengths and Virtues* handbook defines hope and optimism together as "expecting the best in the future and working to achieve it; believing that a good future is something that can be brought about" (p. 30).[4]

The study of optimism and hope in psychology has relied on two questionnaires on optimism and one questionnaire on hope that will help us define them both. Charles Carver and Michael Scheier developed the *life orientation test* which assesses optimism as the general expectation that good things will happen in the future.[5] Rick Snyder has developed a measure of hope that assesses it as having the will and the ways to reach our goals.[6] He developed a theory of hope which asserts that the ability to realize our hopes depends on having a sense of agency which involves motivation and confidence (the will) and identifying realistic pathways (the ways) to reach our goals.

Martin Seligman and his colleagues have taken a different approach to optimism.[7] They have studied what they call "explanatory style," which involves the attributions we make about why the events in our lives have happened. They believe that optimistic people are those who think that bad events are things that (1) aren't their fault, (2) can be changed, and (3) do not generalize to other events; whereas pessimistic people see bad events as things that (1) are their fault, (2) can't be changed, and (3) mean that other things will go wrong, too. They and other researchers have found that having an optimistic explanatory style leads to better outcomes in the future.

I will use a working definition for optimism and hope based on Scheier and Carver and Snyder's work because they focus on distinct aspects of optimism and hope. At the same time, I think it is important to keep Seligman's work on attributional style in mind as a way of understanding how optimism and hope may be expressed in our cognitions and what we can target in trying to increase them both. Thus, I will define optimism as the general expectation that good things will happen in the future and hope as both the confidence to make them happen and an idea of how to make them happen.

What Difference Do Optimism and Hope Make?

Optimism and hope are some of the strongest and most consistent predictors of a variety of positive outcomes. They have been related to better mental health including lower levels of anxiety, depression, and negative emotion and better physical health including better adjustment to chronic pain and illness. They have also both been related to better relationships and higher levels of social support, better functioning at school and work, and better performance in sports and athletics. Finally, they are some of the strongest predictors of happiness, life satisfaction, and the positive emotion, engagement, and meaning elements of Seligman's PERMA model of well-being.[8]

Although people have written about the dangers of false or unrealistic optimism, there is very little evidence suggesting that optimism and hope are bad things. One exception is what has been called the "optimism bias," which is the belief that most of us have that we are less at risk of experiencing a negative event compared to other people. For example, this may make it more likely that we would not engage in safe sex or that we would engage in risky activities such as gambling or riding a motorcycle. However, the optimism bias may not be related to generally being optimistic or hopeful, which may actually make one less likely to engage in risk taking activities because optimism and hope are usually related to better planning.

In understanding the value of optimism and hope, it is critical to make a distinction between them and "positive thinking." Positive thinking is sometimes used to refer to the general expectation that good things will happen in the future but is also used to mean that just thinking about a positive thing happening will actually cause it to happen. Self-help books may capitalize on the fact that there is often a correlation between thinking about the future in a positive way and something positive actually happening in the future. Optimism and hope, in the way I am defining them, do not imply that just thinking about something will itself cause it to occur.

Why Do Optimism and Hope Make a Difference?

Why do we often find positive correlations between optimism and hope and a variety of good outcomes in the future? You may remember Shelley Taylor's experiment that I talked about in Chapter 7 when we discussed self-efficacy.[9] She compared the effect of just thinking about getting an A on a test to thinking about studying for a test. She found that those who thought about studying did better on the test and that it was related to the fact that they studied more. One reason that optimism and hope may make a difference is that they make it more likely that you will be able to do what you need to do to practice and prepare for the task. The danger in assuming that all you need to do is think about the outcome, as in positive thinking, is that it may make it less likely to do what it takes to make it happen.

The other reasons why optimism and hope may make positive outcomes more possible are that you may be more likely to try to reach your goal in the first place and more likely to persist in the face of obstacles. Carver and Scheier developed their measure of optimism because they believed that it was important in working towards goals.[10] They found that people who are more optimistic are more likely to continue to try even when the going gets tough. They have also found that optimistic people use more active approaches in dealing with stress including planning and problem-solving rather than the avoidant approaches that pessimists use such as denying, drinking alcohol, and using drugs.

Rick Snyder's theory of hope brings the value of positive expectations to another level by breaking down what is involved in reaching a goal.[11] First, there is a need to identify an important goal. No matter how positive your expectations are about the future, you may drift aimlessly through your life if you have no sense of where you want to go. Second, there is a need to have the will, which includes the confidence or self-efficacy that it takes to reach the goal. Third, there is a need to identify a way, or maybe even several alternative ways, to reach the goal. So while some kinds of positive thinking in self-help books only stress having the goal, it is also important to identify how you might be able to reach your goal and how to build your confidence for the journey.

There is also sometimes a false dichotomy between optimism and realism. Some of the most vocal critics of the positive psychology movement equate it with the kind of positive thinking that denies some of the harsh and negative realities of life. While some who claim to be positive thinkers or positive psychologists may do this, there is no reason why it is not possible to look even the most disturbing realities square in the eye and work for something better in the future. In fact, the belief that there is a possibility for something better may actually make it more likely that you will be able to face a harsh reality.

How Can Optimism and Hope Be Fostered?

Here is where I think it can be particularly useful to focus on the three factors in Rick Snyder's theory and tie them in with what we have talked about with other strengths and elements of well-being from the rest of this book. If we can increase our will and ways to reach our goals, as Snyder defines hope, we will also naturally come to expect good things to happen in the future. Here are three ways we can increase optimism and hope:

1. *What is our goal?*

The first thing that is critical for increasing our hope and optimism is to identify some goals and start with one goal that is particularly important to us. Again, it should follow the SMART acronym and be something that is Specific, Measurable, Achievable, Relevant, and Time-bound.[12] Some of the things we have discussed so far that can provide perspective for this may be to clarify your values, identify your top strengths, and understand which elements of well-being are most important to you. Nelson Mandela's goal while he was in prison was at first to simply survive and the goal of many undergraduate students reading this as a textbook may be to graduate from college.

2. *What are the possible pathways to our goal?*

The second thing that is critical for increasing our hope and optimism is to identify possible ways to achieve our goals. This can involve the two-step process we talked about in relation to creativity where you begin by using divergent thinking to brainstorm different ideas and then use convergent thinking to decide upon the first one to try. To help generate new ideas, you can learn how others like you have done it by reading and talking to other people. If your goal is to graduate from college, there are excellent books on how college students have faced specific challenges that may provide good ideas about possible pathways. When he was in prison, Mandela discovered the idea of not allowing being in prison to change who he was, which helped him meet his initial goal of surviving.

3. *How do we increase our confidence in doing what it takes?*

The third thing that is critical for increasing our hope and optimism is to build our confidence that we can achieve our goal. Here, the research about self-efficacy is wonderfully instructive and useful. The kind of self-efficacy that may be most helpful is not the confidence that we can reach our goal, but the confidence that we can do what it takes to reach the goal. It also may be important to have a certain amount of confidence in ourselves just to imagine the goal in the first place and then to imagine possible pathways.

But once we have done both of these things, we don't have to believe that we have to jump like Michael Jordan and do everything—all we need to do is to focus on taking the next step. As we saw in Chapter 7, the ways to learn self-efficacy are well-established and include practicing doing the task, observing others like us doing it, imagining ourselves doing it, finding people who can support us, and simply learning to relax by breathing or practicing meditation. As for graduating from college, this could mean finding successful students who can be mentors and practicing the study habits they can teach us. We could learn relaxation techniques to help us deal with test anxiety and get tutoring for learning to write better.

As for Nelson Mandela, he found a simple and more elegant way to boost his confidence and increase the will he needed to answer his call to adventure in a poem by William Ernest Henley:

> Out of the night that covers me,
> Black as the pit from pole to pole,
> I thank whatever gods may be
> For my unconquerable soul.
>
> In the fell clutch of circumstance
> I have not winced nor cried aloud.
> Under the bludgeoning of chance
> My head is bloody, but unbowed.

Beyond this place of wrath and tears
Looms but the Horror of the shade,
And yet the menace of the years
Finds, and shall find me, unafraid.

It matters not how strait the gate,
How charged with punishments the scroll,
I am the master of my fate,
I am the captain of my soul.[13]

The movie *Invictus* shows how this poem of the same name became an enduring inspiration for Mandela. It not only enabled him to survive, but thrive, and later become the president who brought hope and unity to a country torn by hatred and racial strife. The way to build optimism and hope is not by avoiding or denying reality. It may be to do what Rick Snyder recommended by clearly identifying what you want and then doing it takes to find the will and the ways to achieve it.

What Can We Do to Practice Optimism and Hope?

1. *Write about your best possible self.*

Imagine that everything has gone as well as it possibly could for you in next five years. Write for at least 15 minutes in detail about what your life would be like. Who would you be with, where would you be living, and what would you be doing?

2. *Identify a time you overcame a challenge and succeeded.*

Write about what enabled you to find the will and the way to do it. What helped you feel confident enough to do what it took to succeed? How did you find your way? Think about how you can use what you learned to face similar challenges in the future.

3. *Choose a goal and brainstorm with a friend about how to meet it.*

Write down three SMART (Specific, Measurable, Achievable, Relevant, and Time-bound) goals that you would like to achieve by one year from today. Choose your favorite goal and ask a friend to help you brainstorm about how to achieve it. Visualize yourself doing what you think it will take.

4. *Use a quote on hope or optimism.*

Identify a quote that inspires you to be more optimistic and hopeful about your future. Write it down, memorize it, and say it out loud when you get up and before you go to bed for one week. Keep it in our wallet or purse and take it out and read it when you get discouraged.

5. *Actively cope with a challenge that you are facing.*

Select a challenge that you are facing in the next couple weeks. Brainstorm about all the different ways that you may be able to deal with it. Then rate the ways that you came up with and choose the best one. Imagine yourself dealing with it that way and then follow through in doing it. Pat yourself on the back for doing it regardless of the outcome.

13.2. Humor

Norman Cousins was a writer and editor of the popular London newspaper the *Saturday Review*. He developed a crippling and usually irreversible disorder called ankylosing spondylitis that left him racked with chronic pain. He had difficulty moving his limbs, his jaws were locked, and he could hardly turn over in bed. He was losing hope of ever finding any relief until he began reading about the negative effects of stress on the body. He wondered if laughter might counteract some of these effects and decided to try watching the funniest things he could think of. He got copies of the old television show *Candid Camera* and

Marx Brothers films sent to his hospital room. His nurse learned how to use the old projector they needed in order to show them.

The nurse pulled down the blinds and turned on the machine and Cousins found out that, "It worked. I made the joyous discovery that ten minutes of genuine belly laughter had an anesthetic effect and would give me at least two hours of pain-free sleep" (p. 39).[14] Although it continued to work for him, he had to move to a hotel to continue because his laughter was disturbing the other patients in the hospital. Being able to laugh was his first big step in finding relief from his painful condition and before long he was completely free of it. Norman Cousins was one of the first people to write about the healing power of laughter in his book *The Anatomy of an Illness* and later became an adjunct professor of Medical Humanities at UCLA.[15]

He thought that humor may be one of our greatest gifts and a hidden force for health and healing. It is a strength that may help us transcend our weaknesses and transport us to a happier place. What is humor and how can we benefit from it?

What Is Humor?

Dictionary.com defines humor as "the faculty of perceiving what is amusing or comical" and "the faculty of expressing the amusing or comical."[16] The *Character Strengths and Virtues* handbook equates humor with playfulness and defines it as "liking to laugh and tease; bringing smiles to other people; seeing the light side; making (not necessarily telling) jokes" (p. 30).[17] Willibald Ruch defines it as three things: (1) the playful recognition, enjoyment, and/or creation of incongruities, (2) a composed and cheerful view on adversity that allows one to see the light side and thereby sustain a good mood, and (3) the ability to make others smile or laugh" (p. 584).[18]

I will define the strength of humor as the ability to playfully recognize and express things that make people laugh. This includes both being able to see and experience what makes people laugh and being able to express this to another person. While this idea of humor does not necessarily involve being able to express humor in a formal way such as telling jokes, it does mean being able to share funny things in a way that can lead others to laugh. Also, while humor often involves the sudden recognition that something is absurd, out of place, or the opposite of what was expected, the key element in this definition is simply the urge to laugh.

Although some animals exhibit behavior similar to laughter, humor appears to be a uniquely human behavior that strongly depends on language and social intelligence. Norman Dixon proposed that humor evolved in humans to enable them to survive living close together after developing larger communities.[19] While ancient writers often viewed humor as a negative thing, more recently physicians and psychologists have begun to appreciate its potential value. Sigmund Freud saw it as a way to release defensive tension and George Valliant views it as a mature defense mechanism.[20-21] Valliant distinguishes between self-deprecating humor that is adaptive and hostile humor that is used to control others.

In thinking about humor as a potential strength that can increase happiness and well-being, Valliant suggests it is important to remember that humor can also be used in harmful ways. Constructive and destructive humor can be distinguished by both the intent and the outcome. Constructive humor often involves the playful discovery of incongruity and absurdity without demeaning or making fun of another person. Destructive humor involves intentionally trying to put down, ridicule, or harm another person. However, humor that involves making fun of or laughing at another's expense may be used for constructive purposes if it is a way of speaking out against the harmful behavior of authority figures or those in power.

What Are the Different Kinds of Humor?

Within these broad distinction between constructive and destructive humor, there are many subtypes of humor and most can be used either for benefit or for harm. There are many forms of verbal humor that involve word play and the use of language. The classic form is a joke which is a short story which ends with a surprising twist. One example of a joke addressing the challenge of talking about humor has been attributed to the American writer E.B. White: "Explaining humor is like dissecting a frog, the subject dies in the process."[22] Banter or repartee is the playful and generally friendly exchange of teasing remarks. The comics Abbott and Costello who did the "Who's on first?" routine often made great use of banter.

Understatement is saying that something is smaller, worse, or less important than it actually is and overstatement or hyperbole is doing the opposite. An example of understatement is to say "it is a little warm outside" after coming in to an air conditioned room on a 120 degree mid-summer day in Phoenix, Arizona. An example of overstatement might be to say your friend who just left the air conditioned room to join you outside, "Welcome to Hell!" Sarcasm involves saying the opposite of what you intended usually in a mocking or ridiculing way such as saying to your friend who invited you to visit you in Phoenix in July: "I sure have enjoyed this weather. In fact, I can't wait to come back next summer!"

Satire and parody are used to criticize and make fun of the vices or shortcomings of other people. Satire is a way of exposing other people to scorn or ridicule. Mark Twain used satire to challenge the political corruption and social ills of his day. It does not always result in laughter and is often used in literature and the arts. The *Onion* is a satirical newspaper that takes the form of traditional news organizations to make fun of the tone and format of real news. Parody is a spoof or take-off of an original work. The 1987 movie *Space Balls* was a parody of *Star Wars* that included a very short statured version of Darth Vader with a very large helmet called Dark Helmet. The never-ending *Scary Movie* series is a parody of the horror film genre.

Aside from verbal humor, there is physical humor, practical jokes, and situational humor. Physical humor involves movement rather than the use of language and can include slapstick and physical violence. Examples are the physical antics of the *Three Stooges*, getting hit with a pie in the face, and the exaggerated physical action in many cartoons. A practical joke is a trick played on another person to surprise them and make them look silly or foolish and make other people laugh. An example might be replacing someone's toothpaste with foot cream as the main character did in the movie *Amelie*. Finally, situational humor simply involves being able to recognize and appreciate the humor in everyday life.

How Is Humor Related to Personality and Health?

People who have a good sense of humor tend to be higher on extraversion, lower on neuroticism, and higher on measures of cheerfulness and optimism. People who are witty tend to be higher in intelligence and creativity. Wittiness is a specific ability that is characterized by the quick and keen ability to see the incongruities and contradictions around them in a way that makes other people laugh. The word "gelotophobe" has been coined to identify those who have a fear of being laughed at, and these people may be higher in humility and prudence and lower in hope, curiosity, bravery, love, and zest.

Research on humor and health has shown that constructive humor appears to have many benefits for mental and physical health and for coping with stress. Higher levels of humor have generally been related to less anxiety, depression, and negative emotion and greater life satisfaction and well-being.[23] Millicent Abel and David Maxwell found that just watching a humorous video reduced anxiety and increased positive affect in both high and low stress situations.[24] Charles Carver and colleagues studied the effects of different coping strategies for women having surgery for breast cancer.[25] They found that the use of humor was related to lower levels of psychological distress before and after surgery and at three, six, and 12 months after the surgery.

Paul McGhee thinks that humor is related to better physical health through its effects on the cardiovascular system, immune system, and the response to painful stimuli.[26] James Rotten and Mark Shats tested what Norman Cousins reported on how humor may relieve pain.[27] They found that orthopedic surgery patients who watched a humorous video of their choice requested less pain medication than patients who watched a dramatic video. Michelle Newman and Arthur Stone found evidence that humor may reduce the effects of stress through cognitive reappraisal.[28] They found that those who created a humorous monologue to go with a stressful film had a lower heart rate and skin conductance response than those who created a serious monologue.

How Can Humor Be Fostered?

Although in Norman Cousin's time it was difficult to get access to copies of funny television shows and movies, it is now much easier to find and repeatedly enjoy the things that make us laugh. Does this really make it easier for us to laugh and increase our sense of humor? Researchers have begun to test the effects of interventions that may increase humor. Fabian Gander and his colleagues tested a "three funny things" intervention where people were instructed to write down the three funniest things they experienced or did every day for a week and include an explanation of why they think these funny things happened. They found that this exercise increased happiness and decreased depression at the end of the week and one month and three months later.[29]

Paul McGhee developed a structured humor intervention called *The 7 Humor Habits Program*.[30] The goals of the program are to show that humor can be strengthened, to increase humor, to increase positive emotions, to decrease negative emotions, and to increase resilience and the ability to cope with stress. There have been several studies showing that the program has increased positive emotions, life satisfaction, cheerfulness, optimism, and self-efficacy and decreased negative emotions, anxiety, depression, and perceived stress. In addition, studies have shown a reduction in clinical levels of depression with one study showing that the rate of depression dropped from 38% to 9.5%. Finally, the studies with follow-up assessments showed that many of these changes were sustained two months after the end of the program.

The *7 Humor Habits Program* includes steps for learning each of the seven habits. There is a rationale for each of the habits and suggestions for how to practice each of them in doing "home play." The seven habits include surrounding yourself with humor, cultivate a playful attitude, laughing more often and more heartily, creating your own verbal humor, looking for humor in everyday life, taking yourself lightly and learning to laugh at yourself, and finding humor in the midst of stress. This is a multi-pronged approach that provides many different strategies that may be effective for different kinds of people. They include both passive activities that involve recognizing the humor that is already there all around us and active techniques for finding and creating new instances of humor.

What Can We Do to Practice Humor?

1. *Remember the funniest lines.*

Search the Internet for your favorite routines by your favorite comedians. Write down the things they say that you think are the funniest. Keep the list in your wallet or purse and review it regularly and repeat them when your stress level is high.

2. *Keep a humor log.*

Use your phone or a notepad to keep track of anything that happens that makes you laugh. Write it down and share it with a friend or family member at the end of the week. If you have time, create a fictional story that includes all of these funny things to help you remember them and continue to laugh.

3. *Get a funny buddy.*

Get one of your friends to exchange funny stories or pictures every day for two weeks. Alternate days with you sending one to your friend one day and your friend sending one to you the next day. Notice how your senses of humor are different and find ways to continue to share funny things.

4. *Memorize three jokes to tell your friends.*

Search lists of jokes to find three jokes that you like and that are short enough to remember. Memorize them and practice telling them to your friends. Even if you don't think you are good at telling jokes, give yourself a chance to find jokes you really like, practice telling them, and see how much your timing and general ability to tell a joke may improve.

13.3. Appreciation of Beauty and Excellence

The year was coming to an end and it had been one of the most tumultuous, disturbing, and tragic years in the history of the United States. It was 1968 and civil unrest and the Vietnam War were getting out of control. Martin Luther King, Jr. was assassinated on April 4 and Robert F. Kennedy was assassinated on June 5. The country needed a little hope. The world needed something special. We got it in what the wilderness photographer Galen Rowell called the most influential photograph ever taken. The photograph was taken on Christmas

Eve by astronaut William Anders as his Apollo 8 spacecraft circled the moon. Soon the picture was shared with everyone on earth.[31] In the picture, you can see the Earth floating peacefully in space, like a blue and white jewel in the sky above the moon. This picture gave us a vision of beauty and unity that we so desperately needed. The photo is called *Earthrise* and it is a prime example of how beauty can make a difference.

What Is the Appreciation of Beauty and Excellence?

Although there is no dictionary definition of "the appreciation of beauty and excellence," Jonathan Haidt and Dacher Keltner say it can also simply be called "appreciation" (p. 537).[32] The Oxford online dictionary gives a definition of appreciation as "the recognition and enjoyment of the good qualities of someone or something."[33] This is close to the definition of the "appreciation of beauty and excellence" in the *Character Strengths and Virtues* handbook as "noticing and appreciating beauty, excellence, and/or skilled performance in various domains of life, from nature to art to mathematics to science to everyday experience."[34]

In essence, appreciation or the appreciation of beauty and excellence is the ability to see, enjoy, and respond to the goodness all around us. This ability to appreciate is echoed in the appreciation of beauty in ancient Greece and in the sense of awe and wonder that most major world religions have associated with the experience of the sacred or the divine. In psychology, William James contrasted what he called "healthy-minded people" who could see the good in almost anything with "sick-minded people" who could not.[35] Similarly, Abraham Maslow contrasted people who could have epiphanies and transforming peak experiences with those who were so rational and materialistic that they could not.[36]

Haidt and Keltner have suggested that there may be three major kinds of goodness to appreciate and three corresponding emotional responses.[37] First, there is the appreciation of physical beauty which may include the visual beauty of the environment and the auditory beauty of music. The appreciation of beauty typically produces the emotion or experience of awe. Haidt and Keltner think that awe consists of both perceiving something to be vast and also having difficulty fully comprehending it. When I took visitors from China to the Grand Canyon they stood in silence with their eyes and mouths wide open, which is a common expression of awe.

Second, there is the appreciation of great skill or talent which might include watching a quarterback rally his football team to victory in the Super Bowl or a lead guitarist improvising during the climactic solo in your favorite song. The appreciation of skill or talent is normally associated with the positive emotion of admiration which is a warm and pleasurable positive emotion that makes us feel closer to others. Third, there is the appreciation of moral goodness or virtue which might include watching a documentary about someone like Mother Teresa, reading a biography of Gandhi, or just seeing someone reach out and comfort someone else in distress. The appreciation of moral goodness is normally accompanied by the emotion Jonathan Haidt called "elevation" which involves a feeling of spreading warmth in the chest and feeling connected with other people.

What Are the Benefits of Appreciation?

Most scientists who study emotions think that they have evolved for a specific purpose that involves a tendency to actually do something. As we learned earlier, negative emotions such as anger may ready us for fighting and fear may ready us for running, while positive emotions may have more delayed effects in helping us broaden and build our resources for the future. Awe and wonder might motivate us to stop and take in all the vastness of what had been a mystery so we can begin to understand it. Admiration might motivate us to achieve the same kind of skill or mastery ourselves. Elevation may inspire us to imitate and follow in the footsteps of those who are kind and compassionate to others.

The ability to appreciate the goodness around us may be a largely hidden key to making the most of our lives. While depreciation involves a reduction in the value of something, appreciation is the means by which something increases in value. Appreciation involves savoring by focusing on something in such a way that we can enjoy it fully and completely. Appreciation is a powerful way of increasing the value of what we already have in our lives without spending a dime. While modern advertising may try to persuade us that we need more to be happy, appreciation is the ordinary magic by which we can see how much happier we can be with what we already have.

Finally, appreciation can even be used in the most painful and difficult situations to help us cope and transform tragedy and stress. There are many experiences in stories and movies of how this may be effective. From one perspective the movie *American Beauty* is about the murder of the main character, but from another the murder is just the backdrop for his transformation from a meaningless life to seeing the goodness and beauty all around him. Another example is from *The Shawshank Redemption* when Andy Dufresne risks getting put into solitary confinement to play a beautiful piece of music over the prison loudspeaker. That he not only played the song but turned it up in the face of the warden is a testament to our human ability to increase our awareness of what is beautiful and good in even the worst circumstances.

How Can Appreciation Be Fostered?

The ways that we can increase appreciation can be thought of as being part of three different phases. We can increase appreciation by seeing and creating more good around us, mindfully paying attention to and savoring things in the present, and thinking about how to respond to and use the emotions of awe, admiration, and elevation.

1. *Recognizing More of the Good*

This has been a primary goal of the positive psychology movement and involves countering our bias to focus only on the negative at the expense of the positive. This includes finding ways to see and recognize good things in the small and seemingly insignificant events of everyday life. You might want to divide this up into physical beauty, great skill or talent, and moral goodness, or just start with one of these categories. Then begin keeping a daily log of new examples as you see or think of them. You might want to write down at least one new thing every day, brainstorm by yourself or with your friends, or surf the Internet for examples. The idea is to develop a growing list and to get better at spotting the good things around you.

2. *Savoring the Goodness*

This is where you take time to just pay attention to and fully experience the good things you have identified. If it is something physically beautiful, give yourself the time and space to relax and pay full attention to what you see and fully experience it with all of your senses. When you find yourself getting distracted or are judging yourself for not doing it right, simply return your attention to the object of beauty. If you are focusing on an act of great skill or talent, take the time to continue to watch it if you have it on video. If you cannot watch it that way, take time to remember and think about what it took to acquire that skill or talent. If you are focusing on an act of moral goodness or virtue, do the same in watching or reading about it and take time to reflect on it.

3. *Responding to the Goodness*

After you have identified and taken the time to appreciate and savor something, then sit with the questions "What do I feel like doing? How can I do justice to the goodness that I have seen and experienced? What can I do to have the experience more, to honor and show my appreciation for it, or to make it possible for another person to experience it? If it is physical beauty, it could be keeping a picture of it in your wallet or sharing it with others through email. If it is skill or talent, it might be using it as a motivation to practice and get better at something similar or something you love to do. If it is moral goodness, it might be doing something similar for someone else or otherwise honoring what you saw someone do.

What Can We Do to Practice Appreciation?

1. *Google "beautiful" pictures.*

Give yourself at least 30 minutes and google the images associated with the word "beautiful." See what you think is most beautiful and refine your search until you have found several pictures you can save and take time to savor every day.

2. *Find examples of moral goodness.*

Think of at least one example from your life and one historical or fictional character you admire for their goodness. Think about why you choose them and identify specific things that they have said and done that help you appreciate them.

3. *Watch extraordinary athletic or musical feats.*

Find a video of an extraordinary athletic or musical performance. Watch the video several times and pay attention to the feelings and thoughts that arise. Think about why you chose the examples you did and what makes them special.

4. *Appreciate your daily life.*

Identify one place or thing in your daily routine that has something beautiful about it. When you see it, take time to fully focus on it, take a few deep breaths, and allow yourself to savor its beauty or goodness. Let it be a reminder to appreciate beauty.

13.4. Gratitude

When I was eight years old I shared a bedroom with my six-year-old brother. I have to admit that I was a little jealous that he seemed to get a lot of my parents' attention and that they seemed to take his side a bit too much when we argued. One night when we were both sleeping I had a dream that he died and I still remember how sad I felt. When I woke up and realized that I may have been dreaming, I looked over and saw him lying in his bed. As fast as I could, I jumped over on his bed and started shaking him. I'm sure he thought I was attacking him but when he opened his eyes I was overjoyed. I don't remember ever taking him for granted again.

The movie *It's a Wonderful Life* was voted by the *American Film Institute* to be number one on the list of all-time most inspiring American movies. It is the story of a man who took his life for granted. George Bailey was so depressed about the possibility of losing his family business that he almost took his life until an angel showed him what would have happened if he had never been born. He realized how much others would miss him and most of all how much he would miss the people he loved. When he was able to go back to his old life, he was overjoyed and had a profound sense of gratitude for being alive and having his family and friends.

The chorus of Joni Mitchell's song *Big Yellow Taxi* begins "Don't it always seem to go that you don't know what you've got till it's gone." That is the way it was for George Bailey and for me after I had the dream about my brother. Fortunately we both got another chance. Nothing had really changed about the external circumstances of our lives. The only thing that changed was our perspective; the gratitude made all of the difference. It is difficult to imagine that anything we could ever learn at *Hogwarts* or from Yoda or Obi-wan could do more to increase our ability to enjoy our lives or make us feel that they are really worth living.

What Is Gratitude?

Dictionary.com defines gratitude as the "quality of feeling or being grateful or thankful" and grateful as being "warmly or deeply appreciative of kindness or benefits received."[38-39] The *Character Strengths and Virtues* handbook defines gratitude as "being aware of and thankful for the good things that happen; taking time to express thanks" (p. 30).[40] Robert Emmons defines it as "a sense of thankfulness and joy in response to receiving a gift, whether the gift be a tangible benefit from a specific other or a moment of peaceful bliss evoked by natural beauty" (p. 554).[41]

Robert Emmons has been a pioneer of the psychological study of gratitude.[42] He thinks that gratitude involves both the acknowledgement of having received a gift and an appreciation and recognition of the value of that gift. He also makes the distinction between personal gratitude which involves feeling grateful to another person and transpersonal gratitude which involves being grateful for something other than another person. This could include being grateful to God or a higher power but could also include gratitude for the universe, nature, or simply for good fortune.

Emmons and others have proposed that gratitude may be an emotion that has evolved to serve social and at least three moral functions. First, it may serve as a moral barometer letting us know when someone else has done something for us. Second, it may serve as a moral motive influencing us to give back to others. Third, gratitude may serve as a moral reinforcer that encourages and rewards us for what we have previously done for other people. While revenge may punish and deter harmful behavior, gratitude may have evolved as the converse to reward and reinforce helpful behavior.

What Are the Characteristics of Grateful People?

There may be several things that are characteristic of people who have gratitude as a strength. First, they are more likely to be higher in personal characteristics such as optimism, empathy, and forgiveness, and lower on narcissism. The sense of entitlement in narcissism naturally makes it harder to see anything as a gift. Second, people who have higher levels of gratitude have better relationships and more positive social interactions that may result from the reciprocally rewarding behavior that gratitude fosters. Third, grateful people are consistently higher in life satisfaction and especially positive emotion and somewhat lower on stress and depression.

In addition, there are several dimensions along which people may vary on gratitude. First, grateful people may have greater gratitude intensity, which is the strength of the emotion of gratitude for a given gift from another person. Second, they may have a greater gratitude frequency, which is how often during a given period of time they feel grateful. Third, they may have a greater gratitude span which is the number of different things they are grateful for at a given time. Fourth, they might have a greater gratitude density which is the number of people they feel grateful to for any one given positive thing. Finally, grateful people tend to attribute gifts from others as being more costly, valuable, and genuine than people who are less grateful.

Do Gratitude Interventions Make a Difference?

There is evidence that at least four interventions can increase gratitude and a variety of positive outcomes. The first has been called "counting blessings" and simply involves writing up to five things down on a daily or weekly basis that you are grateful for. Robert Emmons has examined this by comparing the effect of counting blessings with recording either neutral events, recording daily hassles, or with a no treatment control group.[43] He has found that those who counted their blessings had higher levels of optimism, positive emotions, life satisfaction, engaged in more helping behavior, and even exercised more than those in the control groups.

The original "counting your blessings" intervention has morphed into other forms including the one that was part of a weeklong online intervention done by Martin Seligman and his colleagues.[44] However, rather than counting blessings they had people write down three good things that happened to them during the day and write about why they think they happened. They found that although there were no effects immediately after the interventions, those who did this had higher levels of happiness and lower levels of depression than a control group three and six months after the intervention.

The third gratitude intervention adds a strong social dimension and was also included as an online intervention by Seligman and his colleagues. It has simply been called the "gratitude visit" and involves writing a letter expressing gratitude.[45] The idea is to identify someone who one has not fully or properly thanked and then deliver the letter to them. Although the effects of this intervention only lasted one month and did not extend to three and six months, it had the strongest effect right after the intervention and one month later of all the five interventions in the study

The fourth intervention was an expansion of the counting blessings exercise using a Naikan meditation technique. David Chan did the eight-week online intervention with Chinese school teachers.[46] Although there was no control group, he divided the participants into those who were high or low on gratitude. He had them identify three things in the past week that they were grateful for and spend at least 15 minutes a week reflecting on the questions "What did I receive?" "What did I give?" and "What more could I do?" Both the high and low gratitude groups had increased positive affect and the low gratitude group also had increases in gratitude and life satisfaction.

How Can Gratitude Be Fostered?

From reviewing these interventions and the qualities and characteristics associated with gratitude, it appears that gratitude can be fostered by increasing awareness, personal reflection, and social sharing. First, increasing awareness involves becoming more aware of the full range of things that we can be grateful for. The counting your blessings exercise may enable us to do this by including things in our past and the three good things exercise may help us see more of the good things that occur in our everyday lives. Thus, they may help us increase both the span and the frequency of our gratitude.

Second, personal reflection may enable us to increase both the intensity and the density of our gratitude. This could be done by writing exercises such as the gratitude visit or by meditative reflection with Naikan-like questions. Writing a gratitude letter may help us experience more intense and lasting feelings of gratitude and writing about everyone who helped us with one big thing may help increase our gratitude density. Using Naikan-like questions may also help us understand gratitude's social and moral functions. Finally, it may also be useful to reflect or write about the value, cost, and genuineness of what we receive.

Third, the social sharing of our gratitude may not just intensify the feeling of gratitude and help us to appreciate its value and cost, it may also foster an upward spiral of reciprocity. If gratitude evolved to strengthen the give and take in our relationships, then finding more ways to share it with others may help us take advantage of its benefits. Sharing a gratitude letter may be one good way to share our gratitude but we might increase all four dimensions of gratitude if we make it a habit of sharing what we are grateful for with whomever we can whenever we can.

What Can We Do to Practice Gratitude?

1. *Carry Post-It notes to express your gratitude.*

Keep a pad of Post-It notes with you so you can use them to write brief thank you notes. Either give them to people directly or leave them where they will find them. You don't need to write much. The main thing is just to give them something to show your appreciation.

2. *Write one brief gratitude email every day.*

Make a list of at least seven people you are grateful to and send an email to one every day in the next week. You can simply begin by something like, "I never got the chance to..." or "I really want to make sure I say thank for you for..."

3. *Thank someone who is a public servant or gives you good service.*

Take the time to thank public servants including police, firefighters, garbage collectors, or thank a cashier, waitress, or waiter who gives you good service. Try to be specific about what you appreciate about them and what they did for you.

4. *Create gratitude reminders for yourself.*

Make of list of the things you are most grateful for and find creative ways to give yourself reminders about them when you might need them. For example, send a delayed email to yourself, program the alarm on your phone, or leave notes for yourself.

13.5. Meaning, Purpose, and Spirituality

He was not what you would call a happy guy. He was described by those that knew him as gloomy, sensitive, sorrowful, anxious, and sad—and was often depressed. He was estranged from his father, lost his fiancé, and two of his children died. He failed in business, had a high strung and difficult wife, and some worried about him committing suicide. He also had a very stressful and demanding job—but that job also gave him a sense of meaning and purpose. And that sense of purpose is what helped him keep everything else in perspective. That purpose was keeping the country together and that man was Abraham Lincoln.[47]

He is just one example of what difference it can make to have a sense of meaning and purpose in life. The psychiatrist Viktor Frankl wrote in *Man's Search for Meaning* about how a sense of meaning and purpose helped him survive four concentration camps during World War II when those around him were dying.[48] Abraham Lincoln was burdened with a life-long vulnerability to depression in a time when there was no *Prozac*. But having a higher purpose enabled him to transcend it and give a great gift to others. He is a shining example of stress-related growth in using his own pain and suffering to develop the wisdom and empathy he needed to lead the country. Like Nelson Mandela, he completed his hero's journey with an elixir of wisdom and grace that allowed a whole nation to find hope and begin to heal.

Having a sense of meaning and purpose and being connected with something larger than ourselves is what this final strength is about. In many ways and for many people, it may represent both the overarching goal and the driving force of our most challenging and rewarding journeys. It can be the ultimate call to adventure, the source of both our greatest trials and ordeals and our greatest joy and fulfillment, and it can be the very substance of the gift that we may have to offer back to the world. How can we foster this strength and use its great power to make our life worth living?

What Are Meaning, Purpose, and Spirituality?

This final strength of Transcendence is so rich and multi-faceted that it took three words to describe it. The *Character Strengths and*

Virtues handbook defines them together as "having coherent beliefs about the higher purpose and meaning of the universe; knowing where one fits within the larger scheme; having beliefs about the meaning of life that shape conduct and provide comfort."[49]

Although they may best exist together, they can also be defined separately. Meaning is our understanding of who we are, what the world is like, and how we fit in it. Purpose is having a long-term and overarching goal that brings meaning to our lives and also gives us a sense of direction. Spirituality is having a connection with something larger than ourselves that brings our life meaning and purpose. I will talk first about the value of each and ways to foster them and conclude with talking about how they may best be integrated and sought together.

What Is the Value of Having a Sense of Meaning?

The idea of having a sense of meaning has been closely tied to the idea of seeing your life as part of a coherent narrative or ongoing story that makes sense. In Chapter 5, we talked about narrative psychology and how it builds on the human tendency to understand ourselves in the context of stories. Thinking about our lives as a story enables us to organize our daily experiences, link the past with the present and the possible future, and provides a framework for understanding who we are and how we fit in with the world and other people. It may increase our wisdom and social intelligence, improve our ability to predict what will happen, and have a positive impact on how our life unfolds.

The work of Joseph Campbell, Dan McAdams, and James Pennebaker all support the value of developing a sense of meaning in coming to see and think about our lives as an ongoing story. Campbell's idea of a hero's journey shows us how important it has been for people of different times and cultures to see themselves as part of a story where facing challenges can bring great rewards.[50] McAdam's work has shown us that having a life story with a positive resolution and redemption may be important for psychological well-being.[51] Pennebaker and others who have used writing interventions have found evidence suggesting that forming a coherent narrative in the context of stressful events may be good for mental and physical health.[52]

While having a sense of meaning may have an impact on us, this work also suggests that the nature of the meaning may be critical in determining its effects on our happiness and well-being. Michael Steger has studied the role of life narratives in developing a sense of meaning and comprehensibility about our lives.[53] He and Joo Yeon Shin distinguished between (1) a growth-oriented narrative that involves interpreting the memories of the past and the goals of the future in terms of individual growth and the ability to bring benefit to others and (2) a security-oriented narrative that emphasizes security, protection of the self, maintenance, and acquiring pleasure.[54] McAdams work echoes this as it focuses on the value of a story with a positive resolution as does the growing research on stress-related growth.[55]

How Can We Foster a Sense of Meaning?

Based on the central role of narrative, the sense of meaning may be fostered by finding creative ways to see ourselves as part of a growth-oriented narrative moving toward a positive resolution. McAdams suggests a technique for eliciting life stories that involves low points, high points, and turning points.[56] The first step in constructing a growth-oriented narrative may be to engage in a life review process that involves charting these three kinds of points on a timeline. The second step may be to begin to think about how these important points could be woven into a larger narrative about the past that could be the foundation for growth in the future.

This step and the others to come could incorporate the idea of a hero's journey and draw on specific examples of the successful resolution of the journey in real life and fiction that best speak to the individual. The third step could begin with writing about the most important points in a person's past and then filling in the blanks while being aware of the most relevant hero's journey stories. The final step could involve an exercise like Laura King's best possible self to envision the best ending to the story while also using the PATH process to flesh out the steps to take in working toward the overall goal.[57-58]

What Is the Value of Having a Sense of Purpose?

The idea of having a sense of purpose is closely tied to the idea of having future goals. But while goals are usually thought of as being more short-term and specific, purpose is a long-term overarching goal that is broader and helps to organize our shorter-term goals. As Robert Emmons work suggests, having an overarching purpose may reduce the conflict between competing goals that can sap our energy and strength.[59] Finally, having a sense of purpose means having a goal that can motivate us to persevere in the face obstacles and set-backs. Abraham Lincoln's fierce dedication to keeping the country together may have given him tremendous patience and resilience in striving to reach that goal.

The work of Viktor Frankl and a variety of research supports the value of having a sense of purpose in life. In *Man's Search for Meaning*, he argued that having something to live for enabled him and others to survive the horrors of the concentration camp.[60] When I was in graduate school, I did a study showing that a sense of purpose in life was the most important factor in recovering from total knee replacement surgery in relation to both mental and physical health.[61] A classic study that supports the value of having a sense of purpose is the nursing home study done by Judith Rodin and Ellen Langer.[62]

They found that nursing home patients had better health and lived longer if they were given a plant to care in comparison to a group of patients who were given a plant that the nursing home staff cared for.

There appear to be at least two factors that may help determine the value of a sense of purpose in life. The first is how much the purpose will actually benefit human happiness and well-being. Having a sense of purpose that involves meeting internal goals such as being happy, being a good person, and having good relationships may be more beneficial than external goals such as making a lot of money, being admired by others, and having a lot of material goods. The second factor is how much the purpose is authentic and represents the genuine interests and values of the person versus externally imposed by culture, norms, or other people. The more a person is intrinsically motivated, excited, enthusiastic, and passionate about their purpose, the more likely it is to motivate them and lead to the fulfillment of their own needs and desires.

How Can We Foster a Sense of Purpose?

The ways to foster a sense of purpose in life include both making it possible to identify it and finding ways to sustain it. A good place to begin in finding an authentic sense of purpose in life may be to identify your values, goals, and interests. Values clarification can be used to determine what is most important and short and long-term goals can be listed to provide additional perspective. Interests can be determined by examining how free time is spent or how it might be spent in the future. Once there is clarity about values, goals, and interests, then a process of writing, reflecting, and talking to friends and family members about them can help to identify overarching goals and finally a unifying sense of purpose.

Once a clear and authentic purpose is identified, a next step may be to engage in something like the PATH process and make use of mentors and stories that may provide guidance. As presented in Chapter 6, the PATH process begins with identifying where a person wants to go and then provides steps for enabling them to use their strengths, connect with others, and set goals that will help them stay focused on fulfilling their overarching purpose. Another critical element may be to find other people who are trying to fulfill a similar purpose to act as mentors and provide support for staying on the path. Finally, identifying a hero's journey story that is both inspiring and relevant may help in anticipating and overcoming obstacles in the future.

What Is the Value of Spirituality?

The idea of spirituality involves being connected and engaged with something that is greater than yourself. This could be God or a higher power but it could also be some other kind of ultimate value, cause, or concern such as love and compassion, being a good person, or using your strengths to make the world a better place. While spirituality involves being connected with something greater than yourself, religion is now most often defined as being involved with organized religion. Thus, spirituality is not the same as organized religion and it is possible to be spiritual without being religious.

While most research suggests that spirituality is related to greater happiness and well-being, there are so many different forms and expressions of spirituality that it is important to identify those that may be more helpful and harmful. Many of the things that can make spirituality harmful have been tied to organized religion. These include (1) the suspension of critical thinking, (2) extreme group conformity, (3) leaders manipulating people with fear, (4) using religion to justify hurting others, and (5) rejecting and excluding people with different points of view. When these have been a part of the expression of spirituality, they have generally been harmful and destructive to both the individual and to those who are affected and influenced by them.

There is even stronger and more consistent evidence about the ways that spirituality may be beneficial—whether or not it is tied to organized religion. These include (1) fostering a positive and authentic sense of meaning and purpose, (2) positive social relationships with a variety of people, (3) behavior that promotes social justice and the greater good, (4) better health habits such as a better diet and exercise, and (5) positive emotions in the context of individual and group practices. When one or more of these have been present, the value of spirituality has generally been increased and the benefits greater for both the individuals, their friends and family members, and the larger community.

How Can We Foster Spirituality?

Since spirituality involves a connection with something greater than yourself, the first step may be to identify and think about the things that bring you the greatest value and meaning. The following are some of the questions that may be useful to reflect on and begin to answer: What is most important to me? What do I love more than anything else? What would I be willing to devote myself to more than anything else? What can I do to benefit something outside of myself? What do I care about more than anything else? Addressing these questions can be followed with reading about and getting to know people and groups who share some of the same answers and interests.

Once you have identified something that is larger or greater than yourself and are genuinely motivated to be more connected and involved with it, the next step may be to develop the practices and habits that make it possible to sustain and grow in your chosen form of spirituality. As has been common in organized religion, these practices usually involve both doing things with other people as well as developing ways to practice alone. Social practices might include meeting together regularly with those who share your interests, finding someone who can mentor or guide you, and eventually finding others you can mentor or guide. The solitary practices may involve reading, writing, and taking time for quiet reflection.

How Can We Foster All Three Together?

The words "meaning," "purpose," and "spirituality" were chosen by the founders of the VIA classification because they complement each other and go together so well. In thinking about fostering them together, I want to bring us back to the idea of a common human hero's journey.[63] Meaning, purpose, and spiritualty can all be viewed as different aspects of our own unique journey in making the most of our life and living it to the fullest.

In an attempt to foster all three, rather than starting with meaning, it may make the most sense to proceed in the reverse order. Beginning with spirituality, the first step may be to identify that most important thing that is greater than yourself and that is most inspiring and worthy of your whole-hearted devotion. The second step may be to think about how this might translate into an overarching direction or purpose that fits for your values, goals, and interests and that may make the best use of your strengths and what you have to offer. Once these first two steps are in place, then the rest of the story may begin to reveal itself as you reflect on your history in light of the specific hero's journey stories that speak to you the most.

What Are Ways We Can Increase Them?

1. *Identify what means the most.*

Make a list of the things that are valuable and meaningful to you. Rank them from the first to the last. Make a plan for devoting more time and energy to the one that is most important.

2. *Take a day to devote yourself to a larger goal or purpose.*

Give yourself a day or as much time as you can take during one day. Brainstorm and make a list of your most important goals. Do your best to use the time to work towards your top one.

3. *Think about how you would like to be remembered.*

How would you like your friends and family members to remember you? Think about how you might best complete your life story in a way that might make that come true.

4. *Read about what you think is more important than anything else.*

Think about what may be most important to you. Find an article or a book about it and read it with the question: what can I do to make this more a part of my own life and life story?

5. *Sit quietly and reflect on what you love.*

Write down the things that you love the most. Give yourself 10-15 minutes to just sit and think about one or more of them. Just be still and silently note what thoughts and feelings arise.

Using the Strengths of Transcendence for the Journey

While the strengths of Temperance help keep us grounded, the strengths of Transcendence enable us to fly and reach for the stars. While all of the other virtues are essential for completing the journey, the strengths of Transcendence are unique and special in the way that they enable us to taste, see, and reach for the goal of our hero's journey.

Optimism and hope are the ability to envision that which may bring us the greatest joy and happiness and begin to plot our course for achieving it. Nelson Mandela found the way to have hope and be "the captain of his soul" in the very darkest and most discouraging circumstances. Humor is what enables us to rise above and find joy and laughter even during the most challenging and tedious parts of our journey. Norman Cousins laughed himself to health and paved the way for appreciating humor as a source of health and happiness.

Appreciation and gratitude are what enable us to see, remember, and anticipate the goodness and beauty all around us, so that we need never travel in darkness. My own dream showed me how wonderful it can be to have a brother to share my life with and George Bailey saw that he truly did have a wonderful life when he saw how much he meant to others. Meaning, purpose, and spirituality help us get to the very heart of the matter and create the kind of life that is truly worth living. That depressed and suicidal man who suffered so much heartache and loss found meaning and purpose in bringing healing and hope to a broken nation and to us all.

These strengths hold out the hope of a better tomorrow while also enabling us to experience the joy and fulfillment that we seek right here and now. They help us build the motivation and resources we need for the rest of our journey and are a fitting last step in our examination of the human strengths that can serve us so well. Before our time together comes to a close, there is one final chapter in this positive psychology school of ordinary magic. In this next chapter, I will bring you back to the unique contribution of positive psychology and leave you with some guiding principles for continuing your journey.

Chapter 14

The Hero's Journey for the Rest of Your Life

If you plan on being anything less than you are capable of being,
you will probably be unhappy all the days of your life.

—Abraham Maslow[1]

It was a complete set-up. They got him on a British television show called *That's Life* under false pretenses. He was seated in the middle of the front row with his wife. He was 79 years old and it was a good thing that he had a strong heart when they told him that the show was about him. They showed a clip about the other woman sitting next to him and introduced her as one of the children whose life he saved 50 years earlier. He tried to hold back tears when she was introduced to him and gave him a hug. Soon the woman sitting next to her was introduced as another child he saved and she gave him a kiss. Moments later the announcer asked if there was anyone else there who owed their life to Nicholas Winton. Everyone in the first five rows stood up.

Just before World War II, Nicholas "Nicky" Winton was a young businessman who gave up a business opportunity to start a campaign to rescue Jewish children from Germany as Hitler was coming to power.[2] He was single-handedly responsible for bringing 664 children to Britain and finding families to adopt each of them. He had not told anyone what he had done until his wife found a scrapbook about it in their attic 49 years later. The children who surrounded him at the television show were in their 50s and meeting him for the first time. By the time the movie *Nicky's Family* was made about him in 2009 these 664 children had over 5,000 descendants. The movie shows how many of the children and their descendants dedicated their lives to "paying it forward" in gratitude for the gift of their lives that they received from Nicky.

Nicholas Winton is a supreme example of what can happen when you heed the call and make the hero's journey of positive psychology. He was moved by a great need around him and found a way to creatively use his strengths to make a lasting difference. He never bragged or even talked about it but had the life-long satisfaction of knowing that he did the right thing. But one of the most remarkable things about his story is that he lived to see so much of the effects of what he had done. The leaders in the positive psychology movement have often talked about how the simplest acts of kindness can create ripples of hope and love that continue to spread like gentle waves on a lake. They have talked about how a primary goal of positive psychology is to identify things we can do that result in a virtuous cycle that spirals upward.

It would have been easy for Nicholas Winton to have looked the other way and just focus on his business and making money. It would have been easy for that short little Albanian woman named Teresa to give up on the dying in the streets of Calcutta. It would have been easy for Abraham Lincoln to give up on the daunting task that he was faced with and give in to his depressive disposition. It would have been easy for Maya Angelou to remain the song bird in the cage that never escaped and never sang with such beauty and grace. It would have been easy for Nelson Mandela to give up in the despair of his seven by eight foot cell and become obsessed with revenge for the guards who mistreated him. It would be easy for all of us to give in to our cynicism and doubt that we could ever really make a difference or find any kind of true and lasting happiness.

Positive Psychology Offers Us a New Opportunity

However, just as the science of physics let the genie out of the nuclear bottle by splitting the atom, so the science of positive psychology has let the genie of the most important bottle of all by finally focusing on our happiness and well-being. It is now harder than ever to deny that the power of appreciation and gratitude can bring joy to even the dullest and most discouraging days of our lives. It is now harder than ever to deny that our capacity for resilience and stress-related growth can enable us to learn and grow from some of the worst possible things that can happen to us. It is now harder than ever to deny that we have a capacity for kindness and compassion that can ripple beyond us to people that we do not even know.

We live in such strange and contradictory times. We can be so overwhelmed by our deeply ingrained tendency to only see the negative that we can miss the heroes in our midst. We watch the news that shows us the absolute worst that one out of seven billion people can do to another and never even think about the absolute best. We can fly into a rage if someone cuts us off in traffic but we don't see the kindness in the face of that person who smiles and opens the door for us. We are so obsessed with the endless stories of "breaking bad" that we miss the story of breaking good in our parent, friend, or neighbor who loves us no matter what and who always comes through for us.

But positive psychology has finally shined the light of science on the best of what we are and can be and not only the worst of what we have been in the past. When we look people who are just like us in the eyes and see the better angels of their nature, we can no longer deny the possibility that we may have within ourselves. When we have experienced the power of gratitude in the midst of a great loss or compassion when in great pain, we can begin to open ourselves up to the possibility of something that we may never have thought possible—something that can begin to melt even our greatest cynicism and doubt.

The Choice to Follow Your Hero's Path

When I began teaching positive psychology, I had read the ancient stories of people like Jesus and Buddha, the more recent history of people like Lincoln, Gandhi, and Mother Teresa, and was familiar with fictional stories like *The Lord of the Rings*, *Star Wars*, *Wonder Woman*, and *Harry Potter*. I was sometimes excited and sometimes moved but always soon forgot about them because they seemed so long ago and far away. But I did not fully realize that all of these stories may really be about us until I read *The Hero with a Thousand Faces* by Joseph Campbell. I saw so much of this common story come to life in the challenges and struggles of the people that I admired in my own life. I saw that the call they experienced to make the best of their lives was the very same call that I could respond to in my own life.

But the place where this hero's journey became most real and alive to me was in the lives of my students. There were those who used it to be the first in their family to graduate from college and get into law school or medical school. There were those who used it to overcome a divorce or the loss of a loved one only to make new friends and find new love. There were those who used it to keep their sanity while working multiple jobs and raising children. There were those who used it to deal with their own anxiety and depression and substance abuse so they could become counselors to help others who suffered the same way. There were those who otherwise seemed healthy and happy but used it to go to another level in creating meaningful and fulfilling lives for themselves.

As moving as the stories are of people like Nicholas Winton, I saw that there were those around me who were using what they were learning in positive psychology to do things that often seemed just as moving and inspiring. There was the young man whose parents had abandoned him who decided to become the parent he never had to other abandoned and troubled kids like he had been. There was the woman who suffered a terrible injustice that profoundly affected her life who became a passionate advocate for both justice and compassion. There was the man who grew up in one of the most violent cities in the world and faced down being bullied to realize his dream of playing professional soccer. There was the older woman who experienced unimaginable trauma and grew into a shining example of resilience, kindness, and forgiveness.

I could easily go on with many more examples. But the point is that they are the real heroes and you and I can be too. Not heroes in the sense of being the idealized characters that none of us can ever be, but of being the extraordinary heroes in the same kind of everyday life that we all experience. Not heroes who made use of some fictional magic or force that we can only fantasize about and never hope to really use ourselves. No, these are heroes just like you and me who heeded the call to adventure and exercised the extraordinary ordinary magic that the very powerful and very real force of science is finally shining its light on and revealing. They made the choice to walk the road less traveled in responding to the stress and injustice they experienced by transforming it into gifts for others rather than repeating the cycle of violence and pain.

The hero's journey of positive psychology has presented us with the same choice that George Bailey faced in *It's a Wonderful Life* and Nelson Mandela faced in that prison cell. Positive psychology has dared to study the best of what is possible for us and the stories of the everyday heroes all around us can show us the way. Like George Bailey, we can jump off the proverbial bridge into the icy waters below and deny the world and ourselves of what we can do to make it a wonderful life. Just as Nelson Mandela may have been, we might be tempted to hold onto our resentment and take an eye for an eye and add to the world's blindness. But like both George and Nelson, we can choose something very different. We can realize that this very moment and every moment is our chance to answer that call. We can use what we are learning to begin to create ripples like Nicholas Winton started and discover the same lasting sense of joy, meaning, and fulfillment.

Guidelines for Your Continuing Journey

Finally, I want to leave you with some guidelines for continuing to answer the call in making the most of your life and living it to the fullest. If I had to give my last lecture right now, this is what I would want to say to you and to all of my students. I see it as the best of what positive psychology has to offer to us:

1. *Remember that you are on a hero's journey.*

In the many years that I have taught positive psychology, I have come to see that Joseph Campbell's idea of a hero's journey can be a powerful framework for understanding the potential role of positive psychology in our lives.[3] It can bring it to life in the stories all around us and most of all in our own lives. I defined positive psychology as the application of the scientific method to enable us to make the most of our lives and live them to the fullest. The idea of the hero's journey can help us understand what is involved in seeking this kind of life for ourselves which includes great challenges but also great rewards. The hero's journey also includes the idea that we have the choice to refuse or accept the call. Finally, it includes the notions that our lives can have great meaning, we need not be alone in our journey, and we can continue to be motivated and inspired by our ultimate goal.

2. *Discover what makes you most happy.*

In Chapters 3 and 4, I presented the current theory and research on what is happiness and well-being. I told you that happiness has been defined as having fewer negative emotions, more positive emotions, and high life satisfaction and that the other elements of well-being may include engagement, positive relationships, meaning, accomplishment, autonomy, personal growth, and self-acceptance. I encourage you to continue to think about these as colors on a palette that you can use to paint the picture of the kind of life you would most like for yourself. As you finish this book, I would ask that you continue doing this and suggest that the more you do it, the clearer the picture will become. This picture can serve as a powerful inspiration and motivation for you to continue your journey and map out the specific things you need to do to complete it.

3. *Set clear and specific goals for your journey.*

Set long-term and short-term goals that will enable you to achieve your vision of the life you think will bring you the greatest happiness and well-being. Use the SMART acronym to set goals that are Specific, Measurable, Achievable, Relevant, and Time-bound.[4] You can use the PATH process to begin by identifying a "North Star" to guide you and then chart the intermediate steps and goals for reaching it.[5] You can practice the strength of prudence for helping you balance your future goals with more immediate pleasures and gratifications. You can use Rick Snyder's model of hope to help you plan the three-step process of identifying your goals, finding the "way" or pathways to your goals, and boosting your "will" or your self-efficacy in working towards them.[6] Reaching your smallest initial goals will build self-efficacy and the perseverance that you need to continue and reach your long-term goals.

4. *Learn to practice the strengths at the right places and times.*

The strengths we talked about represent our best hope to meet our goals and live our lives to the fullest. They involve attitudes and behaviors we can practice individually and that can eventually become habits and stable aspects of who we are. We need to develop the wisdom to know when and where to use them. The strengths of wisdom enable us to turn on the light and find our way and the strengths of courage help us face and overcome obstacles and set-backs. The strengths of humanity enable us to make the connections we need with others who can support and encourage us and the strengths of justice enable us to do what is good, fair, and right for the larger community and the world. Finally, the strengths of temperance help us to keep our feet on the ground and stay balanced while the strengths of transcendence enable us to envision and reach for the stars.

5. *Find new ways to use your strengths in reaching your goals.*

Be sure to identify your top strengths using the online *VIA Survey* and review the sections of this book that discuss your top five strengths. Identify the practical exercises at the end of the sections that appeal to you the most and brainstorm about other ways you can use your top strengths. Try to practice your strengths in ways that will enable you to experience flow as much as possible. Remember that finding new ways to use your strengths is like lifting the sails on a sailboat, so using them should eventually feel like sailing with the wind at your back. Once you have found several new ways that you can exercise your top strengths, begin to think about and plan how you can use them in reaching your goals for achieving greater happiness and well-being. Continue to experiment and try different ways of using your strengths to reach your goals until you find the ways that work best.

6. *Address your weaknesses when necessary.*

Remember the negativity bias and be aware of the temptation to focus only on your weaknesses. But also remember that sometimes our weaknesses can be like holes in our boat that we need to pay attention to in order to stay afloat. Use the strengths of wisdom and open-mindedness to determine what weaknesses may really be holding you back. The most common weaknesses for people in most modern cultures involve strengths under the virtue of Temperance, especially self-control and prudence. Remember the story of the movie *The Karate Kid* where Mr. Miyagi teaches the young boy the necessary moves by having him do everyday chores. Working on your weaknesses may require persistent effort but may bring great rewards in the long run. Finally, see if you can find creative ways to use your top strengths to improve your weaknesses.

7. *Focus on what is good and beautiful around you.*

Practicing the strengths of appreciation and gratitude can be incredibly powerful in countering the negativity bias, beating the hedonic treadmill, and adding new value to your life. Try to remember that you have the power to say no to advertising when it says you are not enough or you cannot be happy without what they are selling. Using the simple exercise of writing down good things that happened at the end of the day can increase your ability to recognize what you may have missed in the past. Using the exercise of counting your blessings at the end of the day or the week can make you more aware of all kinds of good things in your life even when they aren't happening at the moment. Writing letters and emails to people you appreciate or are grateful for can start a positive feedback loop and improve your social support and the quality of your relationships.

8. *Find a mentor and enlist the help of your friends.*

Try to find others who can encourage your hero's journey to find or achieve what would make you most happy. See if you can find a good mentor. See if you can identify any stories that have heroes or characters that may serve as an inspiration or a guide for you on your journey. Ask friends and family members who care about you if they would be willing to support you and hold you accountable for reaching your goals. See if you can find other people who may want to go on a similar journey or join you in some of the same activities that you will be doing. It may be helpful to reread the chapter on the virtue of Humanity and think about how you can use the strengths of social intelligence, love, and kindness in building your support team. You could also use the PATH process and draw out the steps with them as they help you articulate each of them.[7]

9. *Be sure to find ways to give it away.*

Not only is positive psychology a participatory sport that you have to put into practice to really understand, it is also a gift that you have to give in order to really receive the full benefit. Finding new ways to perform acts of kindness may be one of the best ways to beat the hedonic treadmill and raise your happiness to a new level. We saw the growing body of evidence that the good we do for others does come back around to us in so many ways. We saw that having a meaningful life, good relationships, and a lasting sense of gratification may depend on what we give to others. We saw that spending money on and doing things for others has a more lasting benefit than just spending money on or doing things for ourselves. The most important thing in giving positive psychology away seems to be to focus on the activities and gifts that fit best with our strengths, values, and interests.

10. *Make the best of your stresses, challenges, and set-backs.*

Positive psychology involves facing the dark, harsh, and negative realities of life head-on and not avoiding or denying them. The ordeal in the hero's journey represents the worst things that can happen to us and the possibility of gaining some of our greatest gifts from them. When bad things happen, learn to practice and develop the strength of resilience to bounce back, and that of stress-related growth to find ways to learn, grow, and benefit from them. If you are discouraged or blaming yourself, take a growth mindset that you can use this to learn something new rather than a fixed mindset that you are destined to fail. When you are afraid to do something, practice wisdom to determine whether it is worth the risk, and if it is, practice courage to do it. Above all, learn to rely on others for support and link your story to heroes in other stories who have faced and overcome similar challenges.

11. *Continue to learn with an open mind.*

Positive psychology is a scientific approach to understanding happiness and well-being and how to achieve them. Though many encouraging discoveries have already been made, positive psychology will continue to develop and evolve as the science progresses. Though there are several exercises that have already been shown to improve happiness and well-being, there will no doubt be new ones and a better understanding of which work best for whom and when. Practice the strengths of curiosity, love of learning, and open-mindedness when it comes to positive psychology. Continue to read new articles and books and watch new TED Talks about positive psychology and what makes life worth living. Most important, continue to work on being aware of your biases and use open-mindedness to challenge selective exposure by actively searching for evidence that may contradict what you now believe.

12. *Develop the focused discipline of regular practice.*

If we think that our hero's journey may involve what seem like great battles, then we can begin to view developing and using our strengths as a kind of martial art. The focused discipline of developing a routine of continued practice may be the core of success in making the most of our lives and living them to the fullest. As I already suggested, we can think of it as analogous to undergoing Jedi training or attending *Hogwarts*. The idea is to become a virtuoso in using and expressing our own unique gifts and strengths to make a difference in the world around us. As a way to help you cultivate this discipline, I included Appendix D with exercises that you can do once a week for 14 weeks. In essence, this could be a 98-day plan to put into practice what you have been reading about. Whether or not you do them all, try those that appeal to you the most and see what works best for you.

Fare Thee Well on Thy Journey

In closing, what is positive psychology? In short, it is the application of the most powerful human tool we have to answer the most important question of how we can be happy and make the most of our lives. What does it have to do with a hero's journey? The goal of positive psychology is the same as our own unique hero's journey and the findings of positive psychology may provide us with our greatest hope for completing it.

Positive psychology has shined a new light on the best of what is around us and the best of what is possible for us. Despite all of the pain and darkness in the world, we can now more clearly see and understand the goodness and beauty that is all around us. Despite all of our weaknesses and failures, we can now better see what is good and beautiful within us and cultivate it for our own benefit and for that of others and the world.

Positive psychology is not a dry academic discipline but the most practical science that offers each of us tools, exercises, and activities for transforming our lives. These tools can enable us to develop the strengths that have served others so well and may be the key to true and lasting happiness and well-being. But the only way to fully understand and appreciate the power of positive psychology is by developing these strengths and putting them into practice.

When I was first called upon to teach positive psychology, I had no idea that it could bring as much as it has to those that I have taught and to myself. I thought we would just go through the motions and do our best to just pass the time and try to stay awake. I never thought that I would come to love and appreciate so many who are on the very same journey to make the most of this one life that we have been given.

I hope that you will give positive psychology the same chance that I almost didn't. I wish you the best on your own noble and sacred journey. I hope it will bring you all of the happiness, joy, meaning, and fulfillment that you seek.

REFERENCES

Preface

1. http://www.quotationspage.com/quote/24004.html

2. Smith, B.W., Ford, G., Phan, A., Stearns, A.L., & Garcia, V. (2017, July). Teaching positive psychology and student well-being: Do undergraduate student PERMA scores increase during a positive psychology course? Presented at *the Fifth World Congress of the International Positive Psychology Association* in Montreal, Canada.

Chapter 1

1. https://www.brainyquote.com/quotes/quotes/j/josephcamp157106.html

2. Seligman, M.E.P., & Csikszentmihalyi, M. (2000). Positive psychology: An introduction. *American Psychologist, 55,* 1, 5-14.

3. Gottman, J.M. (1999). *The seven principles for making marriage work: A practical guide form the country's foremost relationship expert.* New York: Harmony Books.

4. Kahneman, D. (2013). *Thinking, fast and slow.* New York: Farrar, Straus, and Giroux.

5. Frankl, V. E. (1963). *Man's search for meaning.* New York: Pocket Books.

6. Niemiec, R.M. (2014). *Positive psychology at the movies: Using films to build character strengths and well-being* (2nd Ed.). Boston, MA: Hogrefe Publishing.

Chapter 2

1. Seligman, M.E.P., & Csikszentmihalyi, M. (2000). Positive psychology: An introduction. *American Psychologist,* 55, 1, 5-14.

2. Maslow, A.H. (1998). *Toward a psychology of being* (3rd Ed.). New York: John Wiley & Sons.

3. Rogers, C.R. (1995). *On becoming a person* (2nd Ed.). New York: Mariner Books.

4. Horney, K. (1950). *Neurosis and human growth.* New York: Norton.

5. Diener, E. (2000). Subjective well-being: The science of happiness and a proposal for a national index. *American Psychologist, 55*, 34–43.

6. Ryff, C. (1989). Happiness is everything, or is it? Explorations on the meaning of psychological well-being. *Journal of Personality and Social Psychology, 57*, 1069–1081.

7. Csikszentmihalyi, M. (1990). *Flow: The psychology of optimal experience.* New York: Harper Perennial.

8. Bandura, A. (1997). *Self-efficacy: The exercise of control.* New York: W.H. Freeman.

9. Frankl, V. E. (1963). *Man's search for meaning.* New York: Pocket Books.

10. Pargament, K.I. (1997). *The psychology of religion and coping.* New York: Guilford Press.

11. Kabat-Zinn, J. (1990). *Full catastrophe living: Using the wisdom of your body and mind to face stress, pain, and illness.* New York: Delta.

12. Watson, D., Clark, L. A., & Tellegen, A. (1988). Development and validation of brief measures of Positive and Negative Affect: The PANAS scales. *Journal of Personality and Social Psychology, 54*, 1063-1070.

13. Seligman, M.E.P., & Maier, S.F. (1967). Failure to escape traumatic shock. *Journal of Experimental Psychology, 74*, 1–9.

14. Seligman, M.E.P., & Csikszentmihalyi, M. (2000).

15. Seligman, M.E.P. (2011). *Flourish: A visionary new understanding of happiness and well-being.* New York: Free Press.

16. Diener, E. (2000). Subjective well-being: The science of happiness and a proposal for a national index. *American Psychologist, 55*, 34–43.

17. Csikszentmihalyi, M. (1990).

18. Snyder, C.R. (1994). *The psychology of hope: You can get there from here.* New York: Free Press.

19. Peterson, C., & Seligman, M.E.P. (2004). *Character strengths and virtues: A handbook of classification.* New York: Oxford University Press.

20. Fredrickson, B.L. (2001). The role of positive emotions in positive psychology. *American Psychologist, 56*, 3, 218–226.

21. Lyubomirsky, S. (2007). *The how of happiness: A new approach to getting the life you want.* New York: Penguin Books.

22. Emmons, R.A., & Crumpler, C.A. (2000). Gratitude as a human strength: Appraising the evidence. *Journal of Social and Clinical Psychology, 19*, 56-69.

23. McCullough, M.E., Sandage, S.J., & Worthington, E.L. (1997). *To forgive is human: How to put your past in the past*. Downers Grove, IL: IVP Books.

24. Wong, P. T. P. (2011). Positive psychology 2.0: Towards a balanced interactive model of the good life. *Canadian Psychology, 52*, 69-81.

25. Ivtzan, I., Lomas, T., Hefferon, K., & Worth, P. (2016). *Second wave positive psychology: Embracing the dark side of life*. New York: Routledge.

26. Kabat-Zinn, J. (1990).

27. Peterson, C. (2013). *Pursuing the good life: 100 reflections on positive psychology*. New York: Oxford University Press.

28. Ibid.

29. https: //www.ted.com/talks/shawn_achor_the_happy_ secret_to better_work

Chapter 3

1. https://www.goodreads.com/work/quotes/2332650-the-how-of-happiness-a-scientific-approach-to-getting-the-life-you-want

2. Lyubomirsky, S. (2007). *The how of happiness: A new approach to getting the life you want*. New York: Penguin Books.

3. Diener, E. (2000). Subjective well-being: The science of happiness and a proposal for a national index. *American Psychologist, 55*, 34–43.

4. Baumeister, R. F., Bratslavsky, E., Finkenauer, C., & Vohs, K. D. (2001). Bad is stronger than good. *Review of General Psychology, 5*, 323-370.

5. Sapolsky, R.M. (1998). *Why zebras don't get ulcers: An updated guide to stress, stress-related diseases, and coping*. New York: W.H. Freeman and Company.

6. Ellis, A. (2009). *Rational emotive behavior therapy: It works for me - It can work for you*. New York: Prometheus Books.

7. Beck, A.T., Rush, A.J., Shaw, B.F., & Emery, G. (1979). *Cognitive therapy of depression*. New York: The Guilford Press.

8. Pinker, S. (2011). *The better angels of our nature: Why violence has declined.* New York: Penguin Books.

9. Hanson, R. (2013). *Hardwiring happiness: The new brain science of contentment, calm, and confidence.* New York: Harmony Books.

10. Fredrickson, B. L. (2004). The broaden-and-build theory of positive emotions. *Philosophical Transactions of the Royal Society B: Biological Sciences, 359,* 1367–1378.

11. Isen, A.M. (2001). An influence of positive affect on decision-making in complex situations: Theoretical issues with practical implications. *Journal of Consumer Psychology, 11,* 75-85.

12. Fredrickson, B.L., & Branigan, C. (2005). Positive emotions broaden the scope of attention and thought-action repertoires. *Cognition and Emotion, 19,* 313-332.

13. Gable, S.L., Gonzaga, G.C., & Strachman, A. (2006). Will you be there when things go right? Supportive responses to positive event disclosures. *Journal of Personality and Social Psychology, 91,* 904-917.

14. Fredrickson, B.L., Cohn, M.A., Coffey, K.A., Pek, J., & Finkel, S.M. (2008). Open hearts build lives: Positive emotions, induced through loving-kindness mediation, build consequential personal resources. *Journal of Personality and Social Psychology, 95,* 1045–1062.

15. Fredrickson, B.L. (2001). The role of positive emotions in positive psychology: The broaden-and-build theory of positive emotions. *American Psychologist, 56,* 218-226.

16. Lyubomirsky, S., King, L., & Diener, E. (2005). The benefits of frequent positive affect: does happiness lead to success? *Psychological Bulletin, 131,* 803-55.

17. Lyubomirsky, S., Sheldon, K.M., & Schkade, D. (2005). Pursuing happiness: The architecture of sustainable change. *Psychological Bulletin, 131,* 803-855.

18. http://worldhappiness.report/ed/2017/

19. Diener, E., Weiting, N., Harter, J., & Arora, R. (2010). Wealth and happiness across the world: Material prosperity predicts life evaluation, whereas psychosocial prosperity predicts positive feeling. *Journal of Personality and Social Psychology, 99,* 52-61.

20. Howell, R.T., & Hill, G. (2009). The mediators of experiential purchases: Determining the impact of psychological needs satisfaction and social comparison. *The Journal of Positive Psychology, 4,* 511-522.

21. Dunn, E.W., Aknin, L.B., & Norton, M.I. (2008). Spending money on others promotes happiness. *Science, 319,* 1687-1688.

22. Lyubomirsky, S. (2013). *The myths of happiness: What should make you happy, but doesn't what shouldn't make you happy, but does.* New York: Penguin Press.

23. Brickman, P., & Campbell, D. (1971). Hedonic relativism and planning the good society. In M.H. Apley (Ed.), *Adaptation level theory: A symposium.* (pp. 287-302). New York: Academic Press

24. Brickman, P., Coates, D., & Janoff-Bulman, R. (1978). Lottery winners and accident victims: Is happiness relative? *Journal of Personality and Social Psychology, 36,* 917-927.

25. Diener, E., Lucas, R.E., & Scollon, C.N. (2006). Beyond the hedonic treadmill: Revising the adaptation theory of well-being. *American Psychologist, 61,* 305-314.

26. Haidt, J. (2006). *The happiness hypothesis: Finding modern truth in ancient wisdom.* New York: Basic Books.

27. Lutz, A., Greischar, L.L., Rawlings, N.B., Ricard, M., & Davidson, R.J. (2004). Long-term meditators self-induce high-amplitude gamma synchrony during mental practice. *Proceedings of the National Academy of Sciences, 101,* 16369–16373.

28. Diener, E., & Biswas-Diener, R. (2008). *Happiness: Unlocking the mysteries of psychological wealth.* Blackwell: Oxford.

29. Lyubomirsky, S. (2007).

30. Parks, A.C., & Schueller, S.M. (Eds.). (2014). *The Wiley Blackwell handbook of positive psychological interventions.* West Sussex, UK: John Wiley and Sons.

Chapter 4

1. https://www.goodreads.com/quotes/215395-happiness-is-not-a-goal-it-is-a-by-product-of-a-life

348

2. Seligman, M.E.P. (2002). *Authentic happiness: Using the new positive psychology to realize your potential for lasting fulfillment.* New York: Free Press.

3. Ibid.

4. Frankl, V. E. (1963). *Man's search for meaning.* New York: Pocket Books.

5. Baumeister, R.F., Vohs, K.D., Aaker, J.L., & Garbinsky, E.N. (2012). Some key differences between a happy life and a meaningful life. *The Journal of Positive Psychology, 8,* 505-516.

6. Ryff, C. (1989). Happiness is everything, or is it? Explorations on the meaning of psychological well-being. *Journal of Personality and Social Psychology, 57,* 1069–1081.

7. Seligman, M.E.P. (2011). *Flourish: A visionary new understanding of happiness and well-being.* New York: Free Press.

8. Seligman, M.E.P. (2002).

9. Seligman, M.E.P. (2011).

10. Fredrickson, B. L. (2004). The broaden-and-build theory of positive emotions. *Philosophical Transactions of the Royal Society B: Biological Sciences, 359,* 1367–1378

11. Haidt, J. (2003). Elevation and the positive psychology of morality. In C. L. M. Keyes & J. Haidt (Eds.), *Flourishing: Positive psychology and the life well-lived* (pp. 275-289). Washington DC: American Psychological Association.

12. Keltner, D. (2010). The compassionate instinct. In D. Keltner, J. Marsh & J.A. Smith (Eds.), *The compassionate instinct* (pp. 8-15). New York: W.W. Norton.

13. Csikszentmihalyi, M. (1990). *Flow: The psychology of optimal experience.* New York: Harper Perennial.

14. Nakamura, J., & Csikszentmihalyi, M. (2001). Flow theory and research. In C. R. Snyder, E. Wright, & S.J. Lopez (Eds.), *Handbook of positive psychology* (pp. 195-206). New York: Oxford University Press.

15. Csikszentmihalyi, M. (1990).

16. Seligman, M.E.P. (2002).

17. Dunbar, R.I.M. (1992). Neocortex size as a constraint on group size in primates. *Journal of Human Evolution, 22,* 469–493.

18. Seligman, M.E.P. (2011).

19. Butler, J., & Kern, M. L. (2015). The PERMA-Profiler: A brief multidimensional measure of flourishing. Available from http://www.peggykern.org/questionnaires.html

20. Seligman, M.E.P. (2011).

21. White, R. W. (1959). Motivation reconsidered: The concept of competence. *Psychological Review, 66,* 297-333.

22. Diener, E. (2000). Subjective well-being: The science of happiness and a proposal for a national index. *American Psychologist, 55,* 34–43.

Chapter 5

1. https://www.goodreads.com/author/quotes/20105.Joseph_Campbell

2. Billig, M. (2013). *Learn to write badly: How to succeed in the social sciences.* Cambridge, MA: Cambridge University Press.

3. Bruner, J. S. (1991). The narrative construction of reality. *Critical Inquiry, 18,* 1-21.

4. McAdams, D. (1993). *The stories we live by: Personal myths and the making of the self.* New York: Guilford Press.

5. Pennebaker, J.W., & Smyth, J.M. (2016). *Opening up by writing it down: How expressive writing improves health and eases emotional pain* (3rd Ed.). New York: Guilford Press.

6. Smyth, J.M., True, N., & Souto, J. (2001). Effects of writing about traumatic experiences: The necessity for narrative structure. *Journal of Social and Clinical Psychology, 20,* 161-172.

7. Wilson, T. (2011). *Redirect: Changing the stories we live by.* New York: Little, Brown and Company.

8. King, L.A. (2001). The health benefits of writing about goals. *Personality and Social Psychology Bulletin, 27,* 798-807.

9. Campbell, J. (1949). *The hero with a thousand faces.* Princeton, N.J.: Princeton University Press.

10. Campbell, J. (2004). *Pathways to bliss: Mythology and personal transformation.* Novato, CA: New World Press.

11. Vogler, C. *A Practical Guide to Joseph Campbell's The Hero with a Thousand Faces.* An online copy of the memo.

12. Vogler, C. (2007). *The writer's journey: Mythic structure for writers* (3rd Ed.). Studio City, CA: Michael Wiese Productions.

13. McAdams, D. (1993).

14. https://www.quora.com/What-was-J-K-Rowlings-inspiration-for-dementors-in-Harry-Potter

15. https://www.mindbodygreen.com/0-2957/Gandhi-Your-Beliefs-Lead-to-Your-Destiny.html

16. Worth, P. (2016). The hero's journey. In I. Ivtzan, T. Lomas, K. Hefferon, & P. Worth (Eds.), *Second wave positive psychology: Embracing the dark side of life* (pp. 175-196). New York: Routledge.

17. http://quoteinvestigator.com/2010/06/29/be-kind/

Chapter 6

1. https://www.goodreads.com/quotes/15579-what-lies-behind-us-and-what-lies-before-us-are

2. Prochaska, J.O., & DiClemente, C.C. (2005). The transtheoretical approach. In J.C. Norcross & M.R. Goldfried (Eds.), *Handbook of psychotherapy integration* (2nd Ed.) (pp. 147-171). New York: Oxford University Press.

3. Pearpoint, J., O'Brien, J., & Forest, M. (2011). *PATH: A workbook for planning positive possible futures.* Toronto, CA: Inclusion Press.

4. Doran, G. T. (1981). There's a S.M.A.R.T. way to write management's goals and objectives. *Management Review, 70,* 35–36.

5. Beck, A.T., Rush, A.J., Shaw, B.F., & Emery, G. (1979). *Cognitive therapy of depression.* New York: The Guilford Press.

6. Ellis, A. (2009). *Rational emotive behavior therapy: It works for me - It can work for you.* New York: Prometheus Books.

7. Ochsner, K. N., Bunge, S. A., Gross, J. J., & Gabrieli, J. D. E. (2002). Rethinking feelings: An fMRI study of the cognitive regulation of emotion. *Journal of Cognitive Neuroscience, 14,* 1215-1229.

8. Burns, D. (2008). *Feeling good: The new mood therapy*. New York: Harper.

9. Lomas, T., Froh, J.J., Emmons, R.A., Mishra, A., & Bono, G. (2014). Gratitude interventions: A review and future agenda. In A.C. Parks & S.M. Schueller (Eds.), *The Wiley Blackwell handbook of positive psychological interventions* (pp. 3-19). West Sussex, UK: John Wiley and Sons.

10. King, L.A. (2001). The health benefits of writing about goals. *Personality and Social Psychology Bulletin, 27,* 798-807.

11. Jacobson, N.S., Dobson, K.S., Truax, P.A., Addis, M.E., Koerner, K., Gollan, J.K., Gortner, E., & Prince, S.E. (1996). A component analysis of cognitive-behavioral treatment for depression. *Journal of Consulting and Clinical Psychology, 64,* 295–304.

12. Lewinsohn, P.M. (1975). The behavioral study and treatment of depression. In M. Hersen, R.M. Eisler, & P.M. Miller (Eds.), *Progress in behavioral modification* (Vol. 1, pp. 19–65). New York: Academic.

13. Fredrickson, B. L. (2004). The broaden-and-build theory of positive emotions. *Philosophical Transactions of the Royal Society B: Biological Sciences, 359,* 1367–1378

14. Campbell, J. (2004). *Pathways to bliss: Mythology and personal transformation.* Novato, CA: New World Press.

15. Abramowitz, J.S., Deacon, B.J., Whiteside, S.P.H. (2010). *Exposure therapy for anxiety: Principles and practice.* New York: Guilford Press.

16. http://www.mcescher.com/gallery/back-in-holland/no-45-angel-devil/

17. https://www.goodreads.com/quotes/31631-we-are-not-enemies-but-friends-we-must-not-be

18. Peterson, C., & Seligman, M.E.P. (2004). *Character strengths and virtues: A handbook of classification.* New York: Oxford University Press.

19-24. Ibid.

25. https://www.viacharacter.org/survey/account/register

26. http://www.actionforhappiness.org/media/52486/340_ways_to_use_character_strengths.pdf

27. Niemiec, R.M. (2014). *Positive psychology at the movies: Using films to build character strengths and well-being* (2nd Ed.). Boston, MA: Hogrefe Publishing.

28. Niemiec, R.M. (2017). *Character strengths interventions: A field guide for practitioners.* Boston, MA: Hogrefe Publishing.

29. Wood, A.M., Linley, P.A., Maltby, J., Kashdan, T.B., & Hurling, R. (2011). Using personal and psychological strengths leads to increases in well-being over time: A longitudinal study and the development of the strengths use questionnaire. *Personality and Individual Differences, 50,* 15-19.

30. Rust, T., Diessner, R., & Reade, L. (2009). Strengths Only or Strengths and Relative Weaknesses? A Preliminary Study. *The Journal of Psychology, 143,* 465–476

31. Hanson, R. (2013). *Hardwiring happiness: The new brain science of contentment, calm, and confidence.* New York: Harmony Books.

Chapter 7

1. http://www.imdb.com/character/ch0000015/quotes

2. https://www.brainyquote.com/quotes/quotes/c/caseykasem 664691.html

3. Kabat-Zinn, J. (1994). *Wherever you go, there you are: Mindfulness Meditation in Everyday Life.* New York: Hyperion.

4. Ibid.

5. Mumford, G. (2015). *The mindful athlete: Secrets to pure performance.* Berkeley, CA: Parallax Press.

6. Hanh, T.N. (1999). *The miracle of mindfulness: An introduction to the practice of meditation.* Boston, MA: Beacon Press.

7. Kabat-Zinn, J. (1990). *Full catastrophe living: Using the wisdom of your body and mind to face stress, pain, and illness.* New York: Delta.

8. Hanh, T.N. (1999).

9. Niemiec, R.M. (2014). *Mindfulness and character strengths: A practical guide to flourishing.* Boston, MA: Hogrefe Publishing.

10. Ivtzan, I., Niemiec, R.M., & Briscoe, C. (2016). A study investigating the effects of Mindfulness-Based Strengths Practice (MBSP) on wellbeing. *International Journal of Wellbeing, 6,* 1-13.

11. Kabat-Zinn, J. (1990).

12. Kabat-Zinn, J. (1994).

13. Mumford, G. (2015).

14. Bandura, A. (1997). *Self-efficacy: The exercise of control.* New York: W.H. Freeman.

15. Bandura, A., & Adams, N.E. (1977). Analysis of self-efficacy theory of behavioral change. *Cognitive Therapy and Research, 1,* 287-310.

16. Moritz, S.E., Feltz, D.L., Fahrbach, K.R., & Mack, D.E. (2000). The relation of self-efficacy measures to sport performance: A meta-analytic review. *Research Quarterly for Exercise and Sport, 71,* 280-294.

17. Stajkovic, A.C., & Luthans, F. (1998). Self-efficacy and work-related performance: A meta-analysis. *Psychological Bulletin, 124,* 240-261.

18. Taylor, S.E., Pham, L.B., Rivkin, I.D., & Armor, D.A. (1998). Harnessing the imagination: Mental simulation, self-regulation, and coping. *American Psychologist, 53,* 429-439.

19. Smith, B.W., Dalen, J., Wiggins, K., Tooley, E., Christopher, P., & Bernard, J. (2008). The brief resilience scale: Assessing the ability to bounce back. *International Journal of Behavioral Medicine, 15,* 194-200.

20. Werner, E. E. (1993). Risk, resilience, and recovery: Perspectives from the Kauai Longitudinal Study. *Development and Psychopathology, 5,* 503-515.

21. Taylor, Shelley E.; Klein, L.C., Lewis, B.P., Gruenewald, T. L., Gurung, R. A. R., Updegraff, J.A. (2000). Biobehavioral responses to stress in females: Tend-and-befriend, not fight-or-flight. *Psychological Review, 107,* 411–29.

22. Seligman, M.E.P., & Maier, S.F. (1967). Failure to escape traumatic shock. *Journal of Experimental Psychology, 74,* 1–9.

23. Bonanno, G. A. (2004). Loss, trauma, and human resilience: Have we underestimated the human capacity to thrive after extremely adverse events? *American Psychologist, 59,* 20-28.

354

24. Haidt, J. (2003). Elevation and the positive psychology of morality. In C. L. M. Keyes & J. Haidt (Eds.), *Flourishing: Positive psychology and the life well-lived* (pp. 275-289). Washington DC: American Psychological Association.

25. Kabat-Zinn, J. (1990).

26. Pargament, K.I. (1997). *The psychology of religion and coping.* New York: Guilford Press.

27. Tugade, M.M., & Fredrickson, B.L. (2004). Resilient individuals use positive emotions to bounce back from negative emotional experiences. *Journal of Personality and Social Psychology, 86,* 320–333.

28. Zautra, A.J. (2003). *Emotions, stress, and health.* New York: Oxford University Press.

29. Meichenbaum, D., & Deffenbacher, J.L. (1988). Stress inoculation training. *The Counseling Psychologist, 16,* 69-90.

30. Calhoun, L. G., & Tedeschi, R. G. (Eds.). (2006). *The handbook of posttraumatic growth: Research and practice.* Mahwah, NJ: Lawrence Erlbaum.

31-32. Ibid.

33. Pennebaker, J.W., & Smyth, J.M. (2016). *Opening up by writing it down: How expressive writing improves health and eases emotional pain* (3rd Ed.). New York: Guilford Press.

34. Stanton, A.L., Danoff-Burg, S., Sworowski, L.A., Collins, C.A., Branstetter, A.D., Rodriguez-Hanley, A., Kirk, S.B., & Austenfeld, J. L. (2002). Randomized, controlled trial of written emotional expression and benefit finding in breast cancer patients. *Journal of Clinical Oncology, 20,* 4160-8.

35. McAdams, D. (1993). *The stories we live by: Personal myths and the making of the self.* New York: Guilford Press.

Chapter 8

1. http://www.searchquotes.com/quotation/Happiness_can_be_found%2C_even_in_the_darkest_of_times%2C_if_one_only_remembers_to_turn_on_the_light./37399/

2. http://www.dictionary.com/browse/wisdom

3. Baltes, P.B., & Staudinger, U.M. (2000). Wisdom: A metaheuristic (pragmatic) to orchestrate mind and virtue towards excellence. *American Psychologist, 55*, 122-136.

4. https://www.viacharacter.org/www/Character-Strengths/Perspective

5. Sternberg, R.J. (1998). A balance theory of wisdom. *Review of General Psychology, 2*, 347-365.

6. Baltes, P.B., & Smith, J. (2008). The fascination of wisdom: Its nature, ontogeny, and function. *Perspectives in Psychological Science, 3*, 56-64.

7. Baltes, P.B., & Staudinger, U.M. (2000).

8. Baltes, P.B., & Smith, J. (2008).

9. Baltes, P.B., & Staudinger, U.M. (2000).

10. Baltes, P.G., Gluck, J., & Kunzmann, U. (2002). Wisdom: Its structure and function in regulating successful lifespan development. In C.R. Snyder & S.J. Lopez (Eds.), *Handbook of positive psychology* (pp. 327-347). New York: Oxford University Press.

11. Ibid.

12. Schwartz, B., & Sharpe, K.E. (2006). Practical wisdom: Aristotle meets positive psychology. *Journal of Happiness Studies, 7*, 377-395.

13. Schwartz, B. (2016). *The paradox of choice: Why more is less* (2nd Ed.). New York: Ecco.

14. http://www.dictionary.com/browse/curiosity

15. Kashdan, T.B. (2004). Curiosity. In C. Peterson & M.E.P. Seligman (Eds.), *Character strengths and virtues: A handbook of classification* (pp. 125-141). New York: Oxford University Press.

16. Kashdan, T.B. (2010). *Curious? Discover the missing ingredient to a fulfilling life.* New York: Harper Perennial.

17. Kashdan, T.B. (2004).

18. https://www.viacharacter.org/www/Character-Strengths/Curiosity

19. Kashdan, T.B. (2007). Curiosity and pathways to well-being and meaning in life: Traits, states, and everyday behaviors. *Motivation and Emotion, 31*, 159-173.

20. Spielberger, C.D., & Starr, L.M. (1994). Curiosity and exploratory behavior. In H.F. O'Neil & M. Drillings (Eds.), *Motivation: Theory and research* (pp. 221-243). Hillsdale, NJ: Erlbaum.

21. Kashdan, T.B. (2007).

22. Campbell, J. (2004). *Pathways to bliss: Mythology and personal transformation.* Novato, CA: New World Press.

23. Peterson, C., & Seligman, M.E.P. (2004). *Character strengths and virtues: A handbook of classification.* New York: Oxford University Press.

24. https://www.viacharacter.org/www/Character-Strengths/Judgment

25. Haidt, J. (2012). *The righteous mind: Why good people are divided by politics and religion.* New York: Vintage Books.

26. Peterson, C., & Seligman, M.E.P. (2004).

27. https://www.viacharacter.org/www/Character-Strengths/Love-of-Learning

28. http://www.azquotes.com/author/43588-Brian_Swimme

29. Peterson, C., & Seligman, M.E.P. (2004).

30. https://www.viacharacter.org/www/Character-Strengths/Creativity

31. Kaufman, J.C., & Beghetto, R.A. (2009). Beyond big and little: The four C model of creativity. *Review of General Psychology, 13,* 1-12.

32. Guilford, J.P. (1950). Creativity. *American Psychologist, 5,* 444-44.

33. Fredrickson, B. L. (2004). The broaden-and-build theory of positive emotions. *Philosophical Transactions of the Royal Society B: Biological Sciences, 359,* 1367–1378

34. Isen, A.M., Daubman, K.A., & Nowicki, G.P. (1987). Positive affect facilitates creative problem solving. *Journal of Personality and Social Psychology, 52,* 1122-1131.

35. Csikszentmihalyi, M. (1990). *Flow: The psychology of optimal experience.* New York: Harper Perennial.

Chapter 9

1. https://www.brainyquote.com/quotes/quotes/f/franklind109480.html

2. https://www.brainyquote.com/quotes/winston_churchill_130619

3. https://www.brainyquote.com/quotes/maya_angelou_132601

4. Peterson, C., & Seligman, M.E.P. (2004). *Character strengths and virtues: A handbook of classification*. New York: Oxford University Press.

5. http://www.dictionary.com/browse/courage

6. Peterson, C., & Seligman, M.E.P. (2004).

7. https://www.viacharacter.org/www/Character-Strengths/Bravery

8. Shelp, E.E. (1984). Courage: A neglected virtue in the patient-physician relationship. *Social Science and Medicine, 18*, 351-360.

9. Biswas-Diener, R. (2012). *The courage quotient: How science can make you braver*. San Francisco, CA: Jossey-Bass

10. Kennedy, J.F. (1955). *Profiles in courage*. New York: Harper Perennial.

11. Putnam, D. (1997). Psychological courage. *Philosophy, Psychiatry and Psychology, 4*, 1-11.

12. Biswas-Diener, R. (2012).

13. https://www.goodreads.com/author/quotes/149829.Mary_Anne_Radmacher

14. https://www.viacharacter.org/www/Character-Strengths/Perseverance

15. Peterson, C., & Seligman, M.E.P. (2004).

16. Duckworth, A.L., Peterson, C., Matthews, M.D., & Kelly, D.R. (2007). Grit: Perseverance and passion for long-term goals. *Journal of Personality and Social Psychology, 92*, 1087-1101.

17. Dweck, C. S. (2006). *Mindset: The new psychology of success*. New York: Random House.

18. Peterson, C., & Seligman, M.E.P. (2004).

19. Pausch, R. (2008). *The last lecture*. New York: Hyperion.

20. https://www.goodreads.com/quotes/48122-the-brick-walls-are-there-for-a-reason-the-brick

21. King, L.A. (2001). The health benefits of writing about goals. *Personality and Social Psychology Bulletin, 27*, 798-807.

22. Pearpoint, J., O'Brien, J., & Forest, M. (2011). *PATH: A workbook for planning positive possible futures.* Toronto, CA: Inclusion Press.

23. Baltes, P.B., & Freund, A.M. (2003). The intermarriage of wisdom and selective optimization with compensation: Two meta-heuristics guiding the conduct of life. In C.L.M. Keyes & Haidt (Eds.), *Flourishing: Positive psychology and the life well-lived* (pp. 249-273). Washington, D.C.: American Psychological Association.

24. Eisenberger, R., Kuhlman, D.M., & Cotterell, N. (1992). Effects of social values, effort training, and goal structure on task persistence. *Journal of Research in Personality, 26,* 258-272.

25. Tice, D.M., Wallace, H.M., & Harter, A.C. (2004). Persistence. In C. Peterson & M.E.P. Seligman (Eds.), *Character strengths and virtues: A handbook of classification* (pp. 229-247). New York: Oxford University Press.

26. http://www.dictionary.com/browse/vitality

27. https://www.viacharacter.org/www/Character-Strengths/Zest

28. Peterson, C., & Seligman, M.E.P. (2004).

29. Ryan, R. M., & Deci, E. L. (2000). Self-determination theory and the facilitation of intrinsic motivation, social development, and well-being. *American Psychologist, 55,* 68–78.

30. Ryan, R. M., & Frederick, C. (1997). On energy, personality, and health: Subjective vitality as a dynamic reflection of well-being. *Journal of Personality, 65,* 529-565.

31. Thayer, R.E. (2001). *Calm energy.* New York: Oxford University Press.

32. Thayer, R.E. (1987). Energy, tiredness, and tension effects of a sugar snack versus moderate exercise. *Journal of Personality and Social Psychology, 52,* 119-125.

33. Peterson, C., & Seligman, M.E.P. (2004).

34. https://www.viacharacter.org/www/Character-Strengths/Honesty

35. https://www.enotes.com/shakespeare-quotes/thine-own-self-true

36. https://www.brainyquote.com/quotes/quotes/s/sorenkierk380643.html

37. Rogers, C.R. (1995). *On becoming a person* (2nd Ed.). New York: Mariner Books.

38. Ibid.

39. Brown, B. (2012). *Daring greatly: How the courage to be vulnerable transforms the way we live, love, parent, and lead.* New York: Gotham Books.

40. Rogers, C.R. (1995).

41. Sheldon, K.M., & Elliot, A.J. (1999). Goal striving, need-satisfaction, and longitudinal well-being: The self-concordance model. *Journal of Personality and Social Psychology, 76,* 482-497.

42. Brown, B. (2012).

43. https://www.ted.com/talks/brene_brown_on_vulnerability

Chapter 10

1. http://quoteinvestigator.com/2010/06/29/be-kind/

2. https://en.wikiquote.org/wiki/Will_Rogers

3. http://www.dictionary.com/browse/social-intelligence

4. Peterson, C., & Seligman, M.E.P. (2004). *Character strengths and virtues: A handbook of classification.* New York: Oxford University Press.

5. https://www.viacharacter.org/www/Character-Strengths/Social-Intelligence

6. Gardner, H. (1993). *Multiple intelligences: The theory in practice.* New York: Basic Books.

7. Mithen, S. (2007). Did farming arise from a misapplication of social intelligence? *Philosophical Transactions of the Royal Society B-Biological Sciences, 362,* 705-718.

8. Singer, T., Seymour, B., O'Doherty, J., Kaube, H., Dolan, R.J., & Frith, C.D. (2004). Empathy for pain involves the affective but not sensory components of pain. *Science, 303,* 1157-1162

9. Goleman, D. (1995). *Emotional intelligence: Why it can matter more than IQ.* New York: Bantam Books.

10. Mayer, J. D., Salovey, P., Caruso, D. R., & Sitarenios, G. (2001). Emotional intelligence as a standard intelligence. *Emotion, 1,* 232-242.

11. Mayer, J. D., Salovey, P., & Caruso, D.R. (2002). *Mayer-Salovey-Caruso Emotional Intelligence Test (MSCEIT): User's manual.* Toronto, Ontario: Multi-Health Systems, Inc.

12. Mayer, J. D. (2008). Human abilities: Emotional intelligence. *Annual Review of Psychology, 59,* 507–536.

13. Schutte, N.S., Malouff, J.M., Thorsteinsson, E.B., Bhullar, N., & Rooke, S.E. (2007). A meta-analytic investigation of the relationship between emotional intelligence and health. *Personality and Individual Differences, 42,* 921-933.

14. Gable, S.L., Gonzaga, G.C., & Strachman, A. (2006). Will you be there when things go right? Supportive responses to positive event disclosures. *Journal of Personality and Social Psychology, 91,* 904-917.

15. Peterson, C., & Seligman, M.E.P. (2004).

16. http://www.dictionary.com/browse/love

17. Berscheid, E., & Walster, E.H. (1978). *Interpersonal attraction.* (2nd Ed.). Reading, MA: Addison-Wesley.

18. Hazan, C. (2004). Love. In C. Peterson & M.E.P. Seligman (Eds.), *Character strengths and virtues: A handbook of classification* (pp. 303-324). New York: Oxford University Press.

19. Lee, J.A. (1976). *Lovestyles: How to pick the perfect partner.* London: Abacus books.

20. Bowlby, J. (1969). *Attachment and Loss, Vol. 1. Attachment.* London: Penguin Books

21. Ainsworth, M.D.S., Blehar, M. C., Waters, E., & Wall, S. (1978). *Patterns of attachment: A psychological study of the strange situation.* Hillsdale, NJ: Erlbaum.

22. van den Boom, D.C. (1994). The influence of temperament and mothering on attachment and explorations: An experimental manipulation of sensitive responsiveness among lower-class mothers with irritable infants. *Child Development, 65,* 1457-1477.

23. Hazan, C., & Shaver, P. (1987). Romantic love conceptualized as an attachment process. *Journal of Personality and Social Psychology, 52,* 511-524.

24. Bartholomew, K., & Horowitz, L.M. (1991). Attachment styles among young adults: A test of a four-category model. *Journal of Personality and Social Psychology, 61*, 226-244.

25. Berscheid, E., & Walster, E.H. (1978).

26. Sternberg, R.J. (1986). A triangular theory of love. *Psychological Review, 93*, 119-135.

27. Cronlund, K. (2015). Mindful love. In S. Polly and K. Britton (Eds.), *Character strengths matter: How to live a full life* (pp. 114-116). Positive Psychology News, LLC.

28. Gottman, J.M. (1999). *The seven principles for making marriage work: A practical guide from the country's foremost relationship expert.* New York: Harmony Books.

29. Haidt, J. (2006). *The happiness hypothesis: Finding modern truth in ancient wisdom.* New York: Basic Books.

30. https://quotefancy.com/quote/765020/Aldous-Huxley-People-often-ask-me-what-is-the-most-effective-technique-for-transforming

31. Peterson, C., & Seligman, M.E.P. (2004).

32. Rogers, C.R. (1951). *Client-centered therapy: Its current practice, implications and theory.* Boston: Houghton Mifflin.

33. Miller, W.R., & Rollnick, S. (2012). *Motivational interviewing: Helping people change* (3rd Ed.). New York: Guilford Press.

34. Keltner, D. (2010). The compassionate instinct. In D. Keltner, J. Marsh & J.A. Smith (Eds.), *The compassionate instinct* (pp. 8-15). New York: W.W. Norton.

35. Darley, J.M., & Latané, B. (1968). Bystander intervention in emergencies: Diffusion of responsibility. *Journal of Personality and Social Psychology, 8*, 377-383.

36. Darley, J. M., & Batson, C.D. (1973). From Jerusalem to Jericho: A study of situational and dispositional variables in helping behavior. *Journal of Personality and Social Psychology, 27*, 100-108.

37. Batson, C.D., Duncan, B.D., Ackerman, P., Buckley, T., & Birch, K. (1981). Is empathic emotion a source of altruistic motivation? *Journal of Personality and Social Psychology, 40*, 290-302.

38. Weinstein, N., & Ryan, R. (2010). When helping helps: Autonomous motivation for pro-social behavior and its influence on well-being for the helper and recipient. *Journal of Personality and Social Psychology, 98,* 222-244.

39. Post, S., & Neimark, J. (2007). *Why good things happen to good people.* New York: Broadway Books.

40. Oman, D., Thoresen, C.E., & McMahon, K. (1999). Volunteerism and mortality among the community dwelling elderly. *Journal of Health Psychology, 4,* 301-316.

41. Piferi, R.L., & Lawler, K.A. (2006). Social support and ambulatory blood pressure: An examination of both receiving and giving. *International Journal of Psychophysiology, 62,* 328-336.

42. Pagano, M.E., Friend, K.B., Tonigan, S., & Stout, R.L. (2004). Helping other alcoholics in alcoholics anonymous and drinking outcomes: Findings from project MATCH. *Journal of Studies in Alcohol, 65,* 766-773.

43. Fredrickson, B.L., Cohn, M.A., Coffey, K.A., Pek, J., & Finkel, S.M. (2008). Open hearts build lives: Positive emotions, induced through loving-kindness mediation, build consequential personal resources. *Journal of Personality and Social Psychology, 95,* 1045–1062.

44. Buchanan, K.E., & Bardi, A. (2010). Acts of kindness and acts of novelty affect life satisfaction. *The Journal of Social Psychology, 150,* 235-237.

45. Otake, K., Shimai, S., Tanaka-Matsumi, J., Otsui, K., & Fredrickson, B.L. (2006). Happy people become happier through kindness: A counting kindness intervention. *Journal of Happiness Studies, 7,* 361-375.

46. Lyubomirsky, S. (2013). *The myths of happiness: What should make you happy, but doesn't what shouldn't make you happy, but does.* New York: Penguin Press.

47. Neff, K. (2011). *Self-compassion: The proven power of being kind to yourself.* New York: HarperCollins.

48. Ekman, P. (2010). Global compassion: A conversation between the Dalai Lama and Paul Ekman. In D. Keltner, J. Marsh & J.A. Smith (Eds.), *The compassionate instinct* (pp. 274-282). New York: W.W. Norton.

49. https://www.goodreads.com/quotes/10667-do-i-not-destroy-my-enemies-when-i-make-them

50. https://quotefancy.com/quote/765020/Aldous-Huxley-People-often-ask-me-what-is-the-most-effective-technique-for-transforming

51. http://prayerfoundation.org/mother_teresa_do_it_anyway.htm

52. https://www.brainyquote.com/quotes/quotes/d/dalailama108820.html

53. http://quoteinvestigator.com/2010/06/29/be-kind/

Chapter 11

1. https://www.brainyquote.com/quotes/quotes/m/mahatmagan109075.html

2. https://en.wikipedia.org/wiki/First_they_came_...

3. https://www.ted.com/talks/vs_ramachandran_the_neurons_that_shaped_civilization

4. Brosnan, S.F., & de Waal, F.B.M. (2003). Monkeys reject unequal pay. *Nature, 425,* 297-299.

5. https://www.youtube.com/watch?v=-KSryJXDpZo

6. https://en.oxforddictionaries.com/definition/fairness

7. https://en.oxforddictionaries.com/definition/justice

8. Peterson, C., & Seligman, M.E.P. (2004). *Character strengths and virtues: A handbook of classification.* New York: Oxford University Press.

9. Peterson, C., & Seligman, M.E.P. (2004).

10. Kohlberg, L. (1981). *Essays on moral development, Vol. I: The philosophy of moral development.* San Francisco, CA: Harper & Row.

11. Gilligan, C. (1977). In a different voice: Women's conceptions of self and morality. *Harvard Educational Review, 47,* 481-517.

12. Piaget, J. (1977). Gruber, H.E., & Voneche, J.J. (Eds.). *The essential Piaget.* New York: Basic Books.

13. Kohlberg, L. (1981).

14. Ibid.

15. Gilligan, C. (1977).

16. Damasio, A. (2005). *Descartes' error: Emotion, reason, and the human brain.* New York: Penguin Books.

17. Haidt, J. (2012). *The righteous mind: Why good people are divided by politics and religion.* New York: Vintage Books.

18. http://www.dictionary.com/browse/citizenship

19. Peterson, C., & Seligman, M.E.P. (2004).

20. https://www.viacharacter.org/www/Character-Strengths/Teamwork

21. Rifkin, J. (2009). *The empathic civilization: The race of global consciousness in a world of crisis.* New York: Tarcher Perigee.

22. https://www.brainyquote.com/quotes/john_f_kennedy_109213

23. https://www.theguardian.com/culture/2009/oct/18/racism-psychology-jane-elliott-4

24. http://heroicimagination.org/

25. https://en.wikipedia.org/wiki/I_Have_a_Dream

26. http://www.dictionary.com/browse/leader

27. Peterson, C., & Seligman, M.E.P. (2004).

28. Ibid.

29. Greenleaf, R. (2002). *Servant leadership: A journey into the nature of legitimate power and greatness,* 25th anniversary edition. Mahwah, NJ: Paulist Press.

30. Csikszentmihalyi, M. (1990). *Flow: The psychology of optimal experience.* New York: Harper Perennial.

31. Campbell, J. (2004). *Pathways to bliss: Mythology and personal transformation.* Novato, CA: New World Press.

32. Peterson, C., & Seligman, M.E.P. (2004).

33. Rath, T. (2007). *Strength Finder 2.0.* New York: Guilford Press.

34. Cain, S. (2012). *Quiet: The power of introverts in a world that can't stop talking*. New York: Broadway Books.

35. Stewart, T.L., Laduke, J.R., Bracht, C., Sweet, B.A.M., & Gamarel, K.E. (2003). Do the 'eyes' have it? A program evaluation of Jane Elliott's 'Blue-Eyes/Brown-Eyes' diversity training exercise. *Journal of Applied Social Psychology, 33*, 1898–1921.

36. http://www.actionforhappiness.org/media/52486/340_ways_to_use_character_strengths.pdf

Chapter 12

1. https://www.brainyquote.com/quotes/quotes/v/viktorefr160380.html

2. Peterson, C., & Seligman, M.E.P. (2004).

3. https://www.viacharacter.org/www/Character-Strengths/Self-Regulation

4. Metcalfe, J., & Mischel, W. (1999). The hot/cool system analysis of delay of gratification: Dynamics of willpower. *Psychological Review, 106*, 3-19.

5. Baumeister, R.F., & Tierney, J. (2011). *Willpower: Rediscovering the greatest human strength*. New York: Penguin Press.

6. Shoda, Y., Mischel, W., & Peake, P.K. (1990). Predicting adolescent cognitive and self-regulatory competences from preschool delay of gratification: Identifying diagnostic conditions. *Developmental Psychology, 26*, 978-986.

7. Wegner D.M., Schneider D.J., Carter S.R. & White T.L. (1987). Paradoxical effects of thought suppression. *Journal of Personality and Social Psychology, 53*, 5-13

8. Baumeister, R.F., Vohs, K.D., & Tice, D.M. (2007). The strength model of self-control. *Current Directions in Psychological Science, 16*, 351-355.

9. Hagger, M.S., Chatzisarantis, L.D., Alberts, H., et al. (2016). A multilab preregistered replication of the ego-depletion effect. *Perspectives on Psychological Science, 11*, 546-573.

10. Muraven, M., Baumeister, R.F., & Tice, D.M. (1999). Longitudinal improvement of self-regulation through practice: Building self-control

strength through repeated exercise. *Journal of Social Psychology, 139,* 446-458.

11. Gollwitzer, P. M., & Bargh, J. A. (Eds.). (1996). *The psychology of action: Linking cognition and motivation to behavior.* New York: Guilford Press.

12. Oettingen, G., Mayer, D., & Brinkmann, B. (2010). Mental contrasting of future and reality: Managing the demands of everyday life in health care professionals. *Journal of Personnel Psychology, 9,* 138-144.

13. Bowen, S., & Marlatt, G. A. (2009). Surfing the urge: Brief mindfulness-based intervention for college student smokers. *Psychology of Addictive Behaviors, 23,* 666-671.

14. http://www.dictionary.com/browse/prudence

15. Peterson, C., & Seligman, M.E.P. (2004).

16. Haslam, N. (2004). Prudence. In C. Peterson & M.E.P. Seligman (Eds.), *Character strengths and virtues: A handbook of classification* (p. 477-497). New York: Oxford University Press.

17. Emmons, R.A. (1986). Personal strivings: An approach to personality and subjective well-being. *Journal of Personality and Social Psychology, 51,* 1058-1068.

18. Rokeach, M. (1973). *The nature of human values.* New York: The Free Press.

19. Emmons, R.A. (1999). *The psychology of ultimate concerns.* New York: Guilford Press.

20. Doran, G. T. (1981). There's a S.M.A.R.T. way to write management's goals and objectives. *Management Review, 70,* 35–36.

21. Pearpoint, J., O'Brien, J., & Forest, M. (2011). *PATH: A workbook for planning positive possible futures.* Toronto, CA: Inclusion Press.

22. Allen, D. (2015). *Getting things done: The art of stress-free productivity.* New York: Penguin Books.

23. https://www.washingtonpost.com/opinions/pope-francis-acts-of-humility/2013/07/25/4e7db41c-f49e-11e2-aa2e-088616498b4_gallery.

24. Peterson, C., & Seligman, M.E.P. (2004).

25. https://www.viacharacter.org/www/Character-Strengths/Humility

26. Kachorek, L.V., Exline, J.J., Campbell, W.K., Baumeister, R.F., Joiner, T.E., & Krueger, J.I. (2004). Humility and Modesty. In C. Peterson & M.E.P. Seligman (Eds.), *Character strengths and virtues: A handbook of classification* (pp. 461-475). New York: Oxford University Press.

27. Tillich, P. (1948). You are accepted. In P. Tillich, *The shaking of the foundations* (pp. 153-163). New York: Charles Scribner's Sons.

28. Ellis, A. (2009). *Rational emotive behavior therapy: It works for me - It can work for you.* New York: Prometheus Books.

29. Rogers, C.R. (1951). *Client-centered therapy: Its current practice, implications and theory.* Boston: Houghton Mifflin.

30. http://www.nbc12.com/story/22301562/vcu-professor-forgives-killer-after-losing-his-mother-and-brother

31. http://www.dictionary.com/browse/forgive

32. Peterson, C., & Seligman, M.E.P. (2004).

33. https://en.wikipedia.org/wiki/Phan_Thi_Kim_Phuc

34. https://en.wikiquote.org/wiki/George_Santayana

35. Worthington, E.L. (2001). *Five steps to forgiveness: The art and science of forgiving.* New York: Crown Publishing.

36. McCullough, M.E., Sandage, S.J., & Worthington, E.L. (1997). *To forgive is human: How to put your past in the past.* Downers Grove, IL: IVP Books.

37. Enright, R.D. (2001). *Forgiveness is a choice: A step-by-step process for resolving anger and restoring hope.* Washington, DC: American Psychological Association.

38. Pennebaker, J.W., & Smyth, J.M. (2016). *Opening up by writing it down: How expressive writing improves health and eases emotional pain* (3rd Ed.). New York: Guilford Press.

Chapter 13

1. Henley, W.E. (1888). *A book of verses* (pp. 56-57). London: D. Nutt.

2. http://www.dictionary.com/browse/optimism

3. http://www.dictionary.com/browse/hope

4. Peterson, C., & Seligman, M.E.P. (2004). *Character strengths and virtues: A handbook of classification.* New York: Oxford University Press.

5. Scheier, M.F., Carver C.S., & Bridges, M.W. (1994). Distinguishing optimism from neuroticism (and trait anxiety, self-mastery, and self-esteem): A re-evaluation of the Life Orientation Test. *Journal of Personality and Social Psychology, 67,* 1063-1078.

6. Snyder, C.R. (1994). *The psychology of hope: You can get there from here.* New York: Free Press.

7. Seligman, M. (1998). *Learned Optimism.* New York, NY: Pocket Books.

8. Seligman, M.E.P. (2011). *Flourish: A visionary new understanding of happiness and well-being.* New York: Free Press.

9. Taylor, S.E., Pham, L.B., Rivkin, I.D., & Armor, D.A. (1998). Harnessing the imagination: Mental simulation, self-regulation, and coping. *American Psychologist, 53,* 429-439.

10. Scheier, M.F., Carver C.S., & Bridges, M.W. (1994).

11. Snyder, C.R. (1994).

12. Doran, G. T. (1981). There's a S.M.A.R.T. way to write management's goals and objectives. *Management Review, 70,* 35–36.

13. Henley, W.E. (1888).

14. Cousins, N. (1979). *Anatomy of an illness as perceived by the patient: Reflections on healing and regeneration.* New York: Bantam Books.

15. Ibid.

16. http://www.dictionary.com/browse/humor?s=t

17. Peterson, C., & Seligman, M.E.P. (2004).

18. Ibid.

19. Dixon, N.F. (1980). Humor: A cognitive alternative to stress? In I.G. Sarason & C.D. Spielberger (Eds.), *Stress and anxiety, Vol. 7* (pp. 281-289). Washington, DC: Hemisphere.

20. Freud, S. (1905). Humor and its relation to the unconscious. *Standard edition of the complete psychological works of Sigmund Freud* (J. Strachey, Trans.) (Vol. VIII, pp. 9-236). London: Hogarth Press.

21. Valliant, G.E. (1993). *The wisdom of the ego*. Cambridge, MA: Harvard University Press.

22. https://en.wikiquote.org/wiki/E._B._White

23. Lefcourt, H.M. (2002). Humor. In C.R. Snyder & S.J. Lopez (Eds.), *Handbook of positive psychology* (pp, 619-631). New York: Oxford University Press.

24. Abel, M.H., & Maxwell, D. (2002). Humor and affective consequences of a stressful task. *Journal of Social and Clinical Psychology, 21,* 165-202.

25. Carver, C.S., Pozo, C., Harris, S.D., Noriega, V., Scheier, M.F., Robinson, D.S., Ketcham, A.S., Moffat, F.L., & Clark, K.C. (1993). How coping mediates the effect of optimism on distress: A study of women with early stage breast cancer. *Journal of Personality and Social Psychology, 63,* 2, 375-390.

26. McGhee, P.E. (1999). *Health, healing, and the amuse system: Humor as survival training*. Dubuque, IA: Kendall/Hunt.

27. Rotten, J., & Shats, M. (1996). Effects of state humor, expectancies and choice on post-surgical mood and self-medication: A field experiment. *Journal of Applied Social Psychology, 26,* 1775-1794.

28. Newman, M.G., & Stone, A.A. (1996). Does humor moderate the effects of experimentally induced stress? *Annals of Behavioral Medicine, 18,* 101-109.

29. Gander, F., Proyer, R.T., Ruch, W., & Wyss, T. (2012). Strength-based positive interventions: Further evidence for their potential in enhancing well-being and alleviating depression. *Journal of Happiness Studies, 14,* 1241-1259.

30. McGhee, P.E. (2010). *Humor as survival training for a stressed-out world: The 7 humor habits program*. Bloomington, IN: Author House.

31. https://en.wikipedia.org/wiki/Earthrise

32. Haidt, J., & Keltner, D. (2004). Appreciation of Beauty and Excellence. In C. Peterson & M.E.P. Seligman (Eds.), *Character strengths and virtues: A handbook of classification* (pp. 537-551). New York: Oxford University Press.

33. https://en.oxforddictionaries.com/definition/us/appreciation

34. Peterson, C., & Seligman, M.E.P. (2004).

35. James, W. (1999). *Varieties of religious experience: A study in human nature.* New York: Modern Library. (Original work published in 1902).

36. Maslow, A.H. (1964). *Religions, values, and peak experiences.* New York: Penguin.

37. Haidt, J., & Keltner, D. (2004).

38. http://www.dictionary.com/browse/gratitude

39. http://www.dictionary.com/browse/grateful

40. Peterson, C., & Seligman, M.E.P. (2004).

41. Emmons, R.A. (2004). Gratitude. In C. Peterson & M.E.P. Seligman (Eds.), *Character strengths and virtues: A handbook of classification* (pp. 553-568). New York: Oxford University Press.

42. Ibid.

43. Emmons, R.A., & Crumpler, C.A. (2000). Gratitude as a human strength: Appraising the evidence. *Journal of Social and Clinical Psychology, 19,* 56-69.

44. Seligman, M.E.P., Steen, T.A., Park, N., & Peterson, C. (2005). Positive psychology progress: Empirical validation of interventions. *American Psychologist, 60,* 410-421.

45. Ibid.

46. Chan, D.W. (2010). Thanks, but no thanks: The role of personality responsibility in the experience of gratitude. *Journal of Experimental Social Psychology, 46,* 487-493.

47. Shenk, J.W. (2006). *Lincoln's melancholy: How depression challenged a president and fueled his greatness.* New York: Mariner Books.

48. Frankl, V. E. (1963). *Man's search for meaning.* New York: Pocket Books.

49. Peterson, C., & Seligman, M.E.P. (2004).

50. Campbell, J. (1949). *The hero with a thousand faces.* Princeton, N.J.: Princeton University Press.

51. McAdams, D. (1993). *The stories we live by: Personal myths and the making of the self.* New York: Guilford Press.

52. Pennebaker, J.W., & Smyth, J.M. (2016). *Opening up by writing it down: How expressive writing improves health and eases emotional pain* (3rd. Ed.). New York: Guilford Press.

53. Steger, M.F., Bundick, M., & Yeager, D. (2012). Understanding and promoting meaning in life during adolescence. In R. J. R. Levesque (Ed.), *Encyclopedia of adolescence* (pp. 1666-1677). New York: Springer.

54. Shin, J.Y., & Steger, M.F. (2014). Promoting meaning and purpose in life. In A.C. Parks & S.M. Schueller (Eds.), *The Wiley Blackwell handbook of positive psychological interventions* (pp. 90-110). West Sussex, UK: John Wiley and Sons.

55. McAdams, D. (1993).

56. McAdams, D. (1985). *Power, intimacy, and the life story: Personological inquiries into identity.* New York: Guilford Press.

57. King, L.A. (2001). The health benefits of writing about goals. *Personality and Social Psychology Bulletin, 27,* 798-807.

58. Pearpoint, J., O'Brien, J., & Forest, M. (2011). *PATH: A workbook for planning positive possible futures.* Toronto, CA: Inclusion Press.

59. Emmons, R.A. (1999). *The psychology of ultimate concerns.* New York: Guilford Press.

60. Frankl, V. E. (1963). *Man's search for meaning.* New York: Pocket Books.

61. Smith, B.W., & Zautra, A.J. (2004). The role of purpose in life in recovery from knee surgery. *International Journal of Behavioral Medicine, 11,* 197-202.

62. Rodin, J., & Langer, E. (1977). Long-term effects of a control-relevant intervention with the institutionalized aged. *Journal of Personality and Social Psychology, 35,* 897–902.

63. Campbell, J. (1949).

Chapter 14

1. https://www.brainyquote.com/quotes/quotes/a/abrahammas 159012.html

2. https://www.youtube.com/watch?v=A6FlMLyf0yk

3. Campbell, J. (1949). *The hero with a thousand faces.* Princeton, N.J.: Princeton University Press.

4. Doran, G. T. (1981). There's a S.M.A.R.T. way to write management's goals and objectives. *Management Review, 70,* 35–36.

5. Pearpoint, J., O'Brien, J., & Forest, M. (2011). *PATH: A workbook for planning positive possible futures.* Toronto, CA: Inclusion Press.

6. Snyder, C.R. (1994). *The psychology of hope: You can get there from here.* New York: Free Press.

7. Pearpoint, J., O'Brien, J., & Forest, M. (2011).

APPENDIX A

Recommended Reading

Biswas-Diener, R. (2010). *Practicing positive psychology coaching: Assessment, activities, and strategies for success.* Hoboken, NJ: John Wiley & Sons.

Brown, B. (2012). *Daring greatly: How the courage to be vulnerable transforms the way we live, love, parent, and lead.* New York: Gotham Books.

Burns, D. (2008). *Feeling good: The new mood therapy.* New York: Harper.

Campbell, J. (1949). *The hero with a thousand faces.* Princeton, N.J.: Princeton University Press.

Campbell, J. (2004). *Pathways to bliss: Mythology and personal transformation.* Novato, CA: New World Press.

Cousins, N. (1979). *Anatomy of an illness as perceived by the patient: Reflections on healing and regeneration.* New York: Bantam Books.

Csikszentmihalyi, M. (1990). *Flow: The psychology of optimal experience.* New York: Harper Perennial.

Emmons, R.A. (2013). *Gratitude works: A 21-day program for creating emotional prosperity.* San Francisco, CA: Jossey-Bass.

Enright, R.D. (2001). *Forgiveness is a choice: A step-by-step process for resolving anger and restoring hope.* Washington, DC: American Psychological Association.

Frankl, V. E. (1963). *Man's search for meaning*. New York: Pocket Books.

Froh, J.J., & Parks, A.C. (2013). *Activities for teaching positive psychology: A guide for instructors*. Washington, DC: American Psychological Association.

Haidt, J. (2006). *The happiness hypothesis: Finding modern truth in ancient wisdom*. New York: Basic Books.

Haidt, J. (2012). *The righteous mind: Why good people are divided by politics and religion*. New York: Vintage Books.

Hanson, R. (2013). *Hardwiring happiness: The new brain science of contentment, calm, and confidence*. New York: Harmony Books.

Joseph, S. (Ed.). (2015). *Positive psychology in practice: Promoting human flourishing in work, health, education, and everyday life*. Hoboken, NJ: John Wiley & Sons.

Kabat-Zinn, J. (1990). *Full catastrophe living: Using the wisdom of your body and mind to face stress, pain, and illness*. New York: Delta.

Kabat-Zinn, J. (1994). *Wherever you go, there you are*. New York: Hyperion.

Keltner, D. (2010). The compassionate instinct. In D. Keltner, J. Marsh & J.A. Smith. *The compassionate instinct* (pp. 8-15). New York: W.W. Norton.

Lopez, S.J., & Snyder, C.R. (Eds.). (2009). *Oxford handbook of positive psychology* (2nd Ed.). New York: Oxford University Press.

Lyubomirsky, S. (2007). *The how of happiness: A new approach to getting the life you want*. New York: Penguin Books.

McAdams, D. (1993). *The stories we live by: Personal myths and the making of the self.* New York: Guilford Press.

Miller, W.R., & Rollnick, S. (2012). *Motivational interviewing: Helping people change* (3rd Ed.). New York: Guilford Press.

Miller, W.R., & C'de Baca, J. (2001). *Quantum change: When epiphanies and sudden insights transform ordinary lives.* New York: Guilford Press.

Mumford, G. (2015). *The mindful athlete: Secrets to pure performance.* Berkeley, CA: Parallax Press.

Neff, K. (2011). *Self-compassion: The proven power of being kind to yourself.* New York: HarperCollins.

Niemiec, R.M. (2014). *Mindfulness and character strengths: A practical guide to flourishing.* Boston, MA: Hogrefe Publishing.

Niemiec, R.M. (2014). *Positive psychology at the movies: Using films to build character strengths and well-being* (2nd Ed.). Boston, MA: Hogrefe Publishing.

Niemiec, R.M. (2017). *Character strengths interventions: A field guide for practitioners.* Boston, MA: Hogrefe Publishing.

O'Hanlon, B., & Bertolino, B. (2012). *The therapist's notebook on positive psychology: Activities, exercises, and handouts.* New York: Routledge.

Pearpoint, J., O'Brien, J., & Forest, M. (2011). *PATH: A workbook for planning positive possible futures.* Toronto, CA: Inclusion Press.

Pennebaker, J.W., & Smyth, J.M. (2016). *Opening up by writing it down: How expressive writing improves health and eases emotional pain* (3rd Ed.). New York: Guilford Press.

Peterson, C., & Seligman, M.E.P. (2004). *Character strengths and virtues: A handbook of classification*. New York: Oxford University Press.

Polly, S. & Britton, K. (Eds.). (2015). *Character strengths matter: How to live a full life*. Positive Psychology News, LLC.

Post, S., & Neimark, J. (2007). *Why good things happen to good people*. New York: Broadway Books.

Proctor, C., & Eades, J.F. (2016). *Strengths gym: Build and exercise your strengths*. Channel Islands, GYI 6HL: Positive Psychology Research Centre.

Rogers, C.R. (1995). *On becoming a person* (2nd Ed.). New York: Mariner Books.

Seligman, M.E.P. (2002). *Authentic happiness: Using the new positive psychology to realize your potential for lasting fulfillment*. New York: Free Press.

Seligman, M.E.P. (2011). *Flourish: A visionary new understanding of happiness and well-being*. New York: Free Press.

Snyder, C.R. (1994). *The psychology of hope: You can get there from here*. New York: Free Press.

Wade, J.C., Marks, L.I., & Hetzel, R.D. (2015). *Positive psychology on the college campus*. New York: Oxford University Press.

Worthington, E.L. (2001). *Five steps to forgiveness: The art and science of forgiving*. New York: Crown Publishing.

APPENDIX B

TED Talks for Positive Psychology

These have all been available on YouTube and have been easy to find by searching for the name of the speaker and title listed below.

Achor, Shawn—*The Happy Secret to Better Work*

Allende, Isabel—*How to Live Passionately*

Ariely, Dan—*Self-Control*

Bartholomew, Hailey—*365 Grateful Project*

Beckham, Ash—*Coming Out of Your Closet*

Berlin, Johann—*The Power of Kindness*

Bidlack, Benjamin—*The Hero's Journey in Modern Life*

Bolte Taylor, Jill—*My Stroke of Insight*

Brown, Brené—*The Power of Vulnerability*

Cain, Susan—*The Power of Introverts*

Csikszentmihalyi, Mihaly—*Flow: The Secret of Happiness*

Cuddy, Amy—*Your Body Language Shapes Who You Are*

Doyle, Brian—*365 Days of Thank You*

Duckworth, Angela—*The Power of Passion and Perseverance*

Elias, Ric—*Things I Learned While My Plane Crashed*

Fisher, Helen—*The Science of Love and the Future of Women*

Gilbert, Dan—*The Surprising Science of Happiness*

Gilbert, Elizabeth—*Your Elusive Creativity Genius*

Goleman, Daniel—*Why Aren't We All Good Samaritans?*

Hamilton, Allan—*Prescribing Hope*

Lazar, Sara—*How Meditation Can Reshape Our Brains*

McGonigal, Jane—*Gaming Can Make a Better World*

McGonigal, Kelly—*How to Make Stress Your Friend*

Pasricha, Neil—*The 3 As of Awesome*

Pink, Daniel—*The Surprising Science of Motivation*

Ramachandran V.—*The Neurons that Shaped Civilization*

Rangel, Sammie—*The Power of Forgiveness*

Ricard, Matthieu—*The Habits of Happiness*

Robinson, Ken—*Do Schools Kill Creativity*

Saxe, Rebecca—*How Do We Read Each Other's Minds*

Schwartz, Barry—*Our Loss of Wisdom*

Schwartzberg, Louie—*Gratitude*

Seligman, Martin—*The New Era of Positive Psychology*

Sinek, Simon—*How Great Leaders Inspire Action*

Winkler, Matthew—*What Makes a Hero?*

Winston, Diana—*The Science of Mindfulness*

Zimbardo, Phil—*The Heroic Imagination Project*

APPENDIX C

Movies for Positive Psychology

1. Hero's Journey Movie Series—these three series were used in this book to illustrate the hero's journey in positive psychology.

The Original Star Wars Trilogy: George Lucas directly modeled *Star Wars* after Joseph Campbell's *The Hero with a Thousand Faces* which clearly illustrates the stages of the hero's journey.

> *Star Wars: A New Hope* (1977)
>
> *The Empire Strikes Back* (1980)
>
> *The Return of the Jedi* (1983)

The Lord of the Rings Trilogy: Based on the books of J.R.R. Tolkien who wanted to provide a new mythology to guide human beings through the challenges of the modern world.

> *The Fellowship of the Ring* (2001)
>
> *The Two Towers* (2002)
>
> *The Return of the King* (2003)

The Harry Potter Series: The movies based on J.K. Rowling's books that have become a guiding myth and story that creatively illustrates the challenges and rewards of the hero's journey.

> *Harry Potter and the Sorcerer's Stone* (2001)
>
> *Harry Potter and the Chamber of Secrets* (2002)
>
> *The Prisoner of Azkaban* (2004)

Harry Potter and the Goblet of Fire (2005)

Harry Potter and the Order of the Phoenix (2007)

Harry Potter and the Half Blood Prince (2009)

Harry Potter and the Deathly Hallows 1 (2010)

Harry Potter and the Death Hallows 2 (2011)

2. Hero's Journey Movie Examples: The following movies provide excellent examples of the strengths listed below as well as other aspects of positive psychology.

12 Angry Men (1957)—open-mindedness, fairness, self-control

Amelie (2001)—kindness, humor, creativity, love

Black Panther (2018)—creativity, open-mindedness, fairness

Chariots of Fire (1981)—meaning, purpose, and spirituality

Dead Poet's Society (1989)—authenticity, creativity, meaning

Erin Brockovich (2000)—citizenship, fairness, courage

ET the Extra-Terrestrial (1982)—love, vitality, hope

Field of Dreams (1989)—optimism, hope, forgiveness

Freedom Writers (2007)—love of learning, hope, love

Gandhi (1982)—leadership, forgiveness, kindness

Good Will Hunting (1997)—hope, love, authenticity

Hidden Figures (2016)—courage, open-mindedness, fairness

Invictus (2009)—forgiveness, leadership, wisdom

It's a Wonderful Life (1946)—optimism, hope, gratitude

Life is Beautiful (1997)—creativity, humor, vitality

My Left Foot (1989)—vitality, perseverance, creativity

October Sky (1999)—creativity, hope, curiosity

Pay It Forward (2000)—creativity, kindness, gratitude

Places in the Heart (1984)—love, kindness, fairness

Schindler's List (1993)—courage, fairness, leadership

The Sound of Music (1965)—vitality, creativity, appreciation

The Grapes of Wrath (1940)—courage, perseverance, hope

The Karate Kid (1984)—self-control, prudence, perseverance

The King's Speech (2010)—creativity, humor, courage

The Lion King (1994)—courage, hope, leadership

The Miracle Worker (1962)—creativity, love, perseverance

The Shawshank Redemption (1994)—perseverance, appreciation

The Wizard of Oz (1939)—authenticity, kindness, wisdom

To Kill a Mockingbird (1962)—integrity, open-mindedness

Wonder Woman (2017)—courage, compassion, fairness

3. Documentaries—these provide an excellent explanation of the hero's journey and the value of positive psychology, respectively.

Finding Joe (2011)—the story of Joseph Campbell including segments on the hero's journey and following your bliss.

Happy (2011)—explores happiness around the world and features several leaders of the positive psychology movement.

APPENDIX D

Positive Psychology Exercises

The following are the weekly exercises used in the positive psychology class developed by the author. They were designed as a progressive sequence but can also work well on their own.

1. Identifying What Makes You Happy

The following questions are designed to enable you to begin to reflect and identify what may bring you the greatest happiness and well-being. Ideally, it would be good to provide written responses to them first and also discuss them with a good friend or mentor.

a. What has brought you the most happiness in the past?

b. What do you think would bring the most in the future?

c. Who are the most important people in your life?

d. What do you like to do in your spare time?

e. What would you most like to do for work?

f. What three values are most important to you? Here are some values at you can choose from or you can come up with others on your own: achievement, adventure, authority, autonomy, beauty, caring, comfort, commitment, cooperation, creativity, dependability, duty, faithfulness, family, friendship, fun, God's will, health, honesty, hope, humor, inner peace, leisure, love, mastery, order, purpose, realism, self-acceptance, self-esteem, service, sexuality, spirituality, tolerance, wealth.

g. What has brought the most meaning to your life?

h. What are your top goals for school, work, and relationships?

i. Which of these goals is most important to you?

j. What would you do if you had unlimited time and money?

k. How would you like to be remembered after you are gone?

l. What do you most want out of life?

2. Identifying Your Top Strengths

The purpose of this exercise is to enable you to identify your top personal strengths and think about the times that you have been at your best and used them. The identification and use of your top strengths has consistently been shown to be a strong factor in increasing happiness and well-being.

Go to the following website:

https://www.viacharacter.org/survey/account/register

Take the *Values in Action Survey (VIA Survey)*. The survey is 120 questions and should take 20-30 minutes to complete. You will need to register first and then log in. You can take the survey for free and you will get a top to bottom ranking of all 24 strengths.

Answer the following questions:

a. List the top five strengths identified for you by the VIA survey.

b. Think any other strengths you are aware of that were not on the survey and include them in re-ranking your top five.

c. Make a list of examples of when you expressed each of your top three strengths.

d. Write about one of your best examples of each of your top three strengths and share them with someone else.

3. Finding New Ways to Use Your Strengths

The purpose of this exercise is to enable you to become more creative in how you use your top strengths. Your task is to use one or more of your top five strengths in a new and different way on at least five different days during the coming week.

Before you decide what to do, review the suggestions for each of your top five strengths at the end of the section in this book and google the *340 Ways to Use VIA Character Strengths* by Tayyab Rashid for more ideas. Whether you use any of these or come up with your own, be sure to do things that are new and different and plan to do them at a clearly defined time and place.

4. Using Your Top Strengths to Reach Your Goals

The purpose of this exercise is to help you think about how you can use your top strengths to reach your goals. To do this, you need to begin by identifying three goals using the SMART acronym to make sure that they are Specific, Measurable, Achievable, Relevant, and Time-bound. These should be goals that you would like to work on reaching in the next month.

After you have identified three goals, brainstorm about how you can use your top strengths to make progress in meeting each of these three goals in the next month. Once you come up with a list of how to use your strengths to reach each of the goals in the next month, then develop a schedule for just what you will do and when in order to make progress in reaching each goal.

Be sure to follow through with your plan and find another way to use your strengths whenever you run into an obstacle. Regardless of whether you reach your goals in the next month, be sure to reward yourself for your planning and for any effort that you make in trying to use your strengths to reach your goals.

5. Finding Ways to Experience Flow

The purpose of this exercise is to enable you to experience flow. Flow is the mental state in which a person performing an activity is fully absorbed and immersed in doing the activity. It often involves the use of our top strengths.

For this exercise, try to identify things that are at least moderately challenging and that you may like to do so much that you may lose track of time. You may want to review the section in Chapter 4 on flow to make sure you understand what it is and the conditions necessary for achieving it.

Be sure to plan to do your activity at a clearly defined time and place where you will not be interrupted. Do this activity for at least one hour and try to do at least one other different flow activity in the next week so you can compare them.

6. Learning to See the Good

This exercise is a variation of the counting blessings and three good things exercises that were presented under the gratitude section of Chapter 13. The purpose of this exercise is to enable you to be see and be aware of more of the good things that occur every day. It has been a good way for many people to counter the negativity bias and learn to pay more attention to the good things that we often miss.

At the end of each day for the next seven days, write down at least three good things that happened during the previous day. This can be things that went well during the day or even just things that you thought about if you cannot think of anything that went well during that day. They can be anything, small or large, that you define as good or beneficial from your perspective. You may find it helpful to keep a sheet of paper or smart phone handy to note them as they occur.

7. Learning to Create the Good

As with the previous exercise, this is a variation of the counting blessings and three good things exercises that were presented in the gratitude section in Chapter 13. The purpose of this exercise is to build on your ability to see good things by finding ways to proactively create and increase them.

There are two parts to this exercise. First, as you did last week, at the end of each day for the next seven days, write down at least three good things that happened during the previous day. Second, choose one of the good things that happened during the previous day and write at least one sentence about what you think you could do to make it happen more often in the future.

8. Savoring the Good

Savoring means to take the time to fully appreciate and enjoy something that makes you feel good. The last two exercises were designed to enable you to see and create good things in your life. This exercise is designed to enable you to increase the pleasure, enjoyment, and benefit you receive from good things.

There are two parts to this exercise. First, identify at least 10 things that you think you would enjoy taking the time to savor more in your life. Second, take at least 10 minutes to savor one or more of them on at least five different days during the coming week. Practice fully focusing your attention on what feels good as you savor.

9. Identifying Love and Kindness

The purpose of this exercise is to enable you to identify and reflect on the best ways that people can treat each other. This is another way of learning to counter the negativity bias by seeing and focusing on how people often love and care for each other.

Make a list of ten of the best acts of kindness, compassion, or love that anyone has ever done for you. On two separate days during the following week, take at least 15 minutes to write about two of the tops acts that you have identified.

As you write, be sure to do three things. First, be specific in telling the details of the story of what happened. Second, write about how it has affected or changed you and what you learned from it. Third, write about what you can do to give back, pass on, or honor what was done for you.

10. Expressing Gratitude

The purpose of this exercise is to give you the chance to sincerely express your appreciation to someone that you are grateful for. This is based on the gratitude expression exercise discussed in Chapter 13 in the gratitude section.

There are three parts to this exercise. First, choose someone who has been especially kind to you, but also who you have never properly or fully thanked. Second, write a letter expressing your gratitude saying in detail what you are grateful for and specifically how it affected you.

Third, and most important, read the letter to them in person and then give them the chance to respond to you. If you cannot meet with the person, read it to them using Skype or over the phone.

11. Sharing Strengths with Others

The purpose of this exercise is to give you the chance to talk about your strengths with a friend, family member, coworker, fellow student, or anyone else you would like. First, identify someone who will take the *VIA Survey* to find out their top strengths. Second, meet with them to share your strengths and talk about how you can encourage and support each other in using them.

Third, ask the other person to tell you about a time that they were at their best and practice active constructive responding when they tell you something good that happened. Active constructive responding was discussed in Chapter 9 at the end of the social intelligence section.

Before you try to practice active constructive responding, view the following video to be sure you understand what it involves:

https://www.youtube.com/watch?v=qRORihbXMnA

12. Performing Creative Acts of Kindness

The purpose of this exercise is to give you the opportunity to experiment with finding and trying new and different ways of expressing kindness. First, brainstorm to come up with a list of at least 10 new things you could do to express kindness.

To help you do this, you can review the ways to express kindness at the end of the section on kindness in Chapter 9, google the *340 Ways to Use the VIA Strengths* by Tayyab Rashid to see more examples of kindness, and watch the video *22 Random Acts of Kindness* at:

https://www.youtube.com/watch?v=wskG18saKk0

After you have come up with a list of things that you would like to try, choose at least three that you can do on different days in the coming week. Try to do at least one kind act for someone you know and at least one kind act for someone you don't know so you can compare how they feel similar and different.

13. Writing About Your Best Possible Life

The purpose of this exercise is to give you the opportunity to imagine the best possible life that you could be living five to 10 years from now. This exercise is a variation of the "best possible self" exercise created by Laura King and discussed in the book. For this exercise, take at least 20 minutes to write freely at a time that you won't be distracted.

When you write, think about your life in the future. Imagine that everything has gone as well as it possibly could. You have worked hard and succeeded at accomplishing all of your life goals. Think of this as the realization of all of your life dreams. Where would you be living and what kind of people would you be with? What kind of work would you be doing and what would you be doing for fun? How might you be giving back to others?

14. Charting Your Hero's Path

The purpose of this exercise is to help you bring together what you have learned in this book to begin to move towards the best possible life that you wrote about in the last exercise. There are three steps to this exercise:

a. Briefly review this book and make a list of the most important things you think can help you reach your best possible life.

b. Identify a wise mentor in real life or a fictional hero's journey story that you can use for inspiration. Write down what you think each would suggest you do to reach your goals.

c. Write out a plan for what you need to do during the next year to begin reach your best possible life. Draw on your strengths, what you have learned in this book, what you think your mentors would say, and imagining yourself on a hero's journey.

INDEX

Made in the USA
Coppell, TX
12 August 2022

81391790R10233